Transient Images

Eric Freedman

Transient Images

Personal Media in Public Frameworks

TEMPLE UNIVERSITY PRESS
Philadelphia

TEMPLE UNIVERSITY PRESS
Philadelphia, Pennsylvania 19122
www.temple.edu/tempress

Library of Congress Cataloging-in-Publication Data

Freedman, Eric, 1965-
    Transient images: personal media in public frameworks / Eric Freedman.
        p. cm.
    Includes bibliographical references and index.
    ISBN 978-1-4399-0326-1 (cloth: alk. paper)—ISBN 978-1-4399-0327-8 (pbk.: alk. paper)—
    ISBN 978-1-4399-0328-5 (electronic)
    1. Information technology—Social aspects. 2. Images, Photographic—Social aspects.
3. Social media. 4. Digital media. I. Title.
    HM851.F73 2011
    303.48'33—dc22

                                                                        2010037300

Printed in the United States of America

062111-P

Contents

Acknowledgments

Despite my best efforts, the media landscape would not hold still while I researched, wrote, and revised this book. The technology evolved, my project followed, and while I felt a certain responsibility to pause and consider every artifact and trend, I slowly came to realize the futility of such an exercise. And now, upon reaching closure, of course I have forgotten exactly where I started—not in terms of the research at hand and my original imperative, but in terms of the intellectual communities that helped me along. My research was originally fueled by several mentors at the University of Southern California (USC), including David James, Marsha Kinder, Michael Renov, and Marita Sturken; though not involved in this project per se, they were instrumental in fostering my early intellectual growth during my graduate years, and their own work, however diverse, continues to inform my approach. Over the years, I have occasionally turned to fellow USC graduates for support; while I value the camaraderie of them all, Harry Benshoff, Sean Griffin, Mary Kearney, and James Moran deserve special mention. After leaving the confines of graduate school, I landed first at Duke University, where Jane Gaines and a number of Duke graduates, including Roger Beebe, were my intellectual community. I finally landed at Florida Atlantic University, where I have found support among my colleagues in the School of Communication and Multimedia Studies; most notably, Mike Budd, Susan Reilly, Chris Robé, and James Tracy have been an invaluable sounding board. Among my friends and colleagues, Linda Fuller, Annette Hill, Anna McCarthy, and Tara McPherson have been instrumental supporters and occasional editors of my work, pushing me to clarify despite my penchant for density and brevity. And Heather Hendershot has been a best friend and confidant, and has lent tremendous insight as a perennial presence on the phone, via e-mail, and at early morning conference sessions. I also thank the editors at *Flow*; the on-line journal hosted by the University of Texas at Austin has provided an extremely valuable space to work through several pieces of this manuscript. Of course, the strongest editorial voice came from the superb team at Temple University Press; among them, I am grateful to my editor, Micah Kleit, for his commitment to the manuscript and his enthusiastic support of my work. I extend thanks to my parents, Harriett and Julian Freedman, who have always followed and supported my scholarly and creative pursuits. Finally, I thank my partner, Ryan Ratliff, who has lived with me through the later years of the manuscript and has been one of the best incentives to finish this project and move on to the next.

Transient Images

Introduction

Picturetown, USA

> *So I resolved to start my inquiry with no more than a few photographs,*
> *the ones I was sure existed* for *me. Nothing to do with a corpus: only*
> *some bodies.*
>
> ROLAND BARTHES, *CAMERA LUCIDA*

> *A photograph is only a fragment, and with the passage of time its*
> *moorings come unstuck. It drifts away into a soft abstract pastness,*
> *open to any kind of reading.*
>
> SUSAN SONTAG, *ON PHOTOGRAPHY*

This book began as a study of images; it started as an attempt to understand my personal fascination with a specific type of image production—the visual matter of cyberdating. But the more I indulged my obsession, the more futile were my attempts at any serious structural analysis, as the catalog of images kept expanding. The inventory continued to grow as new participants joined the fray of the online dating network, and those already participating updated or added to their photo albums. Confronted by this ever-widening array, my attention began to drift to the more generalizable and inherently meaningful aspects that exist beyond photographic practice or close textual analysis—the temporal and existential underpinnings that seem to ground the musings of both Roland Barthes and Susan Sontag. After all, within my study, an image was simply an appendage to a profile; more pointedly, it belonged to a trail of signifiers that led back to an individual and was in fact shaped by that individual's psychology. Each marker was not simply a physiognomic trace, but part of a psychological profile. What I found most interesting were not the images themselves, but their orientation. Why did the individual choose this particular image? Why did he or she use this construction of selfhood? Each answer revealed intentionality, even when there did not seem to be a conscious attention to detail.

The question of consciousness leads me to reflect on the variability of the gaze, to consider how we view ourselves and how we view others. Particular social spaces call forth particular forms of gazing; that is to say that context often privileges certain social practices over others, making them more likely, and to suggest that the gaze is not simply self-motivated. Structural analysis is difficult here as well, as the very variability of the gaze suggests it is difficult to speak about a universal experience. Gazing itself is a historically and culturally situated practice; to attend to the gaze is to consider the broader history of cultural influence as well as the narrower incidence of social activities buried within such a generalized chronology. The microsituation may call forth a particular system of signs and reading strategies, a nuance lost in (and perhaps against the grain of) the history of things.

Tourism as Metaphor and Practice

Despite my wholehearted investment in the images that I survey, I often feel like a tourist. But rather than understand my fascination as empty (or worse, exploitative) voyeurism, I embrace tourism as a metaphor for my experience. John Urry opens his study of the tourist gaze by suggesting that tourism, far from being a trivial subject or enterprise, "is significant in its ability to reveal aspects of normal practices that might otherwise remain opaque."[1] Like the typical tourist, I collect signs, and my engagement, as a scholarly activity, positions these fragments as separate from everyday experience, despite the fact that they may form a dynamic part of someone else's life. By attending to the minutiae of everyday life, my goal in this book is to move toward transparency. By opening up overlooked and rather commonplace practices to more deliberate scrutiny, we may begin to understand the social constructs, cultural patterns, and behaviors that structure our lives and birth particular subject positions. I choose to consider cultural practices that are messy; throughout this manuscript, I tackle several distinct activities that depend on media artifacts, but my attention remains largely on praxis, on action itself, a matter that cannot be summed up by a catalog of objects. The objects of my analysis are dynamic, and therefore often exceed their objecthood, circulating but not always existing as fixed commodities; I tend to focus on phenomena and ephemera.

The concept of dynamism returns me to the subject of time, the somewhat romantic or perhaps nostalgic notion of "passage" and "drift" found in the excerpt from Susan Sontag's work at the head of this chapter. Indeed, my reading is inevitably informed by my own nostalgia and personal history. I can trace my engagement with photography back to my role as family photographer during summer vacations in the seventies. I willingly embraced the task, toting my trusty Polaroid OneStep to national parks and monuments across the United States, posing members of my clan in front of token landmarks—the Grand Canyon, Mount Rushmore, Old Faithful. Though my photos have long since turned deep shades of blue, I am still enthralled with these relics of my youth and their shifting evidentiary status—at once a record of a fixed geographic region, a marker of my family's travels, a testament to our conquest of the great frontier, a cultural trace of a decade, a document of each family member during a particular past moment and, on close inspection, a map of our interpersonal dynamics. Perhaps my fascination with images formed over those summers in the seventies, as I longingly watched the chemicals of overheated instant film develop into an exquisite corpus. Fixed in the album, the images do not necessarily speak directly about conflict, typical family strife, the growing disinterest of teenagers in the matter of family vacations, torturous hours spent on the road sandwiched between siblings, or the occasional stench of antifreeze wafting from the overheating engine of the maroon Chevrolet station wagon. But temporality (and, for that matter, spatiality) is not altogether eclipsed by visuality; in fact, my memory may be enhanced by these images, even if it is made over by them. The flat surface of the Polaroid print yields a profound sense of space (the geometric contours of the automobile's interior in contrast to the vast exterior of the western frontier) and activates senses beyond vision (the trace of a dissipating odor in the breeze).

I include this particular autobiographical aside because the focus of this book is on transience and by extension its inverse, which might best be understood as momentary stasis. Transience and stasis seem to describe the conflicted nature of the emerging subject, moving simultaneously toward and away from parental law. Indeed, throughout this text I often return to the family frame, as it is one of the more common forms of prescription. Beyond subjectivity, however, the dueling states of transience and stasis are intertwined explicitly in the matter of technological mediation. We see this in instant photography—both in the physical substrate (the chemicals of film stock) and in whatever contents these chemicals are asked to reproduce. Polaroid, for example, actively exploits a fascination with seeing an otherwise inscrutable semiotic formula—watching sign becoming referent; as the film stock approximates its portrait, becoming yields to being. Despite this apparent fixity, there is a less-visible return toward entropy as the images, lodged in the archive of the family photo album, start to decay while hidden from view. Yet even as they decay, these images still operate as placeholders, and they seem to shirk the subject of transience, displacing it onto their long-passed referents. The events, once so fresh, have moved further and further away from the present moment, and the experience of an image's once-visible state of becoming has long since been eclipsed, replaced by other comings and goings. The photograph is tinged with nostalgia and begins to serve less a purely evidentiary purpose and instead a more romantic function, fixing certain qualities of lived experience but losing others. Its "wow" factor, once a function of a physical process (what chemicals can do), is now attached to a mental process; the mechanics of imaging become subservient to the machinations of memory, yet synesthesia seems too grand a term for what might be a more limited evocation of sensory experience brought on by the still image.

Though I engage with the study of images in this book, my goal is not simply to talk about images, but rather to discuss what they reveal about looking—not in the abstract, but with regard to looking as an embodied term. It seems, therefore, that my interest is in getting down to basics, to explore subjectivity by critically examining the look. Perhaps this is not entirely new terrain, as certainly more than one writer has engaged with looking and with subjectivity. But my focus is on a particular form of looking and of subjectivity made possible through new technology. Indeed, my aim is to meld these terms together by exploring what I call the "life technobiographic"—the life written through technology and approximated by a data trail (a rich record of subjective presence). Technobiography implies a particular form of authorship and calls for an understanding of how the self is situated within social relations that inherently involve engaging with information technologies. I am less concerned with story (the technobiographic artifact) than I am with narrative (the technobiographic process). At the same time, I am not invoking a cyborg arrangement (of classical fusion or postclassical virtualization), nor am I engaging with explicitly cybernetic systems of feedback and self-regulation. Instead, I am attempting to make calm technologies more frenetic. We need to bring technology to the foreground, if only momentarily, to understand the implications of integrating it into everyday life. By speaking of the life technobiographic, I am articulating the manner in which subjectivity is transformed by new technologies, for those very same technologies impact how we translate everyday events into a knowledge system. Subjectivities, knowledges, and technologies are always situated; they all can be appropriated, rehistoricized, and read anew.[2] By linking technology to biography, I am acknowledging the fundamental power of enunciation. To approximate the life technobiographic, we might begin by "googling" ourselves, gathering every self-inflected node. This will produce a rather abstract portrait, allowing us to see how diffuse we have become, determined as we are to infiltrate networked space. Here, diffusion is a sign of success. Then, we might move on to examine our smart devices and consider the personal preferences that we have used to imprint ourselves on them. After that, we might study our more nuanced interactions with the interfaces we encounter every day—recording, communicating, producing, consuming, and transacting. Still, taken together, these tactics, this sum total of signs, will not speak the technobiographic subject. There is more work to do, and these signs are merely symptomatic of a process (of mutual inflection). The concept of authorship is culturally relative. Any singular biographic tactic must be read against the varied modes of referential self-expression that are practiced in contemporary culture.[3] Furthermore, in an age of pervasive computing, we must also read biography against the dominant forms of technological projection and consider how technology too is practiced.

As transiency suggests a trajectory, however overtly purposeful (set in motion by biological or mechanical physics), as a study of the phenomenon, my emphasis is on becoming, as well as on one particular form of rupture along what otherwise might be a rather formulaic path—trauma. Catastrophic trauma shatters norms, overwhelms the psychic system, and often produces fractured subjects. As a media scholar, I evaluate media and media events as deconstructive and reconstructive agents, and agency is most clearly accessed (at least from the critic's vantage point) during moments of failed (or flailing) subjectivity.

The formation of subjectivity suggests a movement through a landscape at once psychological and geographical, and these two aspects can be mapped together along a chronological axis. My study of transient images is a form of tourism, and I return to the term both to acknowledge my critical distance and to restate my approach—reading images. While our attention is often drawn only to our own movements as we journey about the world, images too have a life of their own. Images are subjected to similar movements; they are asked to take on different functions as they move across the terrain. I am interested in the life of images, and intend to consider what their movement tells us about our own desires. In this respect, I too am a tourist; I take on this role as I survey the field and encounter a catalog of images, some of which I am more attached to than others.

The image is a semiotic phenomenon, a poetic record that produces a powerful form of knowledge. It is this very form of transcription (the image as a knowledge system) that Jonathan Culler describes when he argues that the tourist gaze transforms things into complex sign systems, aligned with the real but also imbued with an ideality that informs reality, making it figural. Culler privileges tourism as a field of analysis, for it can provide significant insight into sign relations.[4] My analysis of these relations is not aligned with Jean Baudrillard's influential account of the simulacrum, a rather melancholic view that speaks about the emptying out of meaning and the collapse of stable referents. Rather than attempting to secure the real for its own sake,

I instead follow Gilles Deleuze's account of the simulacrum in *Difference and Repetition*, where the play of the real is important only insofar as it informs any studied attention to identity. Deleuze studies the interplay of his titular terms, repetition and difference, divorced from any melancholic attribution. While Baudrillard follows one trail of simulations, Deleuze chooses another. Baudrillard considers systems of mediation that drift from a singular reference point; he mourns the translation of the world into a semiotic system. Deleuze pushes further, considering the impact of systems of mediation on identity; as such, his analysis is less historical (less attached to the forward movement of history) and perhaps more temperamental (subject to the complexities of subject formation). I am interested in what we do with images; to this end, I am not interested in developing an exhaustive catalog of images but, more pointedly, I offer up several revealing case studies of postproduction praxis.

There is a long tradition of scholarly inquiry into photographic practice; the medium and its object lessons have become a transdisciplinary enterprise, sometimes serving simply as a checkpoint on a larger critical agenda. Following such a discursive path, in *Understanding Media*, Marshall McLuhan tackles a rather broad range of media forms, and as he attempts to illustrate the self-consciousness of the photographic age (the development of what he terms "gestalt culture"), he turns to the following example: "To see a photograph of the local slum makes the condition unbearable. The mere matching of the picture with reality provides a new motive for change, as it does a new motive for travel."[5] This narrative suggests two possible responses—fight or flight. At the same time, it suggests that the optical realm is not a value-neutral terrain, but instead one with decided consequence. The photograph can give concrete form to social categories; however, the process by which it does so is complex and refractive. Oftentimes, action of any sort is superseded by debate over the status of the image. The search for authenticity can be paralyzing.

When nostalgia is invoked in popular discussions of new technology, it suggests a critical position that mourns the loss of authentic experience; and the most common inflection extends this concept of authenticity to speak about the loss of interiority (of personal authenticity) in contemporary life. The refrain here is that commodities yield inauthentic forms of knowledge. Yet to focus on commercialization is to overlook the specific machinations of the culture industry (and perhaps to assume that capitalist exploitation is intrinsic to the operation of contemporary media forms) and to consider in only the most abstract way the link between capitalism and consciousness.[6]

A Preliminary Study in Transience

To move closer to the subject of transience and to illustrate how the term operates in everyday life, I turn to three industrial signs. Each taps the term for its metaphoric power and, by extension, highlights its decided conceptual weight. Our lives are truly saturated by transiency.

In the first instance, consider Kodak. With the rise of the U.S. automobile culture in the early 1920s, Kodak found a way to associate the nascent pleasures of motoring with the joys of amateur photography, born at the end of the previous century.[7] To court the newly mobile consumer, Kodak sent its advertising representatives on a field trip; the company's scouts toured the country's most traveled highways seeking out picturesque views. After their survey was completed, six thousand small signs were erected alongside the nation's roadways to alert travelers that there was a photo opportunity ahead; each exclaimed, "Picture Ahead! Kodak as you go."[8] The slogan effectively turned the company brand into an activity. By the mid-1930s, the typical American vacation involved car travel, and automobile tourism and picture taking became fast friends. Motoring shaped the experience of the landscape for travelers in search of picturesque views; and like the snapshot, driving allowed them to collapse time and explore the world both as a flow and as a series of fragments.[9] But driving also changed what people saw and how they made pictures, for the view from the road and the challenges of its topography were unique; moreover, the journey itself was in part the product of strategic land reclamation. Traffic flowed along the highways and byways that were sanctioned by the Federal Highway Act of 1921 and funded by various federal and state initiatives that followed in subsequent decades. In a symbiotic arrangement, tourists used the highways that in turn made tourist areas accessible.

In the second instance, consider Polaroid, the company that launched the instant camera revolution. Edwin Land, the founder of Polaroid, demonstrated his first camera with self-developing film in 1947 and released the consumer-ready Polaroid Land Camera Model 95 at the end of the following year. In 1972, the company revamped its film process, developing the now-familiar integral print film system with the launch of its SX-70 camera. Popular reports suggest the newly developed process owed its existence to Lady Bird Johnson, wife of President Lyndon B. Johnson. Responding to the First Lady's concern over the growing volume of trash in the country's national parks, Polaroid invented a tidier picture process that eliminated the need for the expended pull tab of its original film. With nothing to pull, the self-contained cartridge also eliminated the need for any intervention from the photographer. The June 26, 1972 issue of *Time* broke the story with its cover

Kodak courts the bourgeoning
tourism industry during the
first part of the twentieth
century by actively framing
the nation's roadways and
engaging with nascent
automobile culture.
(Ellis Collection—Item
#K0485. Duke University
Rare Book, Manuscript, and
Special Collections Library.
http://library.duke.edu/
digitalcollections/eaa/)

image of Land framed by the now-ubiquitous white rectangular mat, an
iconic shape that would become part of Polaroid's legacy. The frame that
bounds the emulsion sets each image off from the world around it in a uniform fashion; the effect is of a rather remarkable aesthetic coherence, at least
at first glance, as every image has the same shape and each a ceremoniously
bounded sense of interiority. The shallow picture box of a frame serves a
practical purpose by forming part of the envelope that contains the film's
caustic gel; in this respect, it binds. But the frame also serves the inverse function of dispersion by providing a space to write and a place to hold the print
(and pass it among friends); in this regard, too, the frame undoes the object's
sense of interiority by encouraging connection and dialogue. Despite the public's fascination with the Polaroid image, the movement to digital photography
ultimately undid the company's leadership in the "now" of instant analog imaging, and in early February 2008, Polaroid announced it was discontinuing
the manufacture of instant film and would be turning its attention to the digital market.[10]

In the third instance, consider Nikon. With the launch of its D40 camera,
Nikon began an applied advertising campaign in May 2007. The print ad tells

Nikon turns Georgetown, South Carolina into its first Picturetown.
(http://www.stunningnikon.com, accessed November 15, 2007; site now revised)

the tale: "People start taking amazing pictures when you hand them the Nikon D40. To prove it, we gave 200 of them to the people of Georgetown, SC. Check out the pictures and see how a whole town was transformed at stunningnikon.com/picturetown." In its approach, Nikon seemed to be engaged in a sincere attempt to move beyond empty rhetoric, providing evidence to back up its pitch. In celebrating the results of its intervention, Nikon dubbed the city "Picturetown," which shaped Georgetown into a fantastical realm. This corporate makeover dwells in the surface of things, shaping a decided place into a series of picture-perfect signifiers offset by white picket fences. Georgetown is introduced as an idyllic yet typical small town in Nikon's video portrait, which frames the Web site's story. The video paints a portrait of diversity that cuts across boundaries of race and class and offers footage that speaks of community and togetherness, producing the neighborhood barbershop, the town hall, the local playground, and the small town fire department, showcasing people gathered at work and at play. And the site speaks of engagement, of civic action, to the point that it erases the world of private consumption and privatized media. One participant remarks: "It's been fun as a parent. We shut off the TV, grab the camera, go outside, and enjoy nature."

The Nikon campaign began as a traditionally empty advertising trope, with the company speaking about the power of photography and, in fact, about empowering a community, but nestling that community neatly inside the campaign's discursive boundaries. Beyond these boundaries, the discourse of empowerment seems to be superseded by one of facile consumption; it is perhaps stating the obvious to suggest that Nikon takes on this civic project in order to promote camera sales, and in particular to expand the digital single lens reflex (SLR) market (with digital SLR cameras seemingly too complex for everyday use, the goal is to make them less intimidating). Nikon melds the old and the new, mapping the latest advances in digital technology onto the most traditional notions of community, and suggests that even ordinary people can take the most extraordinary of pictures. And indeed, following through with this suggestion, in August 2007, Nikon reached through the gates of its planned community to launch "my Picturetown," a free public photo sharing and storage site.

Kodak, Polaroid, and Nikon exhibit a shared concern for distinct yet related aspects of transience. In the case of Kodak, the photographic mile marker is a form of punctuation in otherwise boundless terrain; it yields momentary rupture by producing temporary stasis. Not only do we stop the car to take the picture but also we introduce crop marks on an otherwise infinite horizon line and collapse the road trip into a quantifiable number of signs. Movement is reduced to a semiotic trace.

Polaroid's instant imaging technologies tell a different tale of transience. Here, fixity itself is experienced; it is transformed into a physical process, and our interest in seeing things through the viewfinder is matched by our fascination with seeing the very mechanics of the imaging process. We freeze time and watch it congeal.

Lastly, Nikon embraces transience by enabling the flow of images; indeed, the company suggests that electronic photo sharing is part of our civic duty. It enables and transforms; photographs move and communities materialize and evolve. Yet the goal of sharing, at least when channeled through Picturetown, seems to be rather absolutist; the photo-sharing network is built on a foundational myth (the Eden of Nikon's Georgetown) that is itself counterintuitive to community. To this end, the Web venture is built on a fallacy. The more public venture of Picturetown follows through with the ontological claims of Nikon's capital city—a planned community that serves as an imagined and ever-present limit, a testament to solidarity and diversity, and a yardstick for future community development. Georgetown has been repurposed as an ideal of communion.

Distillation is an ontological process discussed repeatedly in critical examinations of photographic practice. Sontag suggests that with the passage of time, a photograph loses its specificity to become a purely aesthetic object, while Barthes suggests that a photograph can do little more than confirm the existence of an object at some other time. But distillation is also an enterprise and therefore speaks to desire, however real or constructed the need. Whether or not the photograph can actually stand in as a memory image, it can serve as a practical mnemonic aid. We want the image to be an active part of the narrative of memory, even if this desire is simply fleeting (an impulse that drives us to take the image, even if we are only to forget about it later). Though photography is part of commodity culture and may be complicit with traditional economies of circulation (always under the laws of capitalism), it is nonetheless a highly charged psychic endeavor and, as participants in this exchange, we seem to want to insist on the authentic nature of its rituals and the ceremonies it serves to condense, even as we acknowledge our rampant idealism.

Transience and the Traumatized Subject

Let me return to one of the quotations that opens this book, which was left as a dangling modifier of sorts. In his seminal investigation of photography and photographic knowledge, Roland Barthes examines his fascination with a few select images in an attempt to arrive at a universal truth of the general field of photographic objecthood. Yet his very aversion to a science of the image leads him to focus on the state of fascination itself. Reinscribing fascination as an "internal agitation," Barthes comes to understand his preference for particular photographs, identifying those images that give birth to certain interferences that mark the intersection of two forces—what Barthes refers to as the *studium* and the *punctum*. The *studium* emerges from the reader's cultural consciousness and explains the spectator's attraction to the image, exposes its cultural relevance, and is inherently bound to the historical field. The *punctum*, conversely, emerges from the field of the image itself.[11] It is a detail grounded in the visual narrative, but it jogs the memory and carries in it the "power of expansion."[12] It penetrates the cultural layer while moving beyond the immediacy of the detail from which it arises and escaping the coded nature of things. While an image may distill experience and posit an incomplete and unsatisfying fixity, the *punctum* indeed reopens the image to presentness and addresses its incompleteness head-on; stasis yields to transience. Barthes found Polaroid images "fun, but disappointing," and one wonders whether his dissatisfaction is due to the failure of instant photography to maintain the distance between spatial immediacy and temporal anteriority (a distinction that figures significantly into Barthes's suggestion that photography invokes a unique consciousness).[13] The sense of an object's "having-been-there" is undone by an image that materializes in the same space and time as the object it represents.

Paralleling Barthes's study, which moves from the few to the many and from the personal to the social, this volume examines several distinct sites of cultural production, each of which functions here toward the larger goal of considering the role of new media in articulating the public sphere within selected constructions of identity (national, communal, consumer, or otherwise). Each image referenced in this text gains its significance from an attachment to a specific cultural field and practice; at the same time, however, these images speak to the reader's memory as more-obscure curiosities.

Yet memory too occurs within a fixed cultural terrain, and it may be naive to assume that the *punctum* provides a point of exit or escape; it may be as overdetermined as its counterpart. While Susan Sontag reflects on the photograph's slow but steady temporal trajectory, which inevitably leads to a certain "unmooring," she throws out of focus any attention to the relative fixity of subjectivity, itself moored by certain cultural predispositions that reattach the free-floating signifier of the photograph in rather finite ways. And more significantly, Sontag overstates the narrative possibilities of the photographic record and retreats to tell the tale of the power of interpretation, which is itself about narrative but which inherently leaves the photograph behind to do something more or otherwise. Sontag suggests: "Those occasions when the taking of photographs is relatively undiscriminating, promiscuous, or self-effacing do not lessen the didacticism of the whole enterprise. This very passivity—and ubiquity—of the photographic record is photography's 'message,' its aggression."[14]

Photographs do not have a uniform grammar and, perhaps acknowledging this, Sontag locates their meaning in the conditions of either the reading or the recording and the "attitude" present in either moment. But she clings to the notion that this attitude will manifest itself inside the image's borders.

In this volume, I seek to elaborate on the nature of the photographic frame and its relation to the interpretive practices that follow. This is perhaps simply a difference in attention. At the end of their arguments, Sontag and Barthes seem to be intrigued, perhaps haunted, by visual images, and enamored by their affect. My goal is to put the frame back in focus—to examine the framing devices that provide the syntax for images—with attention to those narrative frameworks that are manufactured some time after the image. I use the term "manufactured" here to suggest that the frameworks at the center of my analysis are not simply reading strategies but a whole host of other predeterminations, "physical" constructs that play a syntactical role. It is the constructs that give the images their psychical weight.

What links all of the chapters in *Transient Images* is an interest in examining how media technologies activate particular notions of self and community, and an investment in articulating the means by which a given technological apparatus may be domesticated and ideologically charged. To do so, I undertake an analysis of transitory images that move between public and private and are articulated as such; by studying this process, best understood as a movement, either physical or psychical, I aim to reveal the general processes of inscription by which images take on meaning or through which acquired meanings are discarded and meaning shifts. Meaning is a temporary vestment for these artifacts. Pierre Bourdieu suggests that the psychological explanation of photographic engagement is insufficient; to account for photography as a practice and to understand its rhythms, we must also attend to sociological accounts of production, distribution, and reception.[15] As images move, they become systems of exchange. The transient image serves a greater purpose than (personal) meditation; it is an object of (social) integration. Photography, Bourdieu suggests, is a technology for reiteration; repurposing and restating their evidence, the hardest-working images create a social contract.[16]

I use the notion of transience to evoke movement of a specific sort, a series of stops and starts that elicits rupture. While images may be actively circulated, they are just as often forgotten or discarded, lost in an archive as static relics yet still imbued with the potential to be repurposed and sent back into circulation. I draw a loose distinction between continuous and discontinuous transience (with the latter being my primary concern). Continuous transience is characterized by gradual, linear change of either decay or accretion, whereas discontinuous transience is abrupt and irregular in its transformations, and is marked by fragmentation and impulsive synthesis (aligning it with the pathological discourse of trauma).[17] For this reason, I find theories of trauma useful in considering subjectivity in the digital age because what I am describing is a landscape where fracture is the norm. Trauma theory informs the first four chapters of this book, as these case studies are most explicitly about trauma—both traumatic events and traumatized subjects. And while I move from photography to videography and then to broadcast television and to mobile and Internet-based communications technologies, I skirt the matter of medium specificity. For in the field of trauma and, more pointedly, within the terrain of new media, the multiple and varied frames of moving images are collapsed into single signifiers that acquire a certain object status, in part because they are leveled by the process of digitization. This process makes them register with a certain equivalence. Videography becomes a videographic trace and television a televisual one. The embedded movement of the moving image assumes a form of stasis; what is privileged is the life of the object. Like photographs, videos are something to be exchanged; as we share them, they clearly acquire an object status, even in the most virtual of spaces (as torrents or self-contained and embedded files). However, in this volume, I am acutely attentive to the unique features of any embedded context, better understood as the frame of the apparatus (of distribution and reception, of device and interface), even as distinct media elements become things simply to be shared and whose meaning lies outside of their objecthood, defined by the nature of sharing. The act of exchange is accompanied by the act of translation, and although the process is situated and individualized, it is also collectively mediated; translation is a cultural practice. And as cultural practices commonly rely on material goods and services, we must also consider the varied operational limits of the citizen-consumer in social, political, and economic discourse. The citizen-consumer performs through commodities, choosing and often exceeding them, yet this subject always does so in relation to both a local and a global field and as part of a complex interaction between the two processes of consumption and citizenship.

Desire in Narrative: The Subject of Trauma

Fear is a response that is intimately bound to transience, for beyond the transient image, transiency is a matter of the human condition. The loss of a unified textuality is echoed in the loss of a unified subject position, and this experience gains greater momentum in an age of hypermedia. Psychoanalytic case histories have demonstrated how difficult it is for some to relinquish control over time to the objective world and to admit that time proceeds with or without us; for these individuals, acknowledging the sovereignty of time is experienced as dangerous. Such an acknowledgment threatens the individual with the reexperiencing of early traumatic separations and the resurgence of desires that are inherently beyond the control of the ego. This difficulty, by its very nature, reminds us that a certain amount of narcissistic renunciation is needed to reconcile the concept of objective time. Within this framework, the transient image satisfies a psychic need; the tragedy of our transience disappears from the field of view, however momentarily, as we study the image. This act, as a particular form of dissociation, carries much the same weight as forms of the mechanism that are more broadly defined; dissociation in general allows disavowal and enables individuals to steadfastly hold on to a set of beliefs. The dissociative effect is defensive and may depersonalize ("this isn't about me, it's about someone else") or derealize ("this isn't real") an event or experience. Unfortunately, the effect leads to a certain compartmentalization, to a constructed subjective experience of personal reality and of the self—in clinical terms, understood as the possible development of a pronounced psychopathology. Yet, at the other end, through treatment and synthesis, dissociation may serve a healing function by permitting the development of restorative fantasies that help to redress and undo traumatic psychic injuries.

Trauma theory concerns itself with the unconscious meaning of actual traumatic events and the relative success of restorative fantasies. The goal of psychoanalytic therapy is to unite the pieces of the shattered self, to reconstitute traditional central organizing fantasies of selfhood. While I draw from trauma theory in the first half of this book, as a media scholar, I am more concerned with analyzing a series of objects in their respective cultural fields than I am with the intricacies of treatment and recovery. Nonetheless, I am concerned with fantasy; but rather than turning to psychoanalysis, I draw from narrative theory to more rigorously examine the operation of desire and its relative freedom. Narratology aims to describe the specific system of rules that presides over both the production and processing of narratives and, by extension, to understand the rule-governed ways in which human beings refashion their universe. Narratology exemplifies the structuralist ambition to isolate the necessary and optional components of textual types and to characterize the modes of their articulation. Narratives are found and stories are told in a variety of media and can be transposed from medium to medium. Though narratology in its purest sense argues that the narrative component of a text can and should be studied without reference to the medium in which it occurs, as a media theorist, I am equally invested in reading the formal attributes of the medium in which the narrative activity unfolds because the medium may promote certain forms of narrative coding over others. While traditional narratology—research aligned more closely with the linguistic work of Ferdinand de Saussure and the structuralist pursuits of Claude Levi-Strauss—is devoted to story rather than discourse structure, a number of contemporary theorists such as Mieke Bal have attempted to integrate the study of content and form, an approach that, in Bal's case, reflects her interest in interdisciplinary studies.

Contemporary studies of narrative also have moved beyond more purely structural conceits to consider the context in which narratives occur, taking into account the situation that partly determines their shape and contributes to their meaning, and addressing the pragmatic factors that partly govern their functioning. In this manner, narrative has come to be understood not simply as a product but also as a process. Taking this synthetic approach to narrative, this book locates myth contextually. Yet context should be understood not only as a social setting in which a reading is performed but also as an interface, a formal location from which a reading is extracted. And the interface itself may present the reader with multiple media, each with its own narrative logic.

Transient Images studies the assumptions that underpin the exhibition of personal images, occasional photographs, and amateur video in public domains such as the Internet and considers fundamental questions of community and nation, of public and private, in order to produce a social history that binds together production, distribution, exhibition, and reception. Though this volume aims to understand the movement across these terms, the focus is on exhibition, the most visible of these practices. Close textual analysis provides an appropriate entry point as I am attempting to align my own critical work with the more commonplace and subtle reading practices that inscribe these bodies of evidence. To this end, I am largely concerned with reading the technologies that contain personal photographs and videos; in a Foucauldian framework, these technologies can be understood as social practices that are inevitably implicated in power dynamics, even as they are practices that people enact upon themselves.

Images can be subjected to an array of institutional imperatives, but people also subject images to their own ideologically inflected gazes. For this reason, I am also concerned with reading the images themselves, to the extent that they inform my efforts to identify the structuring tendencies that bear on exhibition and, inevitably, on reception. Scholars such as Patricia Zimmermann and Marianne Hirsch have explored the manner in which select photographic practices, particularly those framed by the family circle, may be infused with the ideologies of domesticity. As I extend these arguments into the terrain of new media, I am not attempting to develop an essential opposition between technologies of representation. Rather, I am interested in articulating the ongoing ability of the cultural field to regulate the use of successive technologies, and I am accepting a certain historical dialectic between mediums for self-representation or home modes. The strength of Zimmermann's and Hirsch's scholarship is their understanding of the ideological assumptions embedded in photographic practices and, in Hirsch's case, her focused attention to strategies for resistance, for using photographs in ways that interrupt the dominant ideological project of cultural myths. Both scholars utilize more or less historically situated models, understanding ideology as something that is not static. Yet Zimmermann and Hirsch nostalgically evoke a period of coding activity—of particular photographic practices—that although not precisely dated is still loosely contoured within certain imagined limits of the very nature of the family photograph; they make reference to a fairly fixed mythology of the family. As such, these models may be less useful for examining specific shifts in the cultural field, where home no longer has the same resonance, the familial has been complicated beyond its adjectival inscription as nuclear, and the images that can be attached to domestic life are more varied in their form.

The primary focus of this volume is not the ontologies of varied visual practices and technologies; however, some review is undertaken of the critical, popular, and industrial discourses that draw distinctions between, for example, photography and videography. This is done as part of an effort to tackle the larger topic of the technological imaginary—cultural projections that shape and sometimes delimit what a technology can and should do in any given historical moment. My attention is drawn to terms and frameworks that are more all-encompassing and central to discourses of the technological imaginary, such as community, identity, family, and nation, as well as to categories more obviously grounded in affect, such as desire, trauma, and fear. Yet cultural projections are not simply affective categories; they are part of an industrial complex, a new plug-in for the all-too-familiar machinations of the culture industry. I use the term "plug-in" purposefully because the landscape charted in this text is one in constant flux and under the sway of a movement toward the computerization (or simply digitization) of culture. This is not a paranoid musing about the digital divide, and I do not operate under the assumption that we can draw a steadfast distinction between visual culture and digital culture as unique enterprises. Indeed, it is the continuities that are explored throughout this text, as new technologies and industries are put in the service of familiar and long-standing ideological imperatives—the newness of new technologies does not necessarily lead to a ground shift in ideology. This is not to suggest that radical thinking is impossible, but only that it is more difficult to isolate because the industrial terrain itself is evolving at light speed, suturing over any apparent ruptures in the surface of things.

Transient Images is therefore a series of readings that highlight those claims that seem to persist despite more obvious changes in the order of things. I begin in Chapter 1 by considering fear as a construct that shapes new technologies. The specific objects are images of missing children, but the larger project is to understand the mechanics of fear production and to connect practices to industrial and social discourses, for exchange is not simply a social phenomenon; it is also a matter of commerce. Looking backward on photographic practice, Jonathan Crary notes: "Photography and money become homologous forms of social power in the nineteenth century. They are equally totalizing systems for binding and unifying all subjects within a single global network of valuation and desire."[18] The abstract relations set in motion within this economy of exchange are still at play; the social world is persistently reconstituted through an evolving series of signs. Visuality, once the domain of science in the age of the camera obscura, has become increasingly mobile and exchangeable, taking truth along with it.[19] To this end, new technology, far from being a matter of invention, can only be understood as an ideological enterprise.

Technology has been a subject of great debate concerning our hopes, fears, and anxieties, and the most common concerns of the digital age center on technologically enabled forms of theft: identity theft, fraud, information loss, hacking, and viruses. These are all virtual losses, aspects of the fiduciary subject. But what of the more troubling thought of physical abduction? Here,

the threat of violence off-line is inevitably connected to the virtual world—
the ever-present paranoia about a crime that may happen (abduction as a
virtual mental construct) and the role that new technologies might play in
linking predators with victims (the virtual presence of imagined predatory
communities that materialize in online communiqués).

Yet, at the same time that technologies are read as unlawful tools for
criminal mischief, they are also positioned as a great new hope, as tools to
dole out justice. One need look no further than NBC's *Dateline: To Catch a
Predator,* a program that alerts viewers to the presence of online sexual predators and at the same time uses the tools and tactics of electronic communication and surveillance to battle criminal conduct. The dystopic and utopic
discourses about new technology converge in the *Dateline* narrative, as we
are at once alerted to the dangers of cyberspace yet told a tale in which technology is deployed as a productive social instrument. Technologies may in-
spire anxiety and fear, but they also carry the promise of salvation.

Chapters 2 and 3 develop one of the underlying assumptions that grounds
the first chapter: the persistence of narrative. The mechanics of fear production provide a useful engine for the generation of larger narrative impulses,
and in Chapters 2 and 3, I examine two distinct tales of terror(ism) that have
been used to reenergize the myth of nationhood. Chapter 2 treats the issue at
a more local level, tracing the echoes that emanated from the September 11,
2001, crash sites. While the events of that day are of international importance, my analysis is limited to a particular media flow—the movement of
images from the streets of Manhattan to the virtual field of CNN's online
missing persons database. Chapter 3 shifts to a more consciously global scale,
linking a series of events and flows from around the world—moving from the
gallows of Kazimain, Iraq, to the transit tunnels of the London underground.
The focus here is on more egregious forms of mobility and the courting of the
mobile consumer. Both Chapters 2 and 3 examine the use-value of cultural
memories and the manner that trauma facilitates the subjugation of the
subject to history; the intent is to consider the stakes involved in this scripting
of memory. Public trauma facilitates the movement of personal documents
into public space, relating the subjects of representation to each other and to
the viewer in a manner that ultimately exceeds the subjectivity of either subject or viewer, and pushing us rather blindly toward communion.

Perhaps I am simply following through with a project undertaken by
Michel Foucault in *The Order of Things,* his most fervent critique of the con-
stitutive limits of discourse (which, he contends, is guided by historically situated epistemes). Foucault's study leads him to ask why we persistently turn to
certain modalities of order to make sense of everyday life. This volume iso-
lates several contemporary modalities and draws attention to the discourse in

order to reveal the rather selective deployment of new technologies and to consider the relative presence and value of alternatives. It does so by excavating the most sacred ground of resemblances, that of self-representation, for it is during those autobiographical moments (speaking out loud about or simply considering ourselves) that we most forcefully insert ourselves into the technological imaginary.

My approach to the matter of self-representation is influenced in part by a question posed by Philippe Lejeune in his seminal work, *On Autobiography*: "What special interest can there be in looking at a self-portrait?"[20] Expanding on this question, Lejeune reveals his own fascination with the object at the center of his query:

> For several years now, in the course of my visits, I have been seeking out self-portraits. Like everyone else, I have been struck by some of the series—that of Rembrandt, for example, scattered to the four corners of the world. At the same instant, at various ages, Rembrandt is looking at himself in Amsterdam, New York, Paris, Florence, in the eyes of hundreds of tourists. From one museum to another, they recognize him; he's an old friend. It's reassuring. We need to be reassured. We can never be too sure of what we're looking at in a museum.[21]

Though Lejeune privileges the value of the autobiographical pact in literature, and even doubts its reproducibility in media such as photography and film, he introduces a number of secondary concerns that are useful to this study. While my project moves beyond the immediate field of autobiography, the ancillary objects surveyed herein are part of the same exercise— elements that are part of a larger picture that illustrates society looking at itself. The value of assurance cannot be overstated, even when we find ourselves questioning the value of seeing images of other people. My students constantly ask me about motives. Why would someone post private images in a public forum? Why develop a publicly accessible blog (Web log) about one's personal obsessions? Is there a use-value that might explain our culture's willful embrace of (and rampant participation in) such private-to-public migrations? Under what conditions are such exchanges transformed into commodities?

To answer these questions, I turn my attention in Chapter 4 to *Intervention*, a reality series now in its ninth season on A&E. *Intervention* profiles people whose dependence on drugs and alcohol or other substances and behaviors has led them into personal crisis. The program makes rather liberal use of the family photo album, playing through a nostalgic photomontage (in search of an origin story that grounds the addictive persona) before navigating toward a final meeting with friends and family. Each episode continues past the confrontational climax, following these addicts as they move into and through recovery. Some succeed and others do not. *Intervention* raises the rather complex issue of motivations in a genre that is an already charged arena where private and public collide. The urgency of the tale of recovery rushes us by any deliberate attention to truth and reality, to the commercialization of the real, and to the contouring of lived experience to television's narrative economy. The stakes seem to be too high to allow such critical scrutiny or to argue about the integrity of what might be a heavy-handed dramatic construction. Yet *Intervention* calls our attention to the manner in which television (more properly understood as television viewing and the situation of television in everyday life) is often discussed as a social abstraction, as the program refuses to be understood as such. The pressing testimonial narrative cannot entirely shirk the uncertainty of its address. Who is benefiting here? Who is the principal subject of the intervention? In speaking to and about the addict, the addict's family, and the viewing public, the program positions the tale as both particular (an individual's story) and universal (positioning the addict as a statistic and a sum total of clinical facts), and it opens up difficult questions about observing and affect. There is an inherently troubling relay here that becomes all the more unsettling when one considers how trauma and addiction are intimately connected. It is fairly common for trauma to lead to addiction and for addiction to lead back to trauma. My analysis looks to answer what I consider a fairly urgent question. Does the program successfully open up the family circle and break the cycle of addiction? It seems that this particular narrative impulse, however benevolent or benignly governmental, might actually open up rather caustic psychic wounds.

On Difference: Making the Personal Public

With these stakes in mind, I seek to bridge the familial and social readings of photography and videography to follow personal images as they migrate outside their usual places of residence in photo albums and family rooms, on office desks and refrigerator doors. As images produced in the home circulate beyond its borders, they can expose cracks in the foundation of domestic architecture, but they can also signify something beyond the domestic; it is too prescriptive to always bind family photos and home videos back to their original contexts of production and consumption. I highlight this migratory process precisely because it leads to questions about the power dynamics evoked by relative positions of authority and ownership of the image, of imaging technologies, and of image interfaces. How is production socialized? How self-evident are the disciplinary methods at play? To what degrees are the processes of socialization unilaterally controlled? And whose desire is acted out in the process? I might pose these questions about power as a series of simple binaries that contrast the personal with the social, the private with the public, and the amateur with the professional. But these terms themselves are not useful for reading contradictory relations as processes; they are too static and seem to evoke an *a priori* system of correlatives that makes no allowances for dialecticism and potential transgression or for thinking historically. The general pathway I am tracing is the movement of images from personal spaces to public ones, though these public spaces are oftentimes privately controlled. Perhaps these polarities are better understood as relative positions inside and outside a market economy that urges us to adopt rather homogeneous codes of production. What are the varied commercial practices that frame personal images, and what tensions develop when private photos enter the flow of commerce, subjected to its hegemonic push? To what degree do the commercial imperatives of privately owned, publicly viewable exhibition venues constrain personal images, making them less-open texts by attaching them to new narrative threads? The moments of image production and site/venue construction are remote from each other, both temporally and physically. What is lost and what is gained when the personal image re-emerges in its new context? And why do the manufacturers of secondary image spaces use the rhetoric of community and personal agency to describe their sites and services? Is free play merely a trope?

Different uses of photography and videography suggest different degrees of ideological containment or the "successful" channeling of desire within a governing framework of value following prescribed formal criteria. *Transient Images* takes the form of a number of case studies, "some bodies" that represent what I perceive to be the most notable degree points of such containment. To this end, I am concerned about the possibility of acting out, a possibility that seems increasingly limited as media monopolies take on new heights of vertical integration and as our reading strategies become more institutionally driven (even if it is impossible to institutionalize all avenues of social action within any given system).[22]

Though the devices for acting out—the software and hardware—are themselves the end products of corporate research and development, we should not accept industry rhetoric as evidence of an inescapable and decidedly hegemonic process. Critical work can be accomplished by exploiting the gap between the personal and the public; certain desires can be liberated in this border crossing. There are striking parallels between the battle invoked in the identity politics of the text (as producers choose among formal strategies) and the battle invoked in the general field of identity politics.

What categories of images are privileged enough to move? How exactly do they move, why do they move, and what happens as they move? My goal is to arrive at an understanding of certain migratory patterns; perhaps these form yet another discursive structure with its own distinctive grammar. This would suggest that migration has an evidentiary purpose and is not simply a product of chaos.

Reclaiming the Subject: Narratives of Excess and Recovery

Chapters 1 through 4 of this book are connected by their focus on trauma and, taken together, they recount a series of failures (institutional or otherwise); these four case studies offer up evidence of liberation lost, of difference made marginal, and of the rather forceful return of a prosocial agenda that inscribes the personal images privileged enough to move. Yet Chapter 4 is also a bridge to Chapters 5 and 6, as it speaks (however provisionally) of the potential for resistance and free articulation, and illustrates the ways in which producers and subjects might move beyond the structures that attempt to channel desire into ideologically acceptable forms. Following the lead of Chapter 4, the final two chapters are united by their shared attention to an opposing movement; they focus on recovery and suggest the possibility of expressly positive outcomes, of working through, and perhaps of transgression. In the final chapters of *Transient Images*, I expose a series of operational limits and move forward through these limits to suggest a model for action.

To this end, Chapter 5 speaks about the business of desire and its relative freedom as a commodity. It turns to the contemporary architectures that frame personal advertisement photography on the Internet and the discourses—both utopic and dystopic—that attempt to read personal advertisement sites as contemporary manifestations of community. I consider the assumptions that underpin this particular use of photography, its alignment with other textual markers, and the position of such sites with regard to more fundamental questions and indices of community and its shifting parameters. In order to do so, I survey a number of Internet "dating" sites and social networking sites, each of which conforms personal information and personal photography to a predesigned template and maps these individuated markers onto a conventional layout that is policed by particular rules, regulations, and codes of conduct that make the personal safely public (and consumable).

Chapter 5 examines the multiple architectures of personal advertisement sites, as well as the particular strategies of containment deployed in the manufacture and distribution of images. It also considers the relative free play of desire in Internet architecture, as individuals map their identities onto generic templates designed by vertically integrated Internet-based communication, information, and entertainment companies. And it speaks about the possibility of excess, of identity out of bounds; returning to a concept first developed in Chapter 1, it begins to articulate the fears that drive prescription in an attempt to understand and overturn them.

Chapter 6, revisiting the theoretical arguments sketched out earlier in the volume and following the autobiographical lineage charted throughout, steps back from the individual in the interest of seeing the general contours of the archive, sending the images found throughout this text back into the network. It tracks the movement of autobiography, from the home to the social network and back again, and considers the discourses that shape the technology, practice, and mechanisms of reception—the push and pull of the private and the public. Chapter 6 is about a change in focus; here, I privilege interaction over imaging, even though I understand that these processes are interdependent. What is the structural logic of the social network? Where do its principles come from? And what happens when the fundamental premises of sociality are violated or narrative progress is hindered? The deepest computational layer of the network is the code that structures the database. Yet it is not simple math. Rather, code and data interact as a discursive construct (and each is a discursive construction in its own right) shaped by history, culture, industry, and technology that may encourage certain forms of engagement.

Though the chapters in this book are presented as a series of case studies, taken together they draw out the tensions that accompany both the casual reading of images and more theoretically inflected exercises in close textual analysis. Perhaps the problem is one more generally associated with postmodernity. Images are ubiquitous in our culture, as is the practice of photo taking within the family circle. This very ubiquity makes photographic artifacts both transparent and complex, signifying nothing and everything, easily overlooked or subjected to intense scrutiny. Photographs can give us insight into the constructed nature of subjectivity, if we pause long enough to reflect on them. And this reflection can ultimately give way to a consideration of the moral dimensions of these objects that are so central in shaping personal and cultural memory. How do we learn to take pictures? And how do we learn to read them? Do the same codes govern both enterprises? Are these codes for a medium? Or are they codes for living? *Transient Images* gathers together several sets of images for the purpose of exploring these questions. The book is a theoretical and practical tool for understanding how to read such familiar encounters. My goal is not to replace one master discourse with another, but to reveal the way that discursive practices shape our daily lives and perhaps help the reader interrupt the hegemonic codes that form even the most familiar and private types of personal expression. The ultimate goal is to open up a space for revision—to look but not to subject.

The difficulty of engaging with the rather unremarkable spaces that permeate daily life is the all-too-common problem encountered in media and cultural studies of speaking about things that we are all engaged with, objects and interfaces we have experienced and know so well that we no longer see them but rather look right through them. The difficulty is not in complicating objects that seem in no need of complication, but rather in defamiliarizing objects to understand them as sign systems. The goal here may be aligned with that far grander project undertaken by Foucault, who, by examining classical thought, sought to restore "to our silent and apparently immobile soil its rifts, its instability, its flaws."[23] My history as an educator, video artist, and scholar shapes this study into one that hopefully helps readers understand the tools we take for granted and that seem to be simply naturalized extensions of our self-proclaimed subjectivities. The aim is to dislocate the self to shed some light on what Foucault refers to as the "dark spaces," to temporarily remove the shadows we cast over the technologies we use and the silent artifacts we encounter in our everyday lives.

1

"Have You Seen This Child?"

From Milk Carton *to* Mise en Abyme

Let us proceed in a summary fashion: we will consider a field of experience taken as a real world no longer in relation to a self but to a simple "there is." There is, at some moment, a calm and restful world. Suddenly a frightened face looms up that looks at something out of the field. The other person appears here as neither subject nor object but as something that is very different: a possible world, the possibility of a frightening world. This possible world is not real, or not yet, but it exists nonetheless: it is an expressed that exists only in its expression— the face, or an equivalent of the face. To begin with, the other person is this existence of a possible world. And this possible world also has a specific reality in itself, as possible: when the expressing speaks and says, "I am frightened," even if its words are untruthful, this is enough for a reality to be given to the possible as such.

GILLES DELEUZE AND FELIX GUATTARI, *WHAT IS PHILOSOPHY?*

We are a culture driven by fear, and we tend to assume the worst—our identities will be stolen; our children will be abducted; crime will overtake our neighborhoods; and our borders, both personal and national, will be crossed. Paranoia is a powerful phenomenon, and as often as it is attached to individuals, it is also put in motion in the broader social and historical field (as in cold war paranoia). Paranoia operates most effectively (or more aptly, disastrously) when it can be visualized; in the case of the cold war, the American documentary television movement of the 1960s supplied ample evidence to make the case for reorienting U.S. foreign policy.[1] Paranoia is a force that subordinates—or in sociological terms, a force that individuates—and puts individuals in their place; in the sixties, it did so under the guise of nationalism and national security.[2] From a structural standpoint, paranoia can be used to create an open discursive system where any number of terms can be renegotiated.[3]

Taken together, *Madness and Civilization* and *The Birth of the Clinic* might be considered Michel Foucault's manifesto on the ordering power of vision. I refer to Foucault because I believe that paranoia can be understood as a pathology of the gaze insofar as it signals unsuccessful individuation—the failure of the panopticon. To elaborate, this chapter examines the link between the disciplinary power of vision and the disciplining power of the visual field. My focus is on something slightly askew, yet nonetheless related to the interiorization of the gaze. The concept of interiorization suggests a certain movement, an inward turn by which an outward objectifying gaze leads to self-reflection and self-surveillance. I am, however, exploring a higher order of subordination, adopting a concept that Celia Lury describes as "prosthetic culture," a developmental shift enabled by technology that has had a profound impact on the individual, taking the completed interior mechanism and projecting it outward. Lury describes this as a process of "outcontextualization," where previously naturally or socially determined aspects of self-identity are taken out of context and refashioned. The individual becomes knowable only by the sum of its parts, which may be regrouped, recategorized, and recombined.[4] This reorganization of the body is postpanoptic, a form of secondary revision largely outside the terrain of conventional considerations of visibility (as a trap).

So what is the link between outcontextualization, paranoia, and the visual field? Paranoids mistake the symbolic and mythic for actual events in the spatiotemporal world. The defense mechanism intrinsic to paranoia is projection. The function of projection in the psychic economy of the paranoid individual is self-preservation, to flee from any high-level insight that might otherwise lead to psychic instability. Sigmund Freud recognized that the drive to know and the drive to see are joined in the desire to master the field of knowledge by casting it as a set of discrete objects within a visual field. If, as Kenneth Paradis notes, "the paranoid stands as a parodic image of the autonomous rational individual to which modernity aspires," why does paranoia seem to be such a pervasive and natural aspect of contemporary being?[5] By subjecting the body to a second order of classification—for instance, taking one's physical attributes and teasing them apart in a database, where they may be counted, regrouped, and subjected to the logic of a search engine—we become knowable to ourselves and to each other as projections. This out-of-body experience is commonplace; projection is no longer a sign of pathology but a fundamental condition of existence. We expect to be able to see (despite our hesitancy to be seen) and we become suspicious on those occasions when our view is obstructed. Focusing on the minutiae, we lose sight of the bigger picture and become guilty of taking individuals out of context and assuming that physical traits are suitable surrogates for psychical ones. Life seems more manageable when it can be subjected to such a clear and decided structuralist practice.

   This willful looking, this casual yet strategic browsing, brings me back to the subject of tourism—an occupation, an industry, and a metaphor discussed in the introduction. In the digital age, tourism is no longer simply about surveying the natural landscape. Rather, we use technology to reorganize the terrain, adding our own contextual markers (known in Google Earth as layers), and we commonly find ourselves traveling an entirely new system of roadways—the information superhighway. Here, the mile markers are of a different nature; the signposts are often other individuals. The push toward transience, the apparent need for movement, is part of a general cultural shift. While we willingly send personal artifacts adrift—sometimes knowing the paths they will take and other times allowing them to wander into uncertain channels—the drive toward dispersion is not necessarily self-ordained. While we may be able to ascribe the act to personal agency, why do we feel the urgency to turn ourselves into a network of signs? The answer, I believe, is security.

Sign and Symptom

Reading through a recent issue of *Entertainment Weekly* magazine, I came across a full-page advertisement for the "Canon4Kids" program, a collaboration between Canon U.S.A. and the National Center for Missing and Exploited Children (NCMEC). Canon has collaborated with the NCMEC since 1997, and currently provides digital cameras, printers, and scanners to law enforcement agencies nationwide to help in the recovery of missing children; the technologies Canon provides are integral to the speedy dissemination of photos and other case-related data. Canon's effort also includes an awareness and prevention campaign that stresses the need for parents to have updated digital photos of their children to assist in the search for a missing child. The company's Web site provides a detailed overview to help parents use digital technology to protect their children, and guides them through a multipronged task list:

1. Use the highest resolution setting. Digitally photograph all children under the age of 18 every six months indoors using a flash against a solid white or light-colored background.
2. Photograph children in portrait-style poses, similar to passport headshots.
3. Photograph children from different angles—profile shots facing left, profile shots facing right, straight-on headshots.
4. Save the digital images in an easily located folder on the hard drive in JPEG format in both black-and-white and color formats. (Color

images can be easily converted to black-and-white images using the software that comes with your camera.)

5. Back up all digital images on multiple disks or CDs and e-mail copies to other family members to store on their computers.

6. Print out multiple 5″×7″ hard copies (prints) of all images and store them in a safe folder where they can be easily accessed in the event of an emergency.

7. Bookmark the NCMEC website (www.missingkids.com) so that you can quickly access helpful information on what you can do to help locate your child in the event he/she is reported missing.

8. Use your digital photo printer to create posters, buttons and flyers with your child's portrait.[6]

The list is quite detailed, both in prescribing a set of production tactics and in outlining a postproduction plan that also includes distribution guidelines. Anxiety is channeled through prescription. A digital archive emerges—one that has no practical purpose unless it is called into action. The dormant archive is simply a vessel to contain our fear, for this phantom archive evokes two sets of subjects—those inside the portrait frame and those on the periphery, hidden from view.

The still-image archive is a reliquary to a crisis. The use of video in criminology by commercial enterprise (the "video fingerprint") has created an evidentiary trace, producing a rather unique form of virtual community containing virtual bodies—a community created through the archiving of moving images of potential kidnap victims. And, not surprisingly, an industry has emerged to give us practical aid while assuaging our fears, an economy driven by fear production.

Canon is not alone in turning fear into venture capitalism. One of the key players, Child Shield, U.S.A., emerged as part of a larger cottage industry that developed in the 1990s and began developing privatized solutions to what was deemed a more general public crisis. Child Shield trains people to videotape their own children and stores these tapes in the event that their children are ever missing. Claiming that video provides a "portrait" of a subject that is more accurate and detailed than still photography, Child Shield contrasts its services to photo IDs, milk cartons, and commercial mailers.

DIGIKIDS, a more recent entrant in the child identification and recovery business, has developed a Child ID Kit, a business card–sized CD that contains the child's vital statistics and high-resolution images. With the included proprietary Quick Response software, the child's data can be transferred onto preformatted posters or e-mailed directly to local law enforcement officials. Moreover, DIGIKIDS takes an antidatabase stance; data is stored on the in-

Canon joins forces with the National Center for Missing and Exploited Children.

dividual disc and is not retained on a central network. The company cautions against the database services provided by their competitors, foregrounding the vulnerability of networked data and the susceptibility of an off-site database to criminals and child predators. Yet the rhetoric of DIGIKIDS reeks of one-upmanship and reflects contradictory attitudes toward new technology—touting the virtues of both CD-ROM and software innovation, while simultaneously spinning a frightful tale of the database. And while the company's mission seems filled with virtue, its innovations are available as a profitable venture to those with sufficient capital. The corporate Web site includes the following invitation:

> If you are interested in a unique opportunity to create a great income while providing a valued service for your community, DIGIKIDS could be the ideal franchise opportunity for you.
>
> DIGIKIDS is a full time, home-based business with very low overhead that can be successfully started on a part time basis.
>
> As a DIGIKIDS franchise owner, you will offer the most advanced and effective child ID available anywhere. You will launch your new business with established marketing systems, proprietary patent-pending software, an accepted trademark, national purchasing power, and thorough training and support.[7]

Manufacturing Fear

In *The Culture of Fear,* Barry Glassner suggests: "The short answer to why Americans harbor so many misbegotten fears is that immense power and money await those who tap into our moral insecurities and supply us with symbolic substitutes."[8] Analyzing several case studies of fear production, Glassner locates blame within a complex array of groups, including businesses, advocacy organizations, religious sects, and political parties, positioning media outlets as both producers and allayers of culturally bound anxieties.[9]

Conversations about fear and about analyzing apparent problems in the culture at large reveal just as much about ourselves as they do about any actual problem. When we talk about fear, our emotions take hold, to the point where it becomes almost impossible to engage in an active, positivistic pursuit of knowledge; nor do we typically gain any immediate self-knowledge.

As one subject of analysis, consider the milk carton. Not only do the sides of the carton acknowledge its contents but they also self-reflexively acknowledge its own production, a hierarchy of dairy and distributor. And not only does the product engage in self-analysis (calories, fat, cholesterol, sodium, carbohydrate, and protein—each considered in terms of a percentage of a daily value based on a 2,000-calorie diet), it does so in a mode that acknowledges "you," the consumer (a form of personal address, considering "your" calorie needs, markedly allowing room for an "other" or "others" that require more or less than 2,000 calories a day). At the top is an expiration date, and although I am not certain what relation this date has to the date of production, I can situate this carton of milk temporally; in fact, to make the most of my dollar, I have to consider not only my present patterns of consumption but also those of the near future. How much milk will I be drinking in the coming week? Will I be eating at home or traveling? And if I have a family, how much milk will my kids consume by week's end? As I ask myself these questions, I turn the milk carton around to consider its other face—more often than not in recent years, a literal face. Though the back of the carton that is the subject of my present analysis (a mirror image of the front, with the same product label) bears a printed advertisement for a local radio station, popular memory recalls a time when most of them were populated by photos of missing children.

But the missing children still appear in my home. Now they are stuffed into my mail slot, smiling up at me from the floor of my apartment when I get home in the evening, framed by the all-too-familiar question: "Have you seen me?" Sometimes, the question takes its plural form: "Have you seen us?" Front side or back side, the "other" side of these fliers features advertisements for carpet care services, home-shopping merchandise (such as the Baby Boom Box), the regional Goodyear dealer, and other local merchants. I personally have never responded to these product ads, and I have never responded to the missing children ads on the other side. I have never seen any of these children and have never phoned the 800 number, though presumably others have—the statistics at the bottom of the mailer state that one out of every seven children featured have been recovered. Yet it is unclear what role, if any, these ads have played in their recovery; and the return on these ads from a marketing standpoint—only ninety-nine kids found, when millions of fliers are distributed nationally—is incredibly low. But how can one put a value on the life of a child, or pause to consider probability and statistics?

Threat Levels

Risk is a cultural conception that is repeatedly and perniciously naturalized. Like the term "community," which it often mobilizes (operating "in the best interests of the community"), it is an authorizing discourse that signals the very authority of those who wield it; the term invokes parallel assumptions about security and responsibility. Insurance itself, an agency of risk, responds to perceptual shifts in the public sector, and at the same time, its institutions shape our understanding of individual and social responsibility.[10] François Ewald points to the complicated relay (of thought and action) that begins by calling out the term:

The moment a population is identified as a risk, everything within it tends to become—necessarily becomes—just that. Risk has an allusive, insidious potential existence that renders it simultaneously present and absent, doubtful and suspicious. Assumed to be everywhere, it founds a politics of prevention. The term *prevention* does not indicate simply a practice based on the maxim that an ounce of prevention is worth a pound of cure, but also the assumption that if prevention is necessary it is because danger exists—it exists in a virtual state before being actualized in an offense, injury, or accident. This entails the further assumption that the responsible institutions are guilty if they do not detect the presence, or actuality, of a danger even before it is realized.[11]

As I examine my pile of junk mail, it occurs to me that someone has failed; some institution or institutions are at fault. Children are missing, and Mailbox Values tells me so. But the crisis has been constructed. In his discussion of epidemics—another form of crisis situation—Michel Foucault points out that the determination that a situation is epidemic is typically a political determination made by those with access to statistical data and the authority to make and circulate such determinations.[12] Such an authoritative discourse governs the missing children epidemic, calling forth the dispensation of resources and justifying tactics of surveillance and regulation.[13] Children are indeed being victimized, but the labeling of the situation as a crisis has depended upon the collection of (scientific) data—tabulated and interpreted by "experts." Though anecdotes do not provide scientific evidence, they are nonetheless critical to keeping the crisis alive; they give the epidemic a face. As part of this evidentiary process, visibility is simultaneously a problem and a solution. The campaign's visibility has focused public concern on the crisis (in a sense, bringing the crisis into existence by making it visible—though the campaign is certainly not responsible for the incidents themselves, and is only one flash point for its being called out) and has allowed the authoritative discourse to take hold (made manifest in the mobilization of dollars and resources and the willful embracing of various institutions as protectors of the public interest). Indeed, as part of this movement, citizens willingly surveil each other, though apparently in the interest of recovering lost (or stolen) children.

With such an interest in mind, we have come to privilege particular technological devices that aid us in surveillance; moreover, we are asked to accept surveillance as the principal *raison d'être* of certain new technologies (such as the camcorder). Outside of an immediate use for surveillance, we rely on technology to help us define, identify, and evaluate risks (and preventive mechanisms).[14] These technologies are not simply used by consumers; they are also a formal part of institutional risk assessment. Yet in both scenarios (of observation/data collection and evaluation/assessment), the technology is not politically or ideologically neutral; its implementation and effects commonly have moral, psychological, social, political, and economic dimensions.

To expose the ideological underpinnings of the technology in relation to its use, I focus on risk for, as François Ewald notes, the mere recognition of risk depends on the shared values of the group threatened by it.[15] Though certain objective risks do exist, they are given effective existence only when accepted by a population. We may know a risk exists, but we are faced with the problem of having to choose whether or not to accept it.[16] In line with the science of probability, we reconsider risk as a "quantifiable presence."[17] And any quantifiable risk has its insurance counterpart—a remunerative policy, a legislative act, or a mode of prevention.

Statistical Knowledge

The case for missing children is, in part, built on an inordinate number of statistics that add up to a number of decided pressure points, giving quantity a particular quality of dread and desperation. The results of sophisticated research design are commonly presented in a manner that maximizes their rhetorical effect.[18] Many of the data sets are underanalyzed or oversimplified, and a fairly universal set of vacant yet haunting numbers is repeated in much of the popular and corporate literature on missing children. The claims are urgent, and suggest that every forty seconds another child becomes lost or missing in America. They are alarmingly exponential, and report the rate of increase in missing children since 1982 at 468 percent. They play the odds, betting that one in every forty-two children will become abducted, missing, lost, or runaway. And they speak of time-sensitive efficacy, warning that most abducted children are recovered or killed in the first three hours.[19] These are talking points masked as statistics, yet they are the products of social processes, and they can have significant social consequences. One social problem is foregrounded at the expense of another, as these truisms take on a life of their own.

The birth of the missing child problem has resulted from an intriguing combination of social forces that include: "media attention given to a few spectacular cases, political pressure from influential lobbyists, and a ground swell of sympathy and concern from individuals around the country for victims and families."[20] These forces came together in the late 1970s and early 1980s, shaping the missing child problem into an epidemic of national proportions; what catalyzed the crisis were several sensational crimes that occurred

during both decades, some of which were clear cases of kidnapping and homicide and others that involved child homicide under unclear circumstances.
These cases, though all different, were somehow melded together in media
reports and institutional surveys (and concomitantly in the popular imagination) as missing children cases. The Adam Walsh story is perhaps the most
well-known among the first cases of younger missing children. Adam disappeared on July 27, 1981, while he and his mother were in a Sears store in
Hollywood, Florida. Two weeks later, after a massive search led by law enforcement officials, his partial remains were recovered from a canal about one
hundred miles from the site of his disappearance.

The media have been instrumental in not only informing the general public of the factual events associated with specific cases of missing children but
also in shaping the public's reaction to what would otherwise be individual
acts. In the early 1980s, stories of missing children began appearing in popular magazines such as *Ladies' Home Journal, Reader's Digest,* and *Redbook.*
Although many of these articles had a semblance of newsworthiness, as well
as proactively and productively positioned personal anecdotes alongside preventive tips and evidentiary statistics, most of the hard crime statistics and
figures presented were of unclear origin and were grossly exaggerated.[21] Nonetheless, the net effect of this flurry of coverage in the popular press was to
elevate human interest stories to the status of a social problem. An article in
the December 1985 *Parents* magazine claims that "no one knows exactly how
many children are abducted by strangers each year, but estimates range from
4,000 to 20,000."[22] These statistics were supported by the NCMEC, which,
in one of its early publications, estimated the number of stranger kidnappings as high as fifty thousand per year.[23]

Television, as well, acted to stimulate the public's interest in the "problem." The most widely viewed made-for-TV movie on missing children was
the docudrama *Adam,* based on the Adam Walsh case, which first aired in
October 1983. The program closed with photographs of fifty missing children
and made an appeal to viewers to call local authorities if they had information on the whereabouts of the featured children.[24] The program was aired
on three separate occasions with different children featured each time, and
an estimated fourteen children were located as a result of the broadcasts.
Adam was closely followed by two other television dramas: *Adam, His Song
Continues* and *Missing: Have You Seen This Child?* Missing children were
found elsewhere on television during the same decade. *Child Search* was a
two-minute spot featuring missing children, which aired on NBC affiliates.
Magazine shows such as *Good Morning America* and *Hour Magazine* also featured segments on missing children. Coverage expanded in subsequent years
and spilled over into other television genres, including local news broadcasts,

true-crime shows (including *America's Most Wanted* and *Unsolved Mysteries*), talk shows (such as *Donahue*), and crime dramas (such as *Without a Trace*).[25]

Through print and broadcasting, missing children groups received the media's help in launching a national campaign to publicize the names, faces, and descriptive statistics of missing children. The goals of this campaign were both retrieval and prevention. As groups and individuals in the private sector began to develop strategies to further the campaign, their activities also stimulated political and governmental entities to take action. On May 22, 1985, Senator Howard Metzenbaum introduced "a bill to require that a portion of the mail of Congress and the executive branch include a photograph and biography of a missing child" (S 1195). This act authorized the use of Senate mail to disseminate pictures of and information about missing children. A 1992 report from the Senate Committee on Rules and Administration found no evidence that a child had been recovered as a direct result of his or her picture appearing on a piece of Senate mail. "Nevertheless, the National Center [for Missing and Exploited Children] believes that the widespread dissemination of such pictures on Senate mail produces approximately 20 to 30 leads per photo used." Moreover, "the use of Senate and other official mail keeps the general public aware of the problem of missing children."[26]

One of the most visible strategies organized by private companies involved putting the photographs of missing children on a variety of products. Chicago dairyman Walter Woodbury was the first person to propose the now-familiar photographs of missing children on milk cartons and, in January 1985, Hawthorn Melody Farm Dairy in Chicago began running the ads.[27] By the end of the month, almost four hundred dairies around the country were participating in this program.[28] The milk carton strategy prompted other industries to place photos of missing children on their products—cereal boxes, grocery bags, and egg cartons—and to place displays of these photos in a variety of locations, including supermarkets, airports, post offices, and bus stops, as well as on municipal buses and subway cars, and on junk mail coupons.[29]

ADVO, Inc., the nation's largest direct mail corporation, has been working with the NCMEC since 1985. ADVO executives recount that in the aftermath of the Walsh case, a groundswell of sympathy among the company's workers led them to collaborate with the NCMEC. Its direct mail fliers are sent to sixty million households on a weekly basis. Each flier contains a fixed-inventory postage mark, the cost of which is offset by the advertisement on the reverse of the NCMEC "ad."[30] ADVO's shared-mail advertising program, previously distributed under the Mailbox Values brand, was repackaged as Shop Wise in January 2000.

One of the many missing child mailers sent to U.S. households every day, locating consumption within a series of concentric narratives that includes the uncertain relation between victim and (presumed) victimizer.

More recent publicity efforts have been developed with the assistance of several of the NCMEC's corporate sponsors. Pizza Hut is the official sponsor of the missing children kiosk program; this national program places kiosks in airports, bus terminals, shopping malls, and train stations to provide viewers with pictures of missing children, as well as safety tips and information on community action programs. Polaroid's KidCare ID provides free identification and safety information to families nationwide, with the partnership of Chrysler, Kmart, Sears, and Toys "R" Us. Details of these programs are available on the NCMEC's Web site, which also includes a searchable database of missing children.

Concern for missing children created a new growth industry of its own, with a complete line of products related to missing children. For example, in 1989, Scott Barrows and Lewis Sadler, two medical illustrators at the University of Illinois, Chicago, developed a computer simulation system to project changes in physical appearance over time. The computer system, which utilizes scanning and digitized facial mapping, can create a copy of an original photograph and generate new photographs of what a child would look like at any time after his or her disappearance. In its earliest configuration, the system was sensitive to the differences between males and females (presumably differences in bone structure), yet did not register racial differences (in mapping facial dimensions, the two illustrators relied on data drawn from a study of Caucasian children in Iowa).[31]

Like the computer industry, the videotaping industry has also benefited from the missing children campaign, expanding its applications and markets.

During the late 1980s, many private studios began offering videotaping services to parents wanting a visual and audio record to help identify their children (in the event of an "incident"). And more recently, through its national
team of independent registered agents, Child Shield, U.S.A. began offering
parents the protection of its unique Videotape Registration Service:

> When a child turns up missing, the ability to positively identify that
> child becomes critical. Our unique Videotape Registration Service
> provides the highest level of identification record available. Unlike a
> still photograph, a properly prepared Identification Videotape gives
> the authorities and concerned citizens so much more to go on when
> searching for a missing child. Familiarity with characteristics of voice,
> manner, motion, and others can greatly improve the likelihood that
> someone may remember having seen the child. Such a recollection
> could be the all-important clue that leads to a reunion of child and
> family.[32]

In toto, the program is based first on preventive education and second on
effective, organized recovery. Parents record their own child's identification
videotape using the easy-to-follow instruction guide. Completed videotapes
are then delivered to the Child Shield headquarters using a protective, pread-
dressed videotape mailer; finally, the tapes are placed in secure storage after
being marked with a unique identification code number known only to the
parents. Child Shield maintains a separate facility outside of its office to ensure the safe storage of all videotapes. For security purposes, only Child
Shield officers, its insurance company, and the chief legal counselor for the
law firm that represents Child Shield know the location of the videotapes. In
the event a child is missing, the parent contacts Child Shield. The agency
duplicates the missing child's tape and proceeds to distribute copies, first to
local and state law enforcement agencies, then to neighboring states, and finally to the FBI. Videotapes are also provided to several national missing
persons organizations and a variety of nationally syndicated and network television news programs. In its press materials, the company foregrounds its
ability to respond swiftly to any crisis, an effort supported by Child Shield's
videotape duplication facilities, which enable the production of more than
one hundred high-quality videotape copies per hour. Blockbuster Video and
local law enforcement agencies offer similar but not equivalent services, providing videography, but not storage and distribution.[33]

The services of Child Shield naturalize the state of emergency that is the
central concern of the NCMEC. Danger exists. The milk carton ad (more
generally, the print ad) is a precedent to the Child Shield ad (the video ad).

The danger exists: the documentation attests to it, the records quantify it, and the photographic evidence is there, to be taken at face value. We are not allowed to consider the still photograph as a site of analysis; some would say we cannot afford the "luxury" of such hesitation. The danger that Child Shield seeks to curtail does not appear to us as virtual, but visible; there is proof—the proof of the still photo. Moreover, the photo is part of a national campaign; images from New York, Michigan, Colorado, Illinois, and Texas resurface in my Florida residence; these are decontextualized images and, on a fundamental level, depict children and families I do not know. My community takes on new dimensions. My family grows. Danger is nowhere and everywhere, as it circulates through the printing presses, along postal routes, and through my front door (not unlike the nowhere and everywhere of the broadcast image). I can see the breach in my nation's security; my home is being invaded.

The Lingering Trace of Ontology: The Codes of Fear Production

The accuracy and detail ascribed to the video image—central to Child Shield's action plan—is perhaps correlated with an assumed mastery of the subject, maintained through particular attention to sound and movement, to unique (vocal) inflections and gestures. Yet this confidence in the video image begs a set of questions: What are the correlative shifts in perception and memory as we move from a static to a moving image and from a filmic medium to an electronic one? On a more general level, what notions are embedded in these tapes themselves and in the minds of those who both create and see a need for their creation? In addition, what can be said of the mapping out of a second imaginary—the potential crime suspect? And what are the possible points of intersection between these two imagined communities of victims and victimizers?

This particular use of video, naturalized within the family circle, is justified by traditional concerns for public interest and public safety. In *The Burden of Representation,* John Tagg historicizes a series of photographic practices, all of which have placed the physical body at the center of a certain political economy and forced it to signify as part of a larger social body. This formation of knowledge is inextricably bound up with power relations ("those who know, can"), and since the late eighteenth century, the refinement of such power relations has been made possible through new technologies that provided the means to secure new forms of knowledge. Tagg notes: "From the eighteenth and nineteenth centuries onward, an immense police text came increasingly to cover society by means of a complex documentary organisation. But this documentation differed markedly from the traditional methods of judicial or administrative writing. What was registered in it were forms of conduct, attitudes, possibilities, suspicions: a permanent account of individuals' behaviour."[34]

Within this critical framework, the standardized image of criminology (proper pose, lighting, and placement) can be understood as both a portrait of the individual (albeit one that punitively inflects its subject) and a signifier of a particular disciplinary method; it is ultimately an index of those devices used to know the body, to contain it within both a social category and a literal image-frame.[35] Reflecting on photographic history in the interest of exploring continuities between past and present, Kevin Robins notes that the uses of positivism are consistently linked to the objectives of industrial capitalism.[36]

In the case of the mailbox ad, there are multiple architectures: the square photo, the rectangular mailer, the postal box. Each of these formal devices in turn forces the image (and figure) to yield up certain truths.[37] Yet these fliers do more than simply showcase a person (or persons) and provide an array of contextual markers (designed to secure a social position, or a more literal geographic position); they also offer a complex narrative relay that operates across these signifiers and along their paths of circulation. The grammar must be intelligible to a broad demographic—the target of the inverse function (the marketing campaign on the flier's other side).

The link between Tagg's history of police photography in the eighteenth and nineteenth centuries, and more contemporary practices of a particular type of portraiture is found in the codes that shape these exercises. Though photos taken by the family are not police photos, are the codes of the family photo of the child nonetheless the same to the extent that they embody a disciplinary method? Are the codes bound up with the act of taking the photo? Or are these photos different (in process) but made to read the same when taken on as police documents (in distribution and exhibition)? Does the family photo look the same as a mug shot, conceived by similar mechanisms, or is it simply reworked to stand in as a mug shot (after the fact of its production)? Is the family photo a form of surveillance and subjugation to the extent that children are told what behavior is appropriate in front of the camera? Are the enforced codes (parenting) of early childhood (experiencing how to sit in front of the camera at Sears and at school) later internalized? Do children learn to willingly surveil themselves?

Returning to traditional ontological claims, Child Shield's information packet reminds parents:

> Please remember that you are shooting a moving videotape with sound, not a silent still photograph. The more your child moves and talks, the

easier it may be for someone to identify him/her from viewing the
tape. It is best to videotape your child while engaged in a game,
hobby, or some other favorite activity. This will allow your child to act
more naturally and it can make the camera seem less imposing. Get
your child talking by asking open-ended questions about familiar topics like school, pets, toys, hobbies, etc. You may even want to ask your
child to sing a song. Many people will remember a voice better than
they can remember a face. Shoot a ten second close up of your child's
face from the front, and another from the side (profile). Also, take
close up shots of any identifying marks or scars.[38]

By referring to the "mechanisms" of production (both physical and psychical),
I am not suggesting that all home modes (of video and photography) are
handed down to the general public, determined by our governing institutions
(to include corporate America). We are not simply told how to shoot and, in
any case, such directives are not simply written into camera manuals (popular television programs bear some of this responsibility). Rather, there is a
form of negotiation at work here. In addition, I do not intend to move away
from arguments about medium specificity, and have perhaps oversimplified
portraiture, eliding for the moment the mode of production (video or photography) and the distinct features of each mode (grounded in the technology
and its prescribed uses). I do want to suggest, however, that certain mechanisms of "fear production" can work to more closely align home modes (in any
medium) with a dominant discourse; and the disciplinary method (and any
negotiation of that method) can be read not only into the relative subjugation
of the actor, but the director as well.

Stylistically, the ADVO photo (on the Mailbox Values flier) and the mug
shot share some basic features. Each is typically a head shot (close-up) with a
neutral background; the framing excludes details that would give the subject an identifiable context. Unable to be situated in space and time, the
subject becomes a free-floating signifier that can be inserted into an endless
assortment of narratives. The criminal (in the photo) is fixed to the crime
scene when recognized by a viewer; his or her identity as a criminal is tied to
the act of recognition. The "wanted" poster must be reattached to a story line.
Likewise, the images on ADVO mailers conjure up a host of suppositions.
When there are two photos—one of the child and the other of the person last
seen with the child—the latter is presumably the guilty victimizer and the
former the innocent victim, though the production codes of each photo are
almost identical (and the conditions of the disappearance are largely unspeci-
fied). It is only the age and physiognomy of the former subject (identified as a
child) that positions him or her as the victim. The narrative cues found in the

photo boxes are bound only to the text below them, which reveals the date and location of the disappearance (letting us know how long the subjects have been missing, and how recently they can be attached to our popular memory), as well as the possible relationship of the two subjects (assessable if, by chance, they share the same last name). What most clearly separates the ADVO photo from the mug shot is the attitude of the sitter: the photo appropriated for the ADVO ad is typically an occasional portrait, with the subject posed accordingly; most are smiling for the camera, and those who are not appear guiltier (if only because of their sour demeanor).

Child Shield has rules of conduct (for taking the video—what the shot should contain and look like). Here, no longer do the police enforce particular attitudes; rather, they are embraced by the family in a form of self-censorship/self-control that is willful. The law is being taken on by commercial enterprises or services that replicate particular codes and bring them to bear on family life. This is all the more acceptable because this form of governance does not read as government, and all the more beneficial for companies like Blockbuster that are being the good parent, caring for families, preserving family values, and developing a kinship base (as family photographer) with their clientele. I may be drawing too forceful a conclusion here about the seamless transference of production tactics from the corporation to the family; unfortunately (as far as my analysis is concerned), as the Child Shield videos have been relegated to the vault, they are not open to further scrutiny. While we may assume that some families are not following Child Shield's guidelines (either being purposefully subversive or characteristically unmindful), we may also assume that the decentralization of fear production—threats loom everywhere in the age of computerized information management, as their networkability makes them decidedly dynamic—leads to a greater investment in controlling variables whenever possible. We might even understand this form of dependence (on rules) as a latent manifestation of Gilles Deleuze's conception of control societies; for here we are exposed to others in ways we cannot control, and we see paranoia, surveillance, and self-regulation (following simple rules to a tee) birthed of an inability to locate the more dangerous forms of discipline and power that pervade our networked culture. As an important caveat, Deleuze notes: "Types of machines are easily matched with each type of society—not that machines are determining, but because they express those social forms capable of generating them and using them."[39]

As a hard sell, the service that Child Shield provides to local resellers is an example of the private sector taking over what is referred to as the government's responsibility—a grassroots action toward preventing and solving child abduction cases. The police are ill-equipped to duplicate videotapes, while missing child agencies are reported to have inferior databases. Yet what information is being recorded in these tapes produced by families throughout the country?

As I pore over the images of missing children on my desk, I notice that most of these kids were last seen with family members, perhaps abducted by family members. What I have found is a crisis of representation as well as the representation of a crisis. What I do not see are the statistics on runaways, those missing on a voluntary basis. What I do not see are the statistics on the number of kids abducted by relatives.

Following the passage of the 1984 Missing Children's Assistance Act, the Office of Juvenile Justice and Delinquency Prevention proceeded with several national incidence studies to measure, among other incident categories, the number of juvenile "victims of abduction by strangers" and the number of "parental kidnappings." While the act provided a statutory definition of "missing children," the expression became a catchall in the public mind. The NC-MEC now differentiates between: (1) attempted abductions of children by nonfamily members, (2) abductions by nonfamily members reported to police, (3) abductions by nonfamily members where the children were gone for long periods of time or were murdered, (4) children abducted by family members, (5) children who ran away, (6) children who were thrown away, and (7) children who were lost, injured, or otherwise missing. In May 1990, the U.S. Department of Justice released the following numbers (for the year 1988): (1) 450,700 children who ran away, (2) 354,000 children abducted by family members, (3) 114,600 attempted nonfamily abductions, (4) 4,600 nonfamily abductions, (5) 300 nonfamily abductions resulting in long-period absence or murder. What these statistics make clear is that the number of children abducted by family members far exceeds the number abducted by nonfamily members (three times as many children were abducted by family members than by nonfamily members), while the number of runaways exceeds both family and nonfamily abductions. Indeed, there seems to be a significant (though only vaguely identified) threat looming inside the family circle.

Yet what I do not see as I examine ADVO mailers are families in crisis, broken homes; one enclosure (the image-frame) fails to speak truthfully about another. However concrete these images are, their circulation yields only an abstraction: a pervasive threat to the American family. Child Shield offers protection from a limitless threat—a threat whose evidence is the still photo. Child Shield distances its product from the still photo and from the threat; as prevention, it cannot signify the threat, though it simultaneously acknowledges its existence—a slippage perhaps made evident only when the videotape is called into action, leaves the security of the vault, and is broadcast and circulated. But still, somehow, its presence—its action—is a distancing mechanism; the aliveness of the image is a testament to the aliveness of the missing child. After all, the still photo would suffice if the child were no longer walking, talking, and playing games. The videotaped image will literally not hold still, will not allow itself to simply stand in as a positive ID. Still photographs and some circulated home video images have the awkward status as private records becoming public domain—images taken innocently at parties and gatherings, which then become the most recent records of children that at a later date are reported missing. The videotapes produced by Child Shield are created specifically for the public domain (though privately stored); issues of family safety are thus relegated to a separate domain and are recorded on different tapes. One can buy peace of mind. "I have done what I should do to ensure the safety of my child. I have detected the danger before it has been realized. I am free from guilt." In much the same way, the ADVO mailer displaces our anxiety; the question in bold type, "Have you seen me?" draws our attention to the fact that something (someone) is indeed missing. Yet at the same time that the mailer asks the question, it draws our attention to a subtler and perhaps selfish concern over absence; the problematic status of the child prompts us to consider our own security. The geographic markers tell us where the child was last seen and, in doing so, tell us our proximity to the underlying threat, localizing the event and the sensation (of anxiety). The mailer calls out a series of proximal relations; its physical presence in our home speaks to the missing child's absence from another home, while that most urgent of relations produces our own sense of security measured in the distance of our home from the particular ground zero noted on the ADVO mailer. The Freudian scenario of paranoid projection is complete. The desire to know a threat, however real or imagined, has produced a series of object lessons, each of which is encapsulated by a number of overtly knowable visual signs that are set in relation to one another—the flier is a sign, its images are signs, and the proximal relations too can be understood as geographic distance visualized and objectified.

It is no coincidence that both the still photograph and the videotape of the missing child circulate along preexisting paths of commerce (in the grocery store or on TV). We are faced with yet another system of distribution guided by the economy. Missing children photos follow the flow of milk, that bone-building staple of the American diet found on breakfast tables across the country, while missing children tapes circulate along the preexisting channels of broadcasting, as the medium dictates their form and content (for images must adhere to the production standards that define "broadcast quality").

The production of the tape secures the child; it dispels the threat and anxiety is displaced. The primary concern of those parents registered with Child Shield does not seem to be the possible disappearance of their children, but rather the disappearance or exploitative use of the videotape (thus the need for it to be locked away in secrecy). Yet the concern for the safety of the tape and the need for its privacy and anonymity is no longer an issue once the child disappears; called into action, the tape fulfills its destiny by becoming public property. What we have are two sites of anxiety—the tape and the child—the latter of which seems, at least on the surface, to be a more appropriate point (or object) of investiture. Yet it is only through a particular commodity fetishism that this duality is realized.[40] While we are disdainful of the need to worry about our children—"the world should be a safer place; child molesters should be locked up"—it is only through a financial investment that the healthy fixation becomes possible. We do not want our children exploited and we do not want their images used for the wrong purposes. Yet when our children disappear, so does the possibility for the misuse of their images (or so we would like to believe), for now the tapes must be removed from the vault, circulated, and seen. What becomes apparent is that the image may either be consumed by no one or everyone—the no one of the vault or the everyone of the public sphere (which we assume can be orchestrated by centralized media forms such as television). What is not allowable is the consumption of the image by a few individuals who are nevertheless read collectively and constitute a (deviant) community engaged in private activities. These individuals are understood as deviant if only because of the privacy of their actions. A community is thought to be appropriately a public body; and in violation of this premise, "we" as the true and healthy community proper feel we have a right to know what others are doing. "They" are guilty not because of what they do, but because of their need to do so without our knowing, even if we are unaware that our knowing, our knowledge, our science, and our truths govern their actions and make them unlawful.[41]

Within this imagined community (of victimizers), abductors and molesters are often linked together; the call to action is strengthened by this vision, as sexual abuse is one of the most radical forms of violation. *Parents* magazine warns that "while kidnapping is terrifying to contemplate, sexual molestation is far more common, and most molesters are known to the child and parents."[42] Abduction and (sexual) violation are fused in the 1995 made-for-TV movie *The Face on the Milk Carton* (a Family Channel production based on Caroline B. Cooney's book of the same title and its first sequel). As the two affected families assess blame, the kidnapper herself, variously described as a cult member, a prostitute, and "God knows what else" remains blameless and largely unrepresented in the text. The kidnapper's mother confesses that her daughter fled the cult and turned the abducted child over to her, for "there were rumors that the cult members were doing things to the children."[43] Though not the face of the film's title, the kidnapper too is a missing person; however, unlike Janie (the face on the milk carton), she is inevitably unredeemable (as perhaps dictated by the conventions of the genre); she turns up dead from hepatitis.

Brian Massumi notes in his preface to *The Politics of Everyday Fear* that: "fear is a staple of popular culture and politics."[44] American social space has been saturated by mechanisms of fear production, a process perhaps hastened by the role mass media has come to assume in this country. From a Foucauldian perspective, the materiality of the body is the ultimate object of technologies of fear, and from a metacritical vantage point it is these technologies that naturalize social boundaries and hierarchies. Moreover, the use of these technologies has itself been naturalized. I share the concern voiced by media activists such as Dee Dee Halleck over the manner in which a uniform home mode (of video production) has been sanctified by *America's Funniest Home Videos* (though this mode has been *appropriated, not created,* by the program); participants all too willingly turn their tapes over to the networks, allowing their lived moments to be narrativized by someone else, while the flow of this narrative is itself determined by product placement.[45] Yet I am more concerned with home modes that more directly simulate control through surveillance and separation, in which we scrutinize ourselves and our neighbors without thinking about a laugh track, and in which the lived moment is taped only to provide a form of evidence. In the worst-case scenario, the tape is a substitute for action or contemplation. It provides evidence but not insight. It is a sign that only someone else can decipher.

Fear and the public sphere are elusive (and intimately bound to one another); and as the statistics on missing children suggest, fear is not simply outside the home, but down the hallway. Felt though not measured, our fears remain more virtual than empirical; and though it is the very (virtual) nature of fear and of the public sphere that drives us toward empiricism, toward our need to know, to see, and to find the predators among us, what we may finally discover is that what we fear most is lying beside us.

Fear in the Archive

The drive toward empiricism takes many forms and the case for missing children has traversed new terrain in the digital age; not only does the NCMEC have a Web presence, but cybercrime itself is a hot button topic, the subject of heated legislative debate and fodder for sensational prime-time television programs. The final section of this chapter should not be misconstrued as a defense of pedophilia, but simply understood as a critical exploration of the mechanisms of quantification and surveillance birthed not simply by new technologies but by newly fueled desires to know.

The still images on the ADVO mailer may enter into their own narrative, but a close analysis of the signifying chain gains greater critical weight only when situated in a larger cultural context, of which other media are a part. We must move from ad text to social text. The mailer is only meaningful if its plea is echoed elsewhere; its text is the product of a dialogue. The flier does not manufacture the missing children crisis, rather it is a response; it is symptomatic of what the culture fears, though it may instigate, furthering the call to action. As I have already suggested, the missing children crisis emerged from a combination of forces, from a broader discussion in the cultural field. And in this vein, it continues to reemerge.

Let me continue this postscript with an anecdote. On the night before Halloween, the local evening news had a brief report on sexual predators, reminding parents to preplan their children's trick-or-treat routes, and urging them to visit the Florida Department of Law Enforcement (FDLE) Web site to identify the homes of known sex offenders, which of course should be avoided. The report also reminded parents (and one assumes the convicts themselves) that sex offenders would have a one-night curfew, during which they were not allowed to answer their doors and were required by law to keep their porch lights off.

Of course, the news report prompted me to go online and search for sexual predators in my neighborhood—not in the interest of tracking them and planning a course of action, but simply in the interest of understanding the knowledge base that was out there, and perhaps simply to add the site to my inventory of unique databases. The FDLE tracks Florida's sexual offenders and predators in a publicly accessible Web site subtitled "Charting a Course for Public Safety."

More than a subtitle, the phrase suggests an active engagement and a collaborative endeavor between law enforcement and the general public or, at the very least, a concerted effort to act in the public interest. The connection between charting and acting is ambiguous. What is the decided relationship between revealing, knowing, and acting? What will knowledge yield? Can we read an archive at a local level to understand the relative degree of prescription that emerges as communal identities are forged from a database?

The FDLE site positions information on sexual offenders and predators under its "citizens" navigational tab, where site users can also find the FDLE's Missing Children Information Clearinghouse. The sexual offenders and predators site features three search engines: an offender search, an e-mail/IM search, and a neighborhood search. The neighborhood search allows users to locate sexual predators by proximity; by simply entering a street address, searchers can retrieve a table or map of sexual offenders and predators within a specified range (in miles) from an origin point (commonly the searcher's home address or neighborhood school). In this virtual Cartesian coordinate system enacted by addresses, the query can produce a table linking the offender's proximity, picture, name, incarceration status, address, and address source information (which also reveals the data's currency), and the results are listed in increasing proximity from the point of origin. The results also can be displayed in map form, locating each offender as a virtual pushpin stuck to the surface of the digital grid of the Tele-Atlas map (powered by Google). Revealed here is an already-burgeoning trend toward the commoditization of geographic information and services, but also the discrete ways in which geography can be marked. Over at Zillow, a real estate valuation site, the same terrain can be marked by home values; and, undoubtedly, the territory can be shaded with other indices. And we can search for corollaries between these maps. Are real estate values affected by the relative presence of sexual predators in any given neighborhood? Certainly, the data can be used by prospective home buyers—criminology becomes market research. The markers yielded by the FDLE site are information nodes, yet definitely not destination points. These are points of warning; their density does not convey a joyous bounty of opportunities (to shop or eat, for instance), but is instead a measure of imminent danger. But any anxiety felt at the local level is compounded or perhaps even birthed by mechanisms of fear production that operate on a grander scale, a transmedia enterprise of national proportions. Fear is not something found happenstance on the Internet or through junk mail, but a planned and determined broadcast affair. While it may be erroneous to equate the sexual predator with the kidnapper, I have already suggested that in the public imaginary (though not supported by statistics), sexual abuse is the greatest threat to child safety and is often simply folded into the generalized danger of abduction; we assume that kidnapping is just the precursor to molestation. Local news stations always seem to have this threat on the back burner, and it is up to national news agencies to periodically turn up the heat, pulling the story front and center. These news stories provide the text for the missing children epidemic; they offer a story that needs a follow-up. Primetime broadcast narratives produce a call to action; they speak the narrative and allow the missing children fliers to simply illustrate, to signify in shorthand. The fliers lack a fully articulated narrative; nevertheless, their details can easily be attached to a plot that has already been elaborated on television. They become intelligible and meaningful largely because of the television text. These technologies of representation are not necessarily in collusion, but they do produce a powerful relay driven by the institutions that govern their use. The fliers are then positioned as a commentary and a response to what is now an obvious epidemic; they serve as feedback to a crisis that now

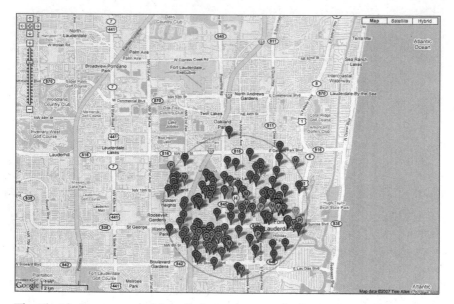

The Florida Department of Law Enforcement sexual offenders and predators map visualizes the proximity of the threat to the family circle. (http://offender.fdle.state .fl.us/offender/homepage.do)

has videographic evidence offered by respected journalists. The news story mobilizes a trail of still images.

To Watch a Predator

For some time now, on the occasional Tuesday night, I have found myself pondering the plight of reality television's latest celebrities—men who are the unsuspecting players in *Dateline: To Catch a Predator,* investigative journalism's response to *America's Most Wanted* and *Big Brother.* Their broadcast debut is always framed by a dramatic dialogic volley between coanchors Ann Curry and Stone Phillips. On the February 13, 2007, episode, their exchange opened with the remark: "Some have seen it, now they're on it, and our hidden cameras are all over it," before moving on to the provocative fragment, "The teacher, the oil man, the ex-cop." NBC's Tuesday-night lineup has become the occasional home of *To Catch a Predator,* which periodically joins the evening's legal drama pairing of *Law & Order: CI* and *Law & Order: SVU.* First aired in November 2004 as a *Dateline* segment titled "Dangerous Web," and with an undercover operation located in New York City, *To Catch a Predator* has since traveled to Washington, D.C., California, Ohio, Florida, Georgia, and Texas in the first ten installments of the investigative series.

My fascination with the series stems from the obvious questions associated with the network's collaboration with law enforcement, and the common legal questions posed about this liaison. Are these participants the victims of a multilayered plan of entrapment that leads from chat room decoys to hired actors to correspondent Chris Hansen? Do these suspects have any right to privacy, or can they be featured freely as part of the flow of network television? In light of the serious nature of the potential offense (the victimization of children), these questions are often assumed to be irrelevant. Yet the show's popularity, borne out by its ratings (*Predator* installments peak the *Dateline* viewership) and its entrance into popular discourse (parodied on YouTube and by Conan O'Brien at the 2006 Emmy Awards, and now in a stage of self-aggrandized historicizing with Chris Hansen's 2007 book culled from his experiences on the series), makes an analysis all the more pressing.[46] What are the cultural implications of a program that circulates information about an assumed public crisis?

The program is part of the general neoliberalist spin that once again turns the public interest over to private industry (consider, for example, the teen lingo cheat sheet on MSNBC.com, written to help parents understand the acronyms their kids use on the Web), and the unsurprising result of a neo-conservative turn that gives information technologies significant leeway as tools of surveillance and discipline in the name of national security—"no privacy, no problem!" *Dateline* calls on the services of Perverted Justice, an organization that exposes men and women who sexually target minors online. Perverted Justice works as a consultant for *Dateline* (and is paid a fee for its services), setting up computer profiles and populating chat rooms with volunteers who pretend to be underage teens interested in sex. There is clearly a conflict of interest here, not simply in the television network's movement from an ideological state apparatus to a decidedly repressive instrument, but also in the confused application of new technology. We are alerted to the dangers of cyberspace, warned of the destructive powers of new media, and told a tale that rallies against surveillance culture (objecting to the ease with which we can see and be seen, and decrying any youthful desire to participate). Yet we are privileged enough to see these very same tools deployed as productive social instruments. The paranoia of online identity as deceptive role play is displaced by the positive yet parallel action of the Perverted Justice decoy, who plays a part to lure the predator. Predator and savior use parallel tactics that have evolved in tandem and are positioned as the yin and yang of the digital age; and we have television to thank for helping us negotiate this contradictory field. The television narrative delivers clarity, a story of decided rights and wrongs, sidestepping ethical quandaries and matters of youthful unrest; whereas the Internet is positioned as a gray zone.

NBC's Dateline: To Catch a Predator *promotes technocratic voyeurism; the program celebrates controlled visibility as it lures both viewer and (alleged) predator into the* Dateline *home.*

Reflecting on *Predator*'s development over its ten investigative installments, Hansen recalls: "The first investigation was very slick. I mean we had five or six cameras. And they set up a mini control room in like a little back room in the house. And they're all huddled in there with the monitors." Tracing the show's development, one of the volunteers with Perverted Justice adds: "We went from Frag [Dennis Kerr, the group's director of operations] and I being perched on a single desk in a hallway at the top of the staircase—to having an entire room set aside where we've got our Web cams up, and we've got our phone verifiers in position. And we've got all these new technologies that we're using. And Frag has gone from having a hallway window to look out of, to having something like seven monitors pyramided around him."[47] The show is a testament to visibility, both in its guiding mission (to put faces on sexual predators) and in its aesthetics of technological oversaturation. The undercover house in Long Beach, California, the set of its February 6, 2007, episode, featured fifteen hidden cameras, while the program itself split the viewing screen repeatedly, at one point offering home viewers four vantage points, plus those additional screens within the televised screen of the surveillance room.

NBC and MSNBC.com have expanded the *Predator* franchise to "Catch an ID Thief" and "Catch a Con Man" and package safety kits for each series. It seems there are many permutations of danger in cyberspace, each of which may be understood as an assault on bourgeois humanism. The body's boundaries can be remapped or penetrated, and desire itself is a dangerous and unruly affair. Both the con and the pedophile speak to unlawful desire, though their acts are vastly different forms of greed. To help us fend off danger (or like a true state apparatus, to keep our desire in check), each series produces its own tool set; the *Predator* safety kit includes a family contract for online safety, culled from Safekids.com, asking parents to pledge, among other things, that they will "not use a PC or the Internet as an electronic babysitter" and reminding kids to "be a good online citizen and not do anything that hurts other people or is against the law."[48]

What *Predator* rather nonchalantly points out, as it produces "the teacher, the oil man, [and] the ex-cop," is that predators are otherwise respectable working-class citizens. Often (though not always), these individuals are identified as family men with wives and children. But the goal here is not to draw a sympathetic portrait; rather, it is to ground the predatory act in the everyday—to make it a commonplace, even widespread nondiscriminatory activity. Predators come from all walks of life, yet they live inside the family circle. What public service is the network doing for their families? Privacy is a problem, even as visibility is a trap. The producers of *To Catch a Predator* do not seem particularly interested in cause or cure; and though abatement and prevention is part of *Predator*'s Internet coverage, the broadcast is most interested in prosecution and punishment.[49]

The public discourse framing the advent of new technologies is complicated by an industry discourse that frames competing yet nonetheless converging technologies. These stories do not neatly align. *Predator* seduces its viewers with several forms of visual pleasure. The first is a voyeurism that is attached to seeing people caught in the act, in watching a performance interrupted and redirected, all from a position of assumed mastery; we all know how this operation works and where this story is going. The second pleasure is a certain technophilia, seeing technology at work, and seeing a lot of it; mastery here comes from knowing the apparatus and seeing more than usual. *Predator* opens up a model home for us to see; much to our delight, it embeds the domestic sphere with technology. This willful violation is integral to the narrative; visibility yields closure.

The missing children epidemic signals absence, a lack of visibility; it is a narrative without closure. In this light, NBC's investigative report seems a better object, even if its narrative impulse is not driven by the exact same phenomenon. These two stories are close enough, and they both involve children, so the slippage here seems easy and willful; it does not require such a big leap of faith to connect these two problems. In her own reading of ADVO mailers, Marilyn Ivy notes: "That a child is missing—not at home—also brings up fears that perhaps we as residents at home are missing something, too."[50] The televisual narrative, like the product ad on the reverse of the missing child mailer, tells us exactly what we are missing. And as it reveals the hidden potentials of other media forms (letting us know about the hazards of life online), it becomes a central instrument in alleviating the very fear it produces; it is a problem solver.

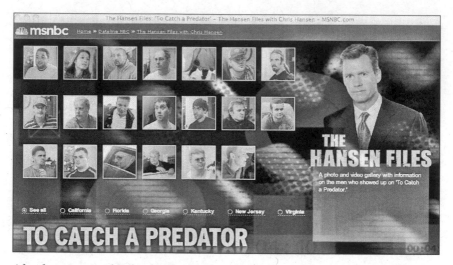

After being exposed individually on network television, the men of To Catch a
Predator *become a visible aggregate on MSNBC.com, where control takes the form
of a user-centered multimedia interface and its governing database logic. The site
prompts visitors to "choose a character" to learn more.* (http://www.msnbc.msn
.com/id/24128499/ns/dateline_nbc-the_hansen_files_with_chris_hansen, accessed
January 29, 2010; site now revised)

Television criticism has positioned commercials as sites of symbolic resti-
tution; in their swift resolution of a crisis, these problem/solution narratives
are more satisfying than the programs they surround. They mark the television text as coherent, for even if closure is absent in the series program, it is
found in the commercial. In the terrain I have charted in this chapter, the
journalistic enterprise and the junk mail flier both function as seductive
problem/solution narratives in their own right; they provide closure. But closure only occurs in those missing children cases that have happy endings,
and even the success stories have arcs that are still distended and angst-
ridden. That media institutions produce fear is concealed by their very calls
to action, and by the seeming consistency of a text that is written across all of
their interfaces. While convergence is still in progress and has led to certain
contradictions, the same cultural myths are being worked out on every platform. Fear seems rather universal and it lingers in the nowhere and everywhere of new media.

2

Private Photos/Public Traumas

National Memories and Moving Images

*When the image of an object changes, the observer must know
whether the change is due to the object itself or to the context or to
both, otherwise he understands neither the object nor its surroundings.
Intertwined though the two appear, one can attempt to tease them
apart, especially by watching the same object in different contexts and
the same context acting on different objects.*

RUDOLF ARNHEIM, *VISUAL THINKING*

Our culture is littered with transitory personal images. Any single
photo can circulate through multiple spaces and be inserted into a
wide array of interfaces, all of which articulate a movement away
from a ground zero of sorts, where the memories elicited by the portrait are
most closely aligned with the occasion of its manufacture. The image's movement gives a spatial and a temporal dimension to an otherwise fixed representation; as the photo traverses space, either virtual or literal, it also evokes a
nostalgic attachment best understood as the workings of the individual memory of each subsequent reader. When the photographic trace is removed, the
personal can still be expressed through an accumulation of surrogate signifiers, if they form a culturally coherent textual system. *Descansos,* or highway
memorials, are one such signifier, and their contested status reveals the tension between two disparate sign systems, one more localized than the other.
The roadside death memorials that populate the roadways of many U.S. cities
are either personal, handmade structures or their mass-produced, governmen-
tally sanctioned equivalents. The form of the standardized highway fatality
marker varies from state to state, often determined by regional departments
of transportation. I suggest that these signposts have a contested status because the local ordinances that govern the erection of official and unofficial
markers of highway deaths are the subject of debates about the limits of freedom of expression at the roadside. The relative presence of ordinances governing highway shrines is itself a marker of the comparative activity of lobbying

efforts and legislation. And more significantly, these debates and decisions reveal that technologies of representation and memory are not ideologically neutral. Rather, these sites of production—as objectified forms of discourse, as symbol systems, and as technologies and institutions—are conflicted pathways.

This chapter considers another set of memorial markers to examine the migration of such conflicts to a new geography. In particular, it examines the circulation of occasional portraits (personal photographs) on CNN.com in the wake of the September 11, 2001, terrorist attacks on America. In the days following the tragedy, CNN posted photos of missing persons in an alphabetized database and, in conforming private images to its predesigned template (positioning cropped images alongside textual cues), made the personal safely public and consumable and attached the individual and privately familial to the collective and publicly familial (the nation). My goal is to unravel some of the assumptions that underpin the exhibition of personal photographs on the Internet and to consider fundamental questions of community and nation, as well as public and private. I turn to this particular category of transient images—images forever imbued with a sense of loss—as I believe the changes here (changes in location, in meaning, and in perspective) might be experienced as the most profound. These images resonate at a deeply felt personal register that might at times help them escape their social attachments. But I also want to draw attention to the more important aspect of any change in perspective—the symbolic attributes of context—for understanding context setting may help us more fully engage with the ideologically laden organizing principles of the technological imaginary.

In the days following 9/11, CNN launched a Web site as part of its coverage of "America's New War" that featured photos of people who were dead, presumed dead, or believed to be missing as a result of the attacks on the World Trade Center. These photos were organized alphabetically by last name and presented as a collection of thumbnails displayed across the page. Photos were submitted to CNN by friends or family of individual victims and, in some cases, gathered by CNN and used with the permission of various media partners. Each name was hyperlinked to a larger profile page of the individual, with an enlarged thumbnail and more extended biographical details, a list of physical traits, and potential locating markers; these details included age, city of residence, employer, physical description, distinguishing characteristics, and information on where the individual was last seen. Personal information was gathered from a variety of sources, including CNN reports, newspaper obituaries, and information submitted by friends and family.

CNN was not alone in creating an online archive. In the days after September 11, reporters from the *New York Times* began compiling profiles of the missing people, culling contact information and details from missing persons

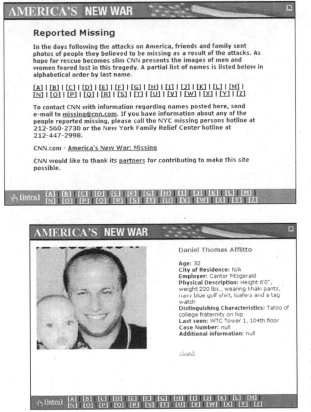

AMERICA'S NEW WAR

Reported Missing

In the days following the attacks on America, friends and family sent photos of people they believed to be missing as a result of the attacks. As hope for rescue becomes slim CNN presents the images of men and women feared lost in this tragedy. A partial list of names is listed below in alphabetical order by last name.

[A] | [B] | [C] | [D] | [E] | [F] | [G] | [H] | [I] | [J] | [K] | [L] | [M] | [N] | [O] | [P] | [Q] | [R] | [S] | [T] | [U] | [V] | [W] | [X] | [Y] | [Z]

To contact CNN with information regarding names posted here, send e-mail to missing@cnn.com. If you have information about any of the people reported missing, please call the NYC missing persons hotline at 212-560-2730 or the New York Family Relief Center hotline at 212-447-2998.

CNN.com - America's New War: Missing

CNN would like to thank its partners for contributing to make this site possible.

[Intro] [A] [B] [C] [D] [E] [F] [G] [H] [I] [J] [K] [L] [M] [N] [O] [P] [Q] [R] [S] [T] [U] [V] [W] [X] [Y] [Z]

AMERICA'S NEW WAR

Daniel Thomas Afflitto

Age: 32
City of Residence: N/A
Employer: Cantor Fitzgerald
Physical Description: Height 6'0", weight 220 lbs., wearing khaki pants, navy blue golf shirt, loafers and a tag watch
Distinguishing Characteristics: Tatoo of college fraternity on hip
Last seen: WTC Tower 1, 104th floor
Case Number: null
Additional information: null

[Intro] [A] [B] [C] [D] [E] [F] [G] [H] [I] [J] [K] [L] [M] [N] [O] [P] [Q] [R] [S] [T] [U] [V] [W] [X] [Y] [Z]

"America's New War: Missing." The CNN. com missing persons database is linked to the war on terror. (http://www.cnn.com)

fliers posted around New York City and interviewing friends and family members of the missing to develop brief narrative sketches. These "Portraits of Grief" were updated daily through the end of 2001, and made available on the Internet. *Times* reporter Janny Scott suggests that: "The portraits were never meant to be obituaries in any traditional sense. They were brief, informal and impressionistic, often centered on a single story or idiosyncratic detail. They were not intended to recount a person's résumé, but rather to give a snapshot of each victim's personality, of a life lived. And they were democratic; executive vice presidents and battalion chiefs appeared alongside food handlers and janitors."[1] Although the portraits are indexed as a searchable database, the interface of the *Times* archive is not a grid; rather, an alphabetized list of hyperlinked names opens up to profiles that are displayed one at a time. Each profile is formatted as a brief news article, with a unique anecdotal header and a biographical narrative laid out alongside a single image of the subject.

The CNN and *New York Times* sites are populated with a wide array of photographic artifacts that, despite their variety, can be categorized; family

photos, vacation photos with marked background vistas, and occasional portraits such as wedding and graduation pictures dominate among those evidentiary photographs included on each site. Some images are formal, some
are informal, some present the subject at work, and others at leisure. Some
are framed as close-ups, others as medium shots or long shots, variably
cropped with or without background detail, representing the featured subject
alone or with others. What further differentiates these individual portraits is
that they are drawn from markedly different original contexts. A few of these
contextual markers can be readily accessed; some of the images are ID photos and others are formal studio portraits, while still others are more casual
images. Each of these contexts subjects the photo-taking process to a different set of codes, loosely understood as distinctions between the amateur and
the professional. But more nuanced distinctions are useful. The varied contexts of the photographic act complicate any simple understanding of the dynamics of public and private. Many of these images are taken by photogra-
phers following industry standards, a series of either overtly legislated or
internalized codes for image taking. The ID photo, for example, is taken with
a series of set standards in mind that govern such variables as background
and framing; yet in the context of the archive or the missing persons flier, the
codes that guarantee a certain degree of homogeneity take a backseat to the
image's ability to signify the uniqueness of the individual.

Clearly, there is a range of portrait files hosted on both servers; some are
direct digital correlatives of an original image of an individual, while others
are remapped files that suggest the image has been cropped to fit the aspect
ratio of the interface's photo box. Still others are more dramatically cropped
from what may have been group shots, trimmed to isolate the victim. Each
image is remapped to make it conform to the specific hypermedia architecture on the local server. Yet this is only one layer of remediation, and there are
more to consider. The CNN site follows and formalizes the geographically
localized actions of individuals in Manhattan who began papering the city
with photos and descriptions of missing persons in the days immediately following the attacks on the World Trade Center. Phone booths and other public
facades throughout lower Manhattan were covered with picture posters in an
ad hoc fashion. Local public service agencies and businesses became identifiable hot spots for community members to post and survey images of the missing.
Subsequently, CNN undertook a doubled representation of loss and recovery,
initially assuming the traditional position of photojournalist, posting photo
essays on its Web site that documented, in an observational mode, the living
gazing at photos of the missing; and in the following week, mounting an
evolving database of the missing persons photos pulled out of their initial essayistic context while immersed in a new frame of reference—that of the

tabularized archive. In this manner, the Web site began to function as a de-territorialized rendering of actual community/material practices. Localized viewing, action, and grief were relegated to a nonspace; in part, these imperatives moved off of particular public streets and onto desktop screens less bound by place. Posters and their embedded images migrated into private homes or semiprivate viewing spaces, the potentially anywhere of the computer and the Internet connection. The relative disarray of public exhibitions gave way to the order of corporate management, made possible in part by a new material practice; images were "removed" from public walls and mapped onto a virtual armature in a digital database on a privately regulated server. The inconsistencies and irregularities of individual photographic practices and the idiosyncrasies of handmade posters were streamlined as they were transcribed to the site's database. This editorializing facilitated the mapping of personal practices onto a standard template—multiple and varied consumer photographs were reduced to selective thumbnail images of particular detail, dimensions, and resolution. In this process, family photographs were unmoored from their specific contexts and reframed as potentially generic signifiers.

The majority of online viewers are inevitably unfamiliar with the immediate familial context of any given snapshot, if indeed contextual details remain in the image as it is cropped for distribution. If we look to hold on to the aura of the image, we find that the immediate family (those individuals through which the image may have circulated) is replaced by a surrogate and more generically inflected conception of the familial. The formal unity of the archive, as Allan Sekula suggests, may be equated with conceptual unity, as photographic resemblances ultimately intimate social cohesion (the honorific possibility of what is nevertheless a territorialized archive).[2] Individual visages yield to the casual viewer simply resemblances. What we are left with, if we do not know the individual, is a curious speculation about how two or more photographs may have similar features, or how any particular portrait may reference our own catalog of images. Through this process of contemplation, the image of an individual body is returned to describe a social aggregate. The site may be understood as both "a socially ameliorative as well as a socially repressive instrument."[3] The viewer's act of speculation is not unrestricted; the site has its own textual markers, formal structures, and principles of organization that delimit the possibilities of narrative interpretation, and as the site's visual structures shift, so do the dominant narrative possibilities.

In the months following its initial launch, the design of the CNN Web site changed, in part reflecting a shift in the discursive strategies of politicians and the news media. "America's New War" was now the "War against

CNN.com

IN-DEPTH SPECIAL In-depth Archive ▾   CNN.com Sections ▾   ☐ CNN Top Stories

September 11 | *A Memorial*

On September 11, four U.S. planes hijacked by terrorists crashed in New York, Washington and Pennsylvania killing more than 3,000 people in a matter of hours. Behind the staggering number of deaths are the individuals, each of whom left behind family, friends and coworkers who feel the national tragedy on a personal level. CNN.com has established this site as an evolving record of those who died and a place for readers to build a living memorial for them.

▸ View Memorial
▸ Send a Tribute
▸ About this Site

Related Sections
▸ War Against Terror
▸ Voices

CNN would like to thank its partners for contributing to make this site possible

---

CNN.com

IN-DEPTH SPECIAL In-depth Archive ⇕   CNN.com Sections ⇕

September 11 | *A Memorial*   ▸ Mainpage ▸ List of names ▸ About this site

HELP   A B C D E F G H I J K L M N O P Q R S T U V W X Y Z
Page: 1 2 3 4 next Δ »

SORT BY > NAME	AGE	EMPLOYER	CITY	STATE	COUNTRY	LOCATION	UPDATED
Gordon McCannel Aamoth Jr.	32	Sandler O'Neill & Partners	New York	NY	United States	World Trade Center	2004-08-23
Edelmiro (Ed) Abad	54	Fiduciary Trust International	New York	NY	United States	World Trade Center	2004-08-23
Maria Rose Abad	49	Keefe, Bruyette & Woods	Syosett	NY	United States	World Trade Center	2004-08-23
Andrew Anthony Abate	37	Cantor Fitzgerald	Melville	NY	United States	World Trade Center	2004-08-23
Vincent Abate	40	Cantor Fitzgerald	New York	NY	United States	World Trade Center	2004-08-23
Laurence Abel		Cantor Fitzgerald	New York	NY	United States	World Trade Center	2004-08-23
William F. Abrahamson	58	Marsh & McLennan Cos. Inc.	Cortland Manor	NY	United States	World Trade Center	2004-08-23
Richard Anthony Aceto	42	Marsh & McLennan Cos. Inc.	Wantagh	NY	United States	World Trade Center	2004-08-23
Heinrich B. Ackermann	38	Aon Corp.	New York	NY	United States	World Trade Center	2004-08-23

"September 11: A Memorial." The CNN.com missing persons site becomes a memorial, as the database is bound to a new interface. (http://www.cnn.com/SPECIALS/2001/memorial)

Terror" and by January 2002, the "Reported Missing" list became a memorial. Individuals previously represented by the text box "photo not available" were now represented by the image of a lit candle—a persistent, uniform, and limited attempt to visualize a memory without an image. These absences beg several questions. Did an image exist? Could an existent image simply not be obtained? And these absences also suggest the limits of photography when it is positioned as the most authoritative trace of memory. Moreover, the site's header reference to "terror" points to the equally horrific fissure opened up by the impossibility of securing an ex post facto image for someone no longer living; the missing image is interpreted as a vacant data field, only to be replaced by an arbitrary placeholder. In this particular incarnation, the technology of memory functions in a rather programmatic yet fundamentally imprecise manner, substituting the individual with the more general register of the vigil (a collective enterprise).

This new database was more rigorously tabularized than its original, with columns organizing the name, age, employer, city, state, country, and location of each victim (expanded beyond the World Trade Center to include all four American Airlines and United Airlines flights, as well as the Pentagon building). This database was searchable by any of these signifiers, all of which could be foregrounded and alphabetized. The individual profiles now included name, age, residence, occupation, location, and tributes. The background graphic was no longer simply red and blue with an image of the American flag, but instead a memorial tableau of candles and flags as a horizontal band that framed the top of each profile.

In this domain, photographic evidence was willingly deployed on behalf of the subject. Most of these images were designed for private consumption, and contained fairly personal (and familial) signifiers; yet they subsequently became part of public discourse. In the movement from the family photo album to the digital domain, from print space to virtual space, notions of geography have been altered. As well, the contextual ground has repeatedly shifted; CNN has since remodeled the space, and (political) history has moved forward while these images have remained stationary.

Public Trauma and the Nature of Events

The terrorist acts of September 11, 2001, in New York, Pennsylvania and near Washington, D.C., resulted in extensive loss of life and tremendous social upheaval, and produced abrupt changes in our social relations—upending the traditional definitions of family, morality, and nation, and creating chaos in a rather brief period of time. Imaged, re-created, and reimagined, these traumatic events produced a new set of cultural memories. Elaborating on the role of representation in the production of collective memory, Marita Sturken suggests: "Cultural memory is produced through representation—in contemporary culture, often through photographic images, cinema, and television. These mnemonic aids are also screens, actively blocking out other memories that are more difficult to represent."[4] Such blocking, or substitution as secondary revision, calls our attention to the formation of sites of erasure that coincide with the very materialization of the national signifier. Citing Andreas Huyssen, Sturken reminds us that objects, images, and representations are technologies of memory, not vessels of memory (nor are they memories themselves). They are bodies through which memories are transmitted. Sturken distinguishes between actively sharing and forming memories (where the object may be understood as an apparatus for meaning production—a technology) and terminally depositing memories (where the object is a lifeless reliquary that does not stimulate a sensory response or foster the production of narrative—a vessel).[5] The vessel may in fact be an impossible figuration, as memory does not occur without articulation. Unavoidably, however, a rift develops between experiencing an event and remembering it, for the technologies of memory cannot shake the suggestion of passage. Roland Barthes pushes further, warning: "Not only is the Photograph never, in essence, a memory (whose grammatical expression would be the perfect tense, whereas the tense of the Photograph is the aorist), but it actually blocks memory, quickly becomes a counter-memory."[6] The emphasis here is on absolute interference rather than an assessment of degree. To consider the stakes involved in this scripting of memory, we must ask if interference has a practical function; and, indeed, it might be best understood as an operation that restores and resocializes. But we are left to consider the impact of new technologies on this process.

Attempts to define the principles of new media by theorists such as Lev Manovich need to be speedily understood as in part allegorical. Any discussion of new media must exceed simply talking about the technological apparatus to consider the way that an apparatus is reshaped by metapsychological codes, and must also admit that every instance of new media is not simply a technological event or passage (however seductive the object or incident), but is at its foundation a multiply determined development, a process wherein technology is deeply enmeshed with other agents.[7] For example, as particular Web sites evolve, they demonstrate the principle of variability, as their underlying data sets can be in part revisualized; the new media object can be defined by the very application of an interface to a multimedia database. But at the same time, the computer layer of the media object, the sum of interface and database, cannot be separated from its cultural layer, its contextual markers, and its historical and psychosocial dimensions. Sites evolve and their evolution is a complex rendering of "keeping up with the times." This adaptive dynamism is consistent with an understanding of technologies as transformative tools. So, in order to analyze the traumatic event, let us shift our focus in this chapter to the content of new media. We should not treat technologies, however convincing their object form, as final resting places for events, nor should we treat them as surrogates for experience, for flux is a norm and technology is merely a passageway.

Despite the obvious nature of technological evolution (new networks emerge, new distributive pathways develop, and images are allowed to continue on their journeys), we must pay closer attention to our use of narrative as a descriptive tool. Narrativity is a process of resistance; it signals a swift and unexamined movement through code to language, as it simultaneously denies the existence of structure and code. If we take a semiotic approach and pause to reflect on the grammatical rules of language and narration, we become open to the impossibility of narrative totality (as narrative cohesion is simply a function of narrative structure). Of course, without closure we are prone to feelings of anxiety. This leads me to certain questions about the nature of events in the digital age. I start from the premise that an event first emerges from virtuality as it becomes knowable, and it becomes knowable only by being narrativized; things happen, yet they need to be ripped out of time and space and given grammatical properties to become speakable and knowable (and capable of being represented). Building from this premise, if an event is extended in time, pushed back into the virtual realm, and read as a string of signifiers, does it become any less unified? Does this process sunder the narrative thread? As images of an event move from one site to the next, leaving a trail in their wake (of varied interfaces, commentary and feedback, and intertextual attachments), do they force the event itself to break apart at the seams, or can these bits be gathered up to simply reinstate our knowledge of things (providing more evidence)? Moving beyond the event, the image, and its associations, I want to consider the unspoken problem that animates the query emerging from these varied signs. Why do we ask images to function in a particular way, encouraging them to produce a singular form of cultural memory? How do we create a stable set of meanings from such an apparent continuum? To answer these questions, I am borrowing from Gilles Deleuze's consideration of the virtual, a concept used to account for the manner in which a discrete entity (an actuality) is the product or effect of a structure or system—a social system, a linguistic system, a kinship system, or other such organizing framework.[8] Trauma creates chaos; it is sudden and shocking. Haunted by such randomness, individuals lose confidence in their abilities to decipher the interconnectedness of events, and can no longer locate their place in history. Chaos raises fundamental questions about the link between our personal lives and historical circumstance. National trauma, unlike personal trauma, depends on a collective consciousness. Yet collectivity depends on the interaction of individuals, either the successful transformation of personal experience into a public crisis or the successful interiorization of public events and their meanings. The cohesive effect of national trauma is best understood as an operation of narrative that at its strongest will not only momentarily bind the nation but also become a collectively ingrained memory. What we must consider are the various systems—ideological or repressive (from ceremonial mourning to martial law, from Freedom Fries to the Patriot Act)—that restore order.

To reflect on structured transformation, one needs only to look at the evidence. In the months since its inception, the CNN.com subsite has been transformed from a database of the dead and missing and a tool for search, recovery, and identification to one of memorial; and in the years since, the site has moved to a lower position in the architecture of the information hierarchy of the general CNN site. The memorial site is no longer hyperlinked to the CNN home page. As the memorial site's function has changed, so has its position and form. The current splash page for the memorial includes a brief paragraph that references the 2001 terrorist acts, recalls the history of a nation in mourning, and establishes the scope and directives of the site. The privileged visual element on the introductory page is a gridlike Flash document. This semirandomized collage includes a number of fixed images that stage a broad iconographic appeal: a fragment of the World Trade Center (the architecturally detailed wall memorialized in postcollapse coverage), an image of a woman in mourning, and a lit candle. The randomized images are portraits culled from the memorial database. In this framework, the portraits are inextricably bound up in the narrative impulse played out across the grid, which is focused on personal and public loss and mourning. In its various incarnations and locations, the inhabitants of the CNN site appear as a community, literally displayed as a thumbnail grouping of individuals, represented collectively as a collage in the domain's image-frame. And this collection of images, of individuals, can be reattached to the World Trade Center itself, as a rearticulation of popular discourses of the familial: the persistent recourse to speaking of the total family of Tower inhabitants, the corporate families of Tower floors, the family of New York City residents, and the family of the Nation, as well as the more immediate familial—those literal families that have been fractured by the loss of relatives.

This collection of images—reassembled momentarily, if only to be once again dispersed at some future time after the site has outlived its function—represents the World Trade Center recollected, though only partially and in radically different spatial terms, within a different architecture, and within a space that melds remote geographies into one localizable arena that places New York, Washington, D.C., and Pennsylvania (tower, building, and air) within the same image-frame.[9] And this collection of images is simultaneously a condensation of the national and a lingering signifier of terrorism. As a memorial, the CNN site is not unlike other contemporary memorials in which the object-status of the reliquary monument is inherently inflected with some evidence of the photographic presence. Late twentieth-century memorial objects seem to demand privatized photographic interventions; in its object form, the memorial cannot shake the residue of latent commodity fetishism. The CNN site is a sanctified form of discourse and it traverses the public and the private; it reads as public architecture that is in some way privately sanctioned. The site is, after all, a privatized discourse, for it is an internal initiative, a corporate undertaking/enterprise made possible in part through the cooperation of IPIX and Kinko's (FedEx Office); the site is scripted and constructed in-house, and its code cannot be altered by its consumers. The site reminds us all too readily of the culture industry and the rift between mass culture and popular culture that the introduction of the personal photograph seems to efface, even though the object is created with the testimonial in mind. In fact, these private/corporate memorials depend upon the insertion of the public/individual, and yet they do so in very prescribed ways. There is a certain order and cleanliness here, codes of conduct that are enforced by the very introduction of a digital conduit; there is no anxiety about the clutter of personal memorabilia at the grave site and there is no anxiety about the misuse of private images. At a time when public safety has shifted from individual to nation, individuals are called to action in a number of ideological ventures in which privacy is willingly yielded. This call to action bears out Sturken's suggestion that memory objects can move between the realms of personal memory, cultural memory, and history, thereby contributing to the obfuscation of these boundaries.[10] Yet each new meaning that accompanies any shift in context is not readily defined in this digital domain; the Internet archive does not function in exactly the same terms as the Hollywood film or the televised program (in terms of ideological bookending or prescription), for it is first and foremost a database, and as such, the images in the database cannot be subsumed into a general script. While they may be located in a general architecture that has a descriptive and prescriptive function, the contours of the narrative pathway are perhaps not as clearly defined and the modes of spectatorial engagement are less fixed. Sturken counters claims of narrative fixity by stating that: "There is nothing politically prescribed in cultural memory."[11] Nevertheless, the atomization of the hypermedia document, a movement away from linearity and from a singular ordering principle and unitary text, is not an inherently political act. While a more general loss of the belief in unitary textuality may be considered liberatory, this textual drift is not innately democratic.

Trauma and the Archive

In *Difference and Repetition*, Gilles Deleuze suggests: "We must always first contemplate something else . . . in order to be filled with an image of ourselves."[12] Public trauma facilitates the migration of personal documents (wedding and vacation photos, intimate family portraits, and the like), ushers them into public space, and encourages the viewer/reader to envision these fragments as part of a "horizontal comradeship," a parasocial relationship with multiple axes. The residues of lived experience as evidenced in the apparently nonfictional enterprise of personal photography are placed at the service of a new narrative; these documents are now part of the public imaginings (however real or fictive) of the nation.

Trauma theory positions those memories associated with traumatic experience in relation to dream logic, recorded not in a linear manner assigned to verbal narrative but in a manner that exceeds words and is fundamentally comprised of vivid sensations and images. The goal of trauma therapy is integrative, to move the victim through stages of safety, mourning, and ultimately reconnection to everyday life.[13] While imaging can serve as a significant component of security and remembrance, personal photos can perhaps overcome the representational limits imposed by photojournalism; print media images are more overtly secured by an agreed-upon grammar and convention, aimed at a form of narrativity that may not be fully productive in posttraumatic integration. Yet quite often, as part of the integrative act, private images intermingle with public images to create a dense fabric of associations that function at the level of allegory.

The CNN profile pages point outward to Legacy.com, a "meta" online memorial site that archives newspaper obituaries from across the country and features searchable records from the Social Security Death Index. Here, the 9/11 victims are scattered among the dead, across the nation and across time; this database intermingles those deaths that have been memorialized as part of national tragedies and those that go relatively unnoticed by the nation at large. Many of the September 11 profiles are reprinted from the *New York Times*, repeating the same anecdotal narrative with its accompanying image, occasionally supplementing it with a standard newspaper obituary. Oftentimes, the placeholder image of a lit candle on the CNN site is filled in by a photo of the person, while a linked guest book mirrors the CNN site's tribute holder. More notable is the photo gallery feature on the Legacy site; each profile has a placeholder for an appended photo gallery that can be played as a slide show. While some of these galleries contain additional personal photos of the deceased, others read as more associative scrapbooks. One such listing contains the following four pictures in sequence: a floral arrangement with the superimposed text, "God Bless America! September 11, 2001"; an appropriated news image of firefighters at Ground Zero standing beneath an iron girder cross; an animation of a red rose dripping blood; and a photo collage of several superimposed elements, including an appropriated news image of the burning World Trade Center, a torn American flag, and text that reads: "that we here highly resolve that these dead shall not have died in vain." This particular photo gallery evokes what Thomas Elsaesser refers to as an inauthentic media history—a second-order memory that is not arrived at through personal artifacts but through national audiovisual media. Referencing the televised documents of the John F. Kennedy assassination and the Challenger disaster, Elsaesser writes: "Such images belong to a different kind of reality: that of obsession or trauma, to which correspond a different kind of action and placing of the self, based on re-telling, repeating, not working-on, but working-through. For this, television is indeed predestined, for otherwise, how to explain its most obvious feature, the compulsion to repeat?"[14] Imaging can be an integral feature of traumatic remembrance, repetition, and working through.[15] Memory itself, at the core of the first step in this process, is part of a signifying chain, for something can only be remembered if and when it is articulated into a chain of knowledge.[16]

Yet the more personal images at the center of my analysis are not inherently aligned with trauma—they are not visual artifacts of such experience. Rather, the images I am considering are the interstitial material of the knowledge chain that has been constructed by event videography of such incidents as building collapse and airline disaster. These images may be part of what Michel Foucault refers to as "subjugated knowledges," those voices that emerge from archives and unlegitimated sources that tangle with the story of (official) history.[17] But what "knowledge" per se is contained in them, and what precisely are the terms of the struggle over memory and history in this domain? Subjugated knowledges, even when they rise to the surface and are "vocalized," may be re-bound and submersed within a superseding narrative; the context of their expression may be overpowering.

The codes of what may be termed loosely as personal advertisement photography embody a particular disciplinary method that is just as likely imposed whether or not the sitter is the photographer. There are multiple architectures of the missing persons/memorial advertisement, and these expand and contract in accordance with a context: the square photo, the text window, the browser window, the computer desktop, and the monitor screen. As with the photographs of missing children discussed in Chapter 1, there are particular strategies of containment deployed in the manufacture of these images, such as what information the director/sitter chooses to include and exclude. And once again, there are particular strategies that govern the distribution of the image, dictating how the image is cropped and inserted into a textual field. Each of these formal devices may shape our understanding of the sitter's physical body, enabling us to read it as part of a larger social body.[18] In her book *Family Frames: Photography, Narrative and Postmemory*, Marianne Hirsch seeks to bring the codes and conventions of family photography to the foreground in order to expose the ideological work of such systems of representation.[19] Superseding the look of the camera and any localized exchange of looks between family members is where Hirsch locates the ideological project of the familial gaze, a culturally and historically specific projection that governs the ideal of family and, by association, the production of its images.[20] It is beyond my scope here to consider at length the unconscious optical chain of family exchanges, but it is important to note that family photographs cannot be understood as a neutral repository of the private; these images too are a contested terrain, subject to a particular set of representational conventions that construct the individual subject inside the family and, by extension, construct the family inside society. Hirsch notes that although the representational system of family photography may seem heterogeneous, it is nonetheless a system.[21]

Individual, Family, and Nation

The CNN.com documents seem to describe the individual and his or her social placement, relationally positioned within (or outside) a social class or community. The individual exists, then, only in relationship to a type, a broader category of being, and the textual markers of the site assist this reading. As these photographic traces are aligned with new textual markers, they become what Deleuze refers to as artificial signs: "Artificial signs . . . are those which refer to the past or the future as distinct dimensions of the present, dimensions on which the present might in turn depend. Artificial signs imply active syntheses—that is to say, the passage from spontaneous imagination to the active faculties of reflective representation, memory and intelligence."[22] Although the photographic act may be commonplace, its codes of conduct are value-laden, now embroiled in the delimiting act of conceptualizing sameness through association—the goal being to make sense of a present that is no longer familiar. The individual is bound up in rethinking the present to secure the nation(al) signifier.

At a fundamental level, the CNN site operates only by transcribing a certain form of desire (for closure, perhaps, or interpersonal association) into a localizable sign necessary for communication. Desire becomes objectified; much in the same way that anxieties about identity politics are squelched through the inscription of rather complex identity formations into a fixed number of visible signs, so too does a culture's anxiety about the potential fluidity of desire manifest itself in the urge to categorize, to delimit specific forms of desire and inscribe each with a relative value. The manifestation of desire that is out of bounds, so to speak, one that is counterintuitive to positivism, speaks to the tenuous fixity of rationality. Though terrorism may not simply be equated with the desire for chaos and anarchy, it suggests a potential interruption in the fabric of dominance; it can denaturalize a dominant ideological position, perhaps only for a moment, by exposing the work required to maintain such a position.

There are inevitably two oppositional motivations fueling the drive toward inscription; the more liberatory impulse is one that produces identification (collapsing distinctions between self and other) for the unleashing of desire, while the more conservative impulse is one that produces distanced identification (identification as nomenclature—naming the "other") in order to eradicate desire. Both of these motives seem inextricably bound together in the CNN site. The identification with innocent victims is part of the operational logic of terror, while the second term of the equation is the distanced "other" or victimizer. The victim and victimizer are critical parts of the same tale, placeholders for the binary opposition essential to any mythology.

The site's drive illustrates an institutional insistence on community. The site engages with the machinations of myth making, and should not be confused with the experience of community in its unadulterated form. The former is an institutional imperative and is simply a simulacrum of community that channels information and desire in rather prescriptive ways, mapping communiqués onto fixed templates. Although a call to a purer notion of community may seem naively nostalgic, we can attempt to distinguish degrees of institutional prescription and consider that community by its very nature may be more fluid and exceed the fixed language of the privately authored and statically coded interface. Community, apart from representing shared physical space (geography), can more abstractly represent shared psychical space.

Individual and cultural memory are bound up in the reconfiguration of the CNN site, as it is transformed from a search engine to a memorial; the individual is not effaced, but embroiled in the fabric of history and the creation of cultural meaning. Families are attached to and stand in as signifiers

of the nation, as private images are circulated, consumed, archived, and woven together in this particular Internet architecture, made literally public
and into metaphors of the public. As Lauren Berlant suggests, in describing
the "national symbolic," the individual is transformed into a subject of a collectively held history. The implications are writ large for the stakes of personal subjectivity in this act of transformation. The individual and the nation
are attached in this domain, as private citizens, their images at least, are
called into service for the nation; the call to community functions as a decidedly counterterrorist act. Thomas Elsaesser concludes that: "Any image
is always more densely packed with information and resonance than the
simple substitution of the one for the many—the icon for the reality—might
suggest."[23] In the context of the CNN site, each image functions to remind
us of the one *and* the many, of the individual *and* the nation, of a private
family *and* a public one. Yet we must be attentive to the relative plasticity
and dynamism of particular hyperspaces and their respective "documents."
Cyberspace has been envisioned as an arena that may facilitate its real-time
restructuring by a community of authors on a network, but it also has been
read as a trap, rendering its subjects immobile. The dynamism of technological and social matrices is compromised by the push toward a stable interface (and the standardization of markup and programming languages).

The social body is defined through individual bodies that adopt its governing *lingua franca*; it would be an oversimplification to suggest, however,
that the bodies that attach themselves to a particular community formation
have simply internalized its ideological trappings. Perhaps these autobiographical artifacts unwittingly embroil their subjects in history. Nevertheless,
to retain the equilibrium between expressive and repressive uses of imaging
in a new media landscape, we must question the assumed truths of traditional photographic and representational practices. We must also question
the privileged and rather monolithic conceptions of representational realism,
and the information hierarchies in which representations are ultimately
inserted.

My goal has been to consider the spatial realignment of experience and
memory in the digital domain, and the contours of the autobiographical act
within a technological system of potentially endless revision. While roadside
descansos are erected at their respective incident sites, standing where loved
ones died in car accidents, online memorial markers have a very different
geographic locus. Certain critical formulations of the autobiographical impulse
in artistic discourse privilege those works that are engaged in a dialogue with
history, which articulate connections between the personal and the social.
This movement is deemed to be revelatory, yet we need to consider precisely
what is being revealed. Not all attachments of the individual to the collective

and not all obfuscations of the private and the public work in the same manner. We need to consider the terms of the attachment and the arena in which it is being staged.

I return to my stated goal of exploring the fissure between an event and its remembrance in an effort not only to understand the stakes involved in scripting memory but also to suggest the possibility that transitory images may evade or exceed their ideological appropriation by any apparatus and interface. Subjectivity is inherently messy, and it is important to dwell on the points of erasure that work to make subjectivity unnaturally sanitary. *Descansos* were originally resting places, points along the walked path to the burial site that served a physical and psychical function, where mourners paused momentarily while carrying the body of the deceased. *Descansos* were erected at these resting points as ad hoc fabrications, culled from whatever materials were available *in situ*. Yet the contemporary roadway is a transitional space that does not encourage us to slow down, and the move toward an industrial logic of memorial production does not encourage us to look closely; what we perceive are simply austere surfaces. The large black lettering on the white circular roadside markers in Florida reads, "Drive Safely," while the deceased is named in the fine print below. Some of these official markers are ringed by garlands or decorated with other unsanctioned mementos such as stuffed animals—evidence that a negotiation is at work. As individuals try to personalize these state-managed sites, we see the tension between two narratives: one that returns the memorialized to the family circle and another that inserts the memorialized into a public-service narrative about auto safety. The tension between private and public does not simply have an active political dimension, but also yields what are often unspoken—yet no less important— divergent narrative threads.

Marianne Hirsch concludes her analysis of family portraiture with a consideration of resistance. Hirsch rereads family photographs to dwell on the discontinuities they produce, as she attempts to intervene with dominant cultural practices. Hirsch cites writer Marguerite Duras: "I believe photographs promote forgetting. . . . The fixed, flat, easily available countenance of a dead person or an infant in a photograph is only one image as against the million images that exist in the mind. And the sequence made up by the million images will never alter. It's a confirmation of death."[24]

Hirsch's project here, via Duras, is to restore the particular, to undo the forced plenitude of the imaginary evoked by a photograph's potential institutional allegiances.[25] Hirsch suggests that the work involved in rereading images might enable resistance and change if any apparent discontinuities are allowed to surface. What stories are told in a particular photo? Why have certain images been selected as representative of an event or an individual?

Roadside memorial markers reveal a subtle tension between private and public sign systems and their narratives. (Photo by Eric Freedman)

What images might complete the sequence? And what has been lost through their omission? What stories are projected onto an image and spoken openly? What stories are left suppressed and unspoken? Rereading may result in a conscious break with cultural positioning by revealing artifacts of memory that cannot be secured into a master narrative; though this deconstructive process may not yield overt social rebellion, it may be liberating for the individual.

To this end, the tributes and information that accompany each profile on the CNN memorial site seem to be central to a less-static notion of identity and community. The numerous repositories for feedback on the CNN site include a brief biographical sketch as well as personal testimonials from friends, family members, coworkers, clients, and even total strangers. Those who never knew the profiled person try to make sense of the individual's life and death. One such contribution reads: "I never knew this man, but his life and tragic death were not wasted. Each victim who gave his or her life died for the future freedom of the free world. Through their tragic death a trusting nation was awakened from a trusting slumber and transformed to the roar of an angry nation that will be heard for 100 years. Through his death and the death of all the victims my children will be free and safe."[26]

Another contribution, positioned alongside testimonials from one victim's friends, reads: "I want to say that I am very sorry about what has happened, and I hope that we get Osama bin Laden and all of his terrorist groups."[27] Still other testimonials return the subject to the familial realm; even if the deceased is not known by the author, the subject can be understood in familiar terms as a wife or husband, mother or father, daughter or son: "After reading the memorial to your husband, I was saddened that he didn't get a chance to realize that he was going to be a father again, but then, realize, YES, he does know and is looking down on you."[28]

The subject can also be read through other cultural signifiers, and can be attached to several distinct frames of reference. Tributes commonly move from the individual to the familial to the nation, responding to very precise textual markers while returning to a far more general narrative, and confessing to the deceased while also being mindful of others:

> Joanne, You don't know me but as a fellow Greek, I feel I lost someone very close to me. It is just a tragedy what happened to you and the rest of the victims of the 9/11 tragedy. Your smile in your picture will always remain forever in my mind, and I hope your smile ensures the terrorist behind this that they have NOT (succeeded) in breaking the spirit of the American people. May your memory be eternal and may your family find the peace one day very soon in dealing with your tragic loss.[29]

The sum of feedback entries on many of the CNN pages positions the profiled individual as a character in multiple narratives. While some entries attach the subject to the nation, others are much more intimate in their attachments, returning the individual back to a more localized family. While both calls to inclusion may be prescriptive and form a part of separate but dependent ideological projects, there is evidence of a certain work or agency involved in these testimonials. The attachments may ultimately read as fleeting, secured only by calling them out. The images on the CNN site seem to exceed any fixed ideological appropriation, if only because the narratives that inscribe them are potentially ever-expandable (and not always readily synthesized). What is evidenced here is a story in progress. Like the body on the path to its final resting place, transient images may rest momentarily. But what they leave in their wake is a trail of discursive shifts; meaning is fleeting rather than fixed. Subjectivity must inevitably be understood as residing in the interstices, in the spaces between the stories and in the gaps between images that are considered part of a larger life's work. And history can only be revised if we continue to rewrite it.

I opened this chapter with what may seem like simply a casual aside about roadside memorials. But reflecting on the events of September 11, what

I have tried to unearth is a more subtle aspect of trauma that is buried be-neath the more accessible and perhaps forceful tragedy—the loss of human life. For there is still an exposed wound in the new geography of Manhattan. The trauma here is the inability to return the landscape to its former state, an anxiety reflected even in the field of popular culture, where producers and critics consider how to treat now-obsolete images of the city's skyline.

3

Trauma and the Cellular Imaginary

*Philosophical concepts are fragmentary wholes that are not aligned
with one another so that they fit together, because their edges do not
match up. They are not pieces of a jigsaw puzzle but rather the
outcome of throws of the dice. They resonate nonetheless, and the
philosophy that creates them always introduces a powerful Whole that,
while remaining open, is not fragmented.*

GILLES DELEUZE AND FELIX GUATTARI, *WHAT IS PHILOSOPHY?*

"Everywhere you go, there you are." *Motorola's vision of Seamless
Mobility is to make your life all about you. It's about devices that share
information so you don't have to remember where the file is. It's about
intelligent networks that automatically know who you are and the
information you need. It's about making your home more connected,
your car more aware, your office more mobile and the world around
you more personal, more predictive, and more accessible. By linking
together every networked device in your life, Motorola wants to make
it possible for you to find everyone and everything, everywhere you are.*

MOTOROLA 2004 ANALYSTS MEETING

At Motorola's 2004 Analysts Meeting at the Westin O'Hare Hotel in
Rosemont, Illinois, the company celebrated two enterprises—making
seamless mobility real and making liquid media real. The realness in
both cases was marked by the materialization of concepts, their embodiment
(taking on physical form) in several distinct software, hardware, and interface
technologies. Reviewing the former of these two pronouncements, Motorola's
press coverage claimed: "Seamless mobility—the interconnection of devices
between operating systems, platforms, and media—was living and breathing at
the Motorola 2004 Analysts meeting."[1]

Seamless mobility is, in part, about marking the terrain, making the general
field a space for autobiographical work; our personal data trails bridge
and brand physical locations. But in commercial discourses, autobiography is
not a privileged term, even though it is trotted out as a powerful conceptual

hook in countless advertising campaigns. Instead, seamless mobility suggests that the consumer is continuously connected to relevant content across devices, networks, and physical environments; and in this series of exchanges, the personalization of protocols is the only trace of the end user's psyche. Autobiography is shaped into a very limited form of self-expression, registered in the myriad ways we engage with and control technology. But how enlightening are such exercises? While my interest is in the autobiographical work accomplished by mobile consumers, "work" may be an inappropriate term here, for it begs the question: "What type of work is actually being performed?"

Motorola's vision of user experience invokes a world where, according to the company's promotional literature, consumers are "mobile, informed, entertained, secured, connected and empowered."[2] Yet this laundry list of actions is displayed as self-evident, and reads as a series of empty slogans, each of which begs any number of inquisitive retorts: Secured against what? Empowered how, exactly? Certainly, Motorola's vision of empowerment does not parallel social movement rhetoric; instead, the company foregrounds the personalization and control of communicative acts. What is evoked is only the most obvious expression of productivity that is in step with the workaday logic of business—not business as usual, but more business than usual. In this chapter, my goal is to explore the terms of productivity more forcefully and to identify moments of activity that seem to be either off-limits or out-of-bounds in order to examine those spaces and actions that seem either unproductive or counterproductive. Empowerment is a forcefully agentive concept, yet it seems a rather passive construct in Motorola's hands, reduced to a matter of conceptualization rather than a call to action.

In the field of contemporary telecommunications, mobile producers and carriers are not simply corporations but acquaintances; we are hailed by such pleasantries as "Hello Moto" and asked to celebrate consumption, value, and technophilia, while being urged to "Get More." Moreover, cellular producers and providers, building on the planned obsolescence inherent to selling technology, call attention to the new and evolving interface with reality—perfecting verisimilitude and integration, measured in megapixels, transmission rates, and other data sets and coded through the familial iconography of their advertising campaigns. Yet in the same moment, the world is being more forcefully reimagined and pointedly reimaged; the relationship between vision and reality is not simply allegorical, especially as the individual and the family are being called into active service for the nation. The selective tethering of the two terms (vision and reality) has material consequences, and we must be attentive to who is constructing the reference frame. The media frame—whether a hardware device, a software interface, or a matter of content creation and management—can contour our imagining of the world beyond the window. We must consider who is reimaging the world and what collaborative partnerships (industrial, governmental, popular, or otherwise) are shaping our knowledge of the public realm of everyday events and actions.

iPhone and the Snuff Film

On December 30, 2006, Saddam Hussein was executed in Iraq after being sentenced to death by hanging for crimes against humanity. Just over one week later, on January 9, 2007, Steve Jobs was introduced on stage to the tune of James Brown's "I Feel Good" and proceeded to unveil the iPhone as part of his keynote address at Macworld in San Francisco. Although these men were on public display for very different purposes, and on quite different stages, they were inevitably bound together by certain cultural logics of new media.

By mid-January 2007, a two-and-a-half-minute clip of Saddam Hussein's execution had been viewed 15,605,630 times on Google Video and had received a rating of four out of five stars (ranking it "above average"). But this clip is just one of many cataloged by Google Video, each of which has a unique title. While most of the entries feature the same video, recorded by a witness to the execution using a cell phone, others take some liberties with the footage, including: a four-minute piece titled "Swinging Saddam Execution Video," described as a "groovy" video "starring GeGe the Go Go girl and her new dance the 'Saddam Swing'!"; and another, "Hanging Saddam," featuring a one-and-a-half-minute still-image montage, a chronology framed by traditional wipe, dissolve, and documentary effects (in the style of Ken Burns), shaped into essayistic form by intertitles, and underscored by Green Day's "Good Riddance (Time of Your Life)."[3]

At the end of June 2007, Apple released its iPhone to consumers in the United States and began to make its first inroads into the telecommunications business. Steve Jobs proudly points out that the company's latest device is not just a mobile phone but also a widescreen iPod and an Internet communicator. The iPhone is, of course, part of a larger industrial history of cellular technology and, like the developments that precede it, the result of a persistent engagement with an evolving and inherently ideologically charged visual interface. The architecture of the mobile phone platform is, after all, a language, and the latest "revolution" in user interfaces marks the degree to which hardware and software are conceptualized in tandem.

In his discussion of cultural transcoding, Lev Manovich suggests that the computer layer and the cultural layer push against and shape each other, to the extent that the general computerization of culture in the digital age gradually substitutes existing cultural categories and concepts with new ones that derive from the computer's ontology.[4] Much in the same manner, geopolitics is bound to spatial politics and reveals the causal relationships between political power and geographic space; natural resources can shape social and political relations, and those very same relations are capable of pushing back against the physical terrain. On the subject of ontological remapping, the shrine city of Kazimain is now home to a Camp Justice franchise, one of several United States military bases in Iraq and one of many such installations across the globe. Law can reclaim fixed points on a compass once claimed by faith; and satellite images reveal the number of distinct institutional footprints that mark the land. Justice can be made elastic and modifiable (the structures at Guantanamo Bay can be ported and erected elsewhere); it can be architected to fit any set of legalistic circumstances, and it can literally remake the political landscape in its own image. Beyond allegory, justice has decided physical properties and consequences; it claims space and has malleable dimensions.

Similarly, computer hardware and software shape culture, and the ability to generate, organize, manipulate, and disseminate data—though part of the developmental trajectory of computer programming—has a much broader impact, influencing how we process the world around us. Computational space has become part of lived space (we live in an interface culture), and computing itself now privileges interaction over computation. However portable and personal, we should not lose sight of the social and political consequences of even the most intimate of new technologies.

A recent Apple press release suggests that the iPhone "completely redefines what you can do on a mobile phone." These pronouncements suggest that Apple has thought through what consumers should do with their mobile phones and has a few ideas about what consumers actually will do, but according to an on-demand delivery logic of production, this purposefully leaves open other possibilities.[5] While the appropriated execution video of Saddam Hussein at the gallows in Kazimain has been subjected to what seems the logic of Apple's already popular iLife suite (embodying the simple material practices of audio and video mixing made possible by consumer-grade desktop editing tools), certainly phone manufacturers do not envision their devices being witness to an execution, nor do consumer-focused software manufacturers dwell on the rhetorical tropes of multitrack editing.

Trauma and the Technobiographic Subject

Given the contested status of the objects I have just considered, this latest push in the pursuit of a digital lifestyle leads me to certain questions about the relationship between two forms of integration—one accomplished and

evidenced by technological convergence and the other associated with the
domain of trauma therapy. The former is of a physical and mechanical nature
and the latter is psychical and biological. What connects these two enterprises (of integration) is the common push toward embodiment, as well as
their mutual dependence on media.[6] As part of a developmental trajectory,
one of the aims of trauma therapy is to localize sensation, delimiting what
was once excessive, and to reattach the subject; this is especially the approach in trauma theories based on dissociation, which emphasize the importance of retrieval, abreaction (the release of emotional tension, often by acting
out), and integration on the path toward psychotherapeutic change. Likewise,
the push toward a singular (and, coincidentally, Cingular, in the case of Apple's United States–locked cellular network provider) manifestation of the
digital lifestyle can be read as a narrative about localizing sensation, investing
in one device, and channeling distinct media along one conduit, though the
change being actuated is a bit more oblique.[7] Is this a change in technology,
character, or culture? As Jobs suggests, the interface itself is fluid and responsive, its malleability an assurance that the iPhone can adapt to changes in the
media landscape and retain its centrality. The "buttons" themselves are virtual
and can be remapped; the hardware of the iPhone is almost as fluid as the
software. Apple's "Instead" campaign shapes the iPhone into a phantasmago-
rical digital hub, touting: "Here's an idea. Instead of carrying an iPod and a
phone, why not carry an iPod, with all your favorite music and your favorite
movies, *in* your phone." The iPhone is imbued with the phantom limbs of its
predecessors. While its functionality may seem rather open, the device is not
simply an empty vessel; it is shaped by our experiences with earlier media
forms and it is launched within a prevailing cultural attitude.

The general trend toward seamless mobility heralded in the research and
development of new technologies (the integration of multiple feature-rich
media devices and operating platforms—in the home, in the car, and at the
office) is part of a larger projection of the future of liquid media (taking media
and shaping it to the various circumstances that people find themselves in)
that also wants to embroil the subject in the technology.[8] New media industries are drafting biographical practices that subsequently can be attached to
individual authors. The aim is to create new media frameworks that replicate
subjectivity and merge the lived context with an apparatus of production,
fostering the development of "technobiographies" that write the self through
the postindustrial logic of new media.[9] Responsive technologies seem to situate end users as unique social actors, as inscribed data (though not governing
code) accumulates and becomes symptomatic of our presence. New technologies may seem to operate freely to the extent that they act intuitively, but
their intuition is by design; it is inherently the result of a script (of a coding

activity brought to fruition by developers). As we become conscious of the possibilities for remapping technology, do we overlook the limits of our own subjectivity, itself the product of an unseen script?

The technobiographic subject is constructed through multiple frameworks. It may be useful, as a start, to outline the following actions that I believe are central to the life technobiographic: (1) anthropomorphizing technology, (2) humanizing technology, (3) fostering dependencies with responsive technologies, (4) using autobiography as a signature content referent, and (5) helping individuals put autobiography into practice. These actions are given form within a number of institutional spaces, narrated by each institution's respective discourse. We see them given form in advertising, industry, and education; they are militarized and often politicized. We see the technobiographic subject celebrated and demonized. In the most general sense, the technobiographic subject may be approximated by examining its encounters with technology; in essence, it is written through them, and recorded and shaped by them. We see this in the life of smart objects that record our personal preferences, as well as in the contouring of smart objects whose interfaces and intelligences have been carefully calibrated with the human subject in mind, making such technologies seem intuitive and responsive. And we see this in the type of fluidity we expect in our engagements with new technologies, a feature we begin to demand rather habitually in our daily lives, regardless of the context.

While I am critical of blind media effects discourse (hypodermic needle theories have been repeatedly upended), I turn to a number of ad campaigns to illustrate how technology is regularly positioned as a technobiographic agent. Most prominent, we see technology consistently anthropomorphized and humanized throughout Apple's multigenerational advertising legacy, beginning with its "1984" ad, a tale of human resistance in a PC-laden Orwellian society. Following through with this impulse several decades later (perhaps as a lighthearted reprisal of the troubling man/machine dyad), a 2002 spot for Apple's redesigned iMac (a flat-screen monitor mounted to a semispherical CPU by a swivel arm) features a man standing outside a store window as he is taunted by an iMac that mimics his every movement. And anthropomorphism segues into humanism in Apple's more recent "Get a Mac" campaign. Opening with the now-familiar greeting, "Hello, I'm a Mac," the spots (created by Apple's advertising mainstay TBWA\Chiat\Day) use actors to play the competing architectures of Mac and PC. Pushing beyond the two platforms, the campaign's later spots expand the human chain. "Network" is designed to highlight Mac's compatibility and casts a Japanese woman as the embodiment of a digital camera. In an effort to familiarize and demystify, and to insert technology into active citizenship (computers are now part of the general population, though clearly cleansed of any dystopic cyborg resi-

*Anthropomorphism emerges
in a 2002 Apple iMac
advertisement.*

due), these ads efface technology altogether—they cast it only as a series of human equivalences.

We see autobiography used as a signature content referent across a range of devices. Apple's "Elope" spot, an advertisement for iDVD, features a Mac-savvy groom who surprises his folks with a DVD of his South Pacific wedding, assembled using iDVD. And the company's "Middle Seat" spot, an ode to Apple's "Think Different" slogan, highlights the rather resourceful actions of a college-age male as he turns his airline seat into an in-flight editing studio and begins to string together clips of his girlfriend and her dog using his iBook and iMovie. In "Elope" and "Middle Seat" (both of which were broadcast in 2001), technology is embedded in a familiar and familial economy that traverses personal geographies and merges different lived contexts (honeymoon and home movie are digitized, migrated, manipulated, and exhibited). Specific places are represented and compressed; events are rescreened at some distance from their points of origin, yet the process is an obvious one. As these advertisements are primarily about a product interface, the act of viewing, scrutinizing, and organizing life's activities is privileged and simplified, even as the private realm is opened up to scrutiny by others (most explicitly in "Middle Seat," as the young man edits while surrounded by his cabinmates). These spots are an invitation to look; we are meant to see both the artifact and the process of manipulation. The goal is to demystify, to couch "ease" and convergence itself in a comfortable metaphor. Commenting on Apple's marketing campaign, advertising analyst Bob Garfield notes: "The 1984 ads did not do one single thing to illustrate or demonstrate the technology. These commercials dramatize in a very engaging way specific features. This is about function and killer apps."[10] Beyond a metaphoric imagining, both "Elope" and "Middle Seat" showcase the interface with noteworthy shots of the desktop screen and the application window, and they willfully explore the production

The iBook is positioned inside a familial economy in a 2001 Apple advertisement.

process to forcefully demonstrate the practical ways that technology can be integrated into everyday life. They move from using autobiography as an empty reference (an advertising trope that simply tugs at our heartstrings) to demonstrating how it might be put into practice.

Following suit, mobile carriers have promoted their own scenarios of integration, literally mobilizing the technobiographic subject. In the 2002 T-Mobile "Baby" advertisement, as people go about their daily routines, a picture of a smiling baby girl starts appearing in the public landscape, embedded in a variety of widely distributed and readily visible media forms (e.g., billboards, bus benches, newspapers, T-shirts, and shopping bags). In these varied contexts, the image functions as news and advertisement, as it follows several commercial flows while maintaining its privatized (though ritualized) function as an image aligned with the family photo album. For T-Mobile, the image announces the birth of a new network of possibilities—a technology in its infancy, though hardly infantilized. Promoting mobile-to-mobile picture messaging, the ad's announcer suggests: "When something great happens, you want everyone to see it. . . . Life's better with pictures."

Likewise, Nokia (in the business of "connecting people") has adopted a campaign that positions its phones as a bridge between "vision" and "reality." The company prompts users to reimagine their worlds, a cultural reimagining made possible only through technology. A 2006 ad campaign for the Nokia N91 features five vignettes. In each, the technology infects its host. The audio tracks from the MP3-capable device play back across each user's body (with each host caught in some act of desiring—dancing, looking, listening, kissing, touching); acoustics become a physical script, a transitory and fluid tattoo that draws itself across each person's skin and gives form to their desire. Nokia gives us an amusing and rather poetic metaphor for embodiment, set to the up-tempo longings of Moby's "In My Heart."

T-Mobile courts consumers in a 2002 advertisement that embeds private family photos in a public urban landscape.

The T-Mobile and Nokia campaigns push technobiographic agency to its logical end; they point to the viral nature of new technologies, but understand the viral as a virile evolutionary enhancement. The technology infiltrates, marking the physical terrain, but what it leaves in its wake is a trail of subject-bound signifiers pronouncing humanity. Or the technology invades, merging with the subject, but it does not efface the subject's presence; rather, it promotes new forms of expressivity, fostering the creative impulse and fueling the desiring engine. At times, technology provides new feedback loops; it reveals our state of being. Here, technological determinism gives way to biomechanical determinism. When Apple unveiled details about its iPhone 3.0 software in March 2009, the company also announced a new class of third-party peripheral development: iPhone-compliant medical devices (a blood pressure cuff and a Johnson & Johnson LifeScan blood glucose meter). These accessories and their respective application suites enable the recording, charting, and transmission of physiological data, connecting patients to their bodies and to their health-care providers. The iPhone is positioned as a fundamental aspect of well-being. Throughout its brief history, the iPhone has been repeatedly framed as a biofeedback device. Continuing a partnership launched by Nike and Apple in 2006, the newest phones can be paired with the Nike+, a wireless in-shoe accelerometer that records the runner's workout statistics. The position of the iPhone as both a popular communicative tool and a personal technobiographic agent is not unique. Microsoft Research introduced the SenseCam in 1999, a wearable digital camera designed to take photos passively, without user intervention. The device has been used in clinical trials for the treatment of patients with a broad range of memory disorders, as a tool to complement the restoration of autobiographical memory. Several Sense-Cam studies have highlighted the relative importance of images to the distinct memory processes of knowing (an act of pure inference) and remembering

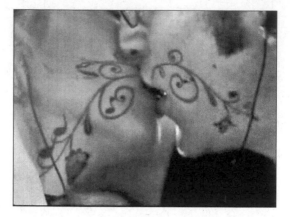

In a 2006 advertisement for the Nokia N91, technology draws itself across its host, becoming a physical script.

(the production of mental re-experience). Like the iPhone, the SenseCam is part of a larger history of the evolution of an apparatus, in this case, of the varied technological practices associated with life-logging (the use of wearable technologies to create person digital archives). These practices bridge the work carried out in research laboratories with the popular deployment of parallel technologies in the commercial sector, and they bridge multiple media forms and object lessons (from the SenseCam and its images, to the Nike+ Sensor and its personal running metrics). These practices reveal the evolving contours of technobiography; they speak to the degree to which the body is a network, experience can be quantified, and life can be lived through data. Yet because of their diversity, these applications also foster a greater understanding of the nature of autobiographical knowledge, and the relative utility of autobiographical exchange. To log is not to blog, though the imperatives to record lived experience are often matched by the imperatives to make the personal data trail public and to connect with others. In this scenario, the community (of other bodies) functions as a yardstick for our wellness, and the online social network becomes part of a corporate supertext that extends the life of material goods. By touting the healthy rewards of its proprietary online social network, Nike, for example, encourages its consumers to share their otherwise personal data networks, and broadens the reach of its sensors.

These various advertising campaigns and research trajectories are signs of the general way that autobiography is being renegotiated in the digital age. Of course, contemporary practices are not simply birthed by industry, nor are they inherently driven by the technology; they are negotiated in the cultural field. For the camera holder, the transient image works as an explicit tool for autobiographical discourse; the mobile producer takes photos as his or her very life unfolds.[11] Yet there is also another strand of autobiographical dis-

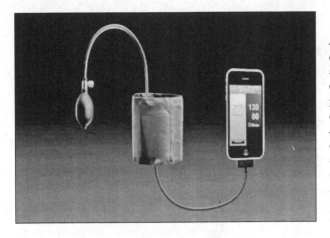

A concept design for an iPhone-compliant blood pressure cuff is one of several third party devices featured at a March 2009 Apple development event. (http://www. apple.com/quicktime/ qtv/preview-iphone-os, accessed January 29, 2010; site now discontinued)

course, a form of secondary revision that is nonetheless autobiographical on very similar grounds (of embroiling the subject in history), yet temporally and spatially distinct (and temporally and spatially open-ended in terms of the possible relation) from the moment and place of its capture. There are at least two primary autobiographical tales: the mobile phone user taking the snapshot while perambulating, and the reader accessing the trail of the photographer. In the context of new media, connected technologies infuse both producer and reader (as in the digital camera's trace in the online social network or the protocols of short message services). The general shift from autobiography to technobiography is a shift in emphasis, and I use the latter term to consider the role that technology plays in both the expression and construction of self. At the same time, I use the term technobiography as a reminder that the interaction between self and technology imbues the technology with a residual trace of the subject; this trace is a lingering trail of subjectivity. It may be found in either a device or in cyberspace; it is a string of signifiers that are forever lodged in the network, in hardware, or in application space, even after the subject departs.

To complicate such apparent seamlessness between self and technology, and in the general birth of the technobiographic subject, I want to examine one potential point of interruption. How might trauma halt the autobiographic project and alter the technobiographic subject? This question is called out with the greatest force in the case of national trauma (rather than personal trauma), when the individual's engagement with technology is reconstituted as something larger than the individual. The lingering trail of subjectivity becomes more diffuse as it is called into service for the nation, and its immediate attachments are purposefully erased or forever lost beneath the chatter. Dispersion seems antithetical to personal synthesis, and indeed it is, but it seems a fundamental part of contouring the nation; diffusion allows the abstraction of national identity to come into being. What I am pointing out are the difficulties and dangers of speaking about a collective consciousness, though such collectivities are constantly proposed by a variety of authorizing institutions—states, churches, and the like. In a new media landscape littered with nonsequiturs, how do we ever see the collective? Isn't the narrative repeatedly derailed by the ceaseless introduction of new points of view?

Referencing Sigmund Freud's work on the formation of subjectivity, E. Ann Kaplan pointedly reminds us that "how one relates to a traumatic event depends on one's individual psychic history, on memories inevitably mixed with fantasies of prior catastrophes, and on the particular cultural and political context within which a catastrophe takes place, especially how it is 'managed' by institutional forces."[12] Trauma opens us up to the willful pursuit of a particular (cohesive) subject position. Not surprisingly, an industry has emerged to fill the drives of this recognizable state of transience and, ultimately, being.[13] In part, by speaking about trauma, I aim to speak about the business of desire and its relative freedom as a commodity. As I have already illustrated, the tenets of the life technobiographic have become principles for aggressive entrepreneurship.

The Event: Convergence, Integration, and Flow

An August 2006 *CNN.com* article on the Israel-Lebanon conflict featured an image, recorded on a cell phone, of a building struck by a Hezbollah rocket.[14] And one year earlier, the *Washington Post* ran an article featuring cell phone images shot by people in the aftermath of the London terrorist attacks, highlighting pictures of transit passengers caught in a tunnel near King's Cross Station.[15] Framed by the popular news media as a form of citizen journalism, from a more immediate vantage point, these sites of imaging shared both locally and across the blogosphere create a fabric of intimate communication that allows photographer and viewer to shape the lexicon of terror.

If the cellular imaginary is in part the product of venture capital, what are the stakes for any photographic act that is not simply a recording, but potentially a working through? Or is working through even possible when diachronic continuity meets an assumed zenith in seamless mobility? These questions are clearly engaged with the role of the individual in convergence culture, where experience is framed not simply by more obvious and centralized media formations (such as commercial broadcasting and its catalog of images and narratives) but also by a host of desired technologies, personal and portable. These technologies, however intimate, are still industrial fabrications. Dissemination is not simply about sending out messages but also about distributing devices. Similarly, a narrative is not simply a self-contained news story but also a protocol for using any given technology (for thinking about its use-value).

Ironically, the battle cry to decentralize the media seems less urgent now that many of us have the necessary tools to communicate. We have gained the freedom to take our own images and forge our own communiqués. With this apparent openness in mind, my goal here is to examine the relative freedom and utility of our exchanges by looking more closely at one of our dominant tool sets—the mobile phone—and consider whether more communication means better communication. To this end, I focus on one particular artifact— the documentation of traumatic events—and, more purposefully, I review a number of incidents that have moved beyond any singular personal register to become signposts of the nation. By reading trauma that has been cellularly transposed, my aim is to study the role of technology at two distinct pressure points—where the individual meets the nation, and where industry meets culture.

Far from simply communicating, sending images across the Internet, the cell phone user at ground zero is both witnessing and translating trauma. As trauma, in critical discourse, has been inherently linked to modernity and its dissociating effects, we must consider the conflicted role of the citizen journalist who is creating cultural memories within the framework of being a traumatized subject. Documenting and transmitting from the field, the citizen journalist is trapped between the spheres of the private and the public. More concretely, the journalistic record may bridge these spheres and be filtered through a number of distinct commercial streams (passed through the cellular network, streamed to the Internet, embedded in a social networking site, or traded and indexed by network news agencies).[16] The moment seems to be a media bonanza; it is an opportune occasion to emote and analyze (or in practical terms, to participate and watch). But this individual also occupies a split-subject position; as analyst and analysand, this field reporter seems to be forever closing off the possibility of secondary revision. Is posttraumatic integration even conceivable when images of terror never serve as meditative points divorced from an original act or as screen memories, but instead as visible, contemporaneous evidence? As the temporal gap between production and distribution is closed, so too is the lag between occurring and witnessing. In the face of immediacy, the role of memory (the ability to recall) is becoming more tenuous, even as the proliferation of visible evidence never lets us forget. Any event seems perpetually lodged in some database, readily retrieved as a subset in a catalog of Google images. I want to draw out what I believe is a subtle but important distinction between remembering (memory in action) and not forgetting (a residue of memory in action). The former seems to call on the individual, while the latter seems to be more firmly ensconced in cultural sanctions that privilege certain events as forever memorable (ascribing a collective value to them).

In the examples scattered throughout this chapter, I have already moved from the gallows to the London underground. However, I am not suggesting that an execution and a bombing are parallel traumatic events. An execution itself is not necessarily a site of public trauma, and the clandestine recording of an execution is not necessarily a journalistic act (though the act has subsequently become part of journalistic discourse). Yet once imaged, the artifact or record itself may become its own site of trauma—this seems to be decidedly the case with the execution, where the act of producing and distributing (of recording and circulating) has created its own cultural rift. And as phones become rich HTML (HyperText Markup Language) Web browsers, no longer are images simply circulated as free-floating artifacts, but rather they are positioned alongside parallel or divergent discursive threads that exist simultaneously on Google Video, YouTube, or other database interfaces. In these frameworks, meaning is anchored by a series of preordained social bookmarks that seem to alter the type of working through that is possible. Saddam Hussein and the Go Go Girl are bound together, and an execution is situated concentrically with the iTunes store.

As the narrator of Apple's 2007 "Instead" campaign concludes his sales pitch, an incoming call presses against the horizontal frame of a Hollywood blockbuster movie playing on the phone's screen. Footage shot and sent from any ground zero might similarly intrude; the recipient might get the urgent call and its attachment while watching or listening to other media. The footage would be immediately inserted into a divergent contextual media flow that is birthed not from the producer's personal experience but from other cultural products. While convergence has been positioned as liberating, media integration may randomly generate cultural discord. What may be produced is an extremely unstable supertext.[17] As the journalistic field expands to include bloggers and cell phone videographers, the new catalog of images produced by these groups poses a conceptual challenge to ethics codes and general notions of newsworthiness. And, at a purely logistical level, as these images stream into already rich media conduits, they can produce semantic chaos.[18] Conversations intersect and media pathways do not simply converge but pass through each other, breaking each other's flow only temporarily. One dialogue yields to another. The music is paused until the talking is over; the film frame is frozen or the image is put away until time permits further viewing. Structural analysis itself becomes an impossible affair, as whole new grammatical systems are invented. Yet despite this complication, the flow is still decipherable and the messages remain meaningful.

Drawing on the work of John Berger, Edward Soja asserts that space is returning with a vengeance in contemporary life, fundamentally changing our modes of narration and forcing us to engage with the prospect of simultaneity:

> We can no longer depend on a story-line unfolding sequentially, an ever-accumulating history marching straight forward in plot and denouement, for too much is happening against the grain of time, too much is continually traversing the story-line laterally. . . . Simultaneities intervene, extending our point of view outward in an infinite number of lines, connecting the subject to a whole world of comparable instances, complicating the temporal flow of meaning, short-circuiting the fabulous stringing-out of "one damned thing after another."[19]

To become more active and engaged with the communicative process, we need to pay closer attention to movement, to migration. What happens as any enunciation traverses space? The haunting underground pictures taken by transit passenger Alexander Chadwick just moments after the July 7, 2005, bombing at King's Cross Station did not simply circulate through the commercial news circuit; they also appeared on the public photo-sharing site Flickr, where they were variably tagged and copied into personal photo albums and became part of the site's larger rubric, finding a home in the "London Bomb Blasts Community" group.[20] Within the group, the images were woven into a broad tapestry, inserted into a composite of terrorism throughout the city, narrated through multiple perspectives, registered as part of a national memorial, and though grouped together in an album, easily redeployed as geographic markers using Flickr's virtual mapping.[21] As part of both traditionally centralized broadcast fare and the more open conduit of Flickr, Chadwick's photos became readily lodged in a narrative web that seems perhaps an all-too-satisfying portrait revealed in ever-increasing detail as it moves us toward meaningful wholeness. We experience this not only in the manner that images are framed (becoming part of a singular narrative trajectory) by broadcast media but also in the manner that publicly malleable image-sharing sites, as openly collaborative endeavors, readily invoke their readers. When hosted on Flickr, each image accumulates a trail of comments and tags that speak to and about an audience. The comments form a temporal trail of annotations, a chronology that moves further and further away from the date of the original post and tends to meander, much like an old-fashioned game of telephone, into tangential terrain; oftentimes, the conversational thread leaves the original object behind to speak to the trail of posts as an object in and of itself. And the tags, part of a new folksonomic logic that is beginning to govern the Web, form an integral part of a

The London Bomb Blasts Community on Flickr houses an archive of images and comments that document and reflect on the events of July 2005. (http://www.flickr .com/groups/bomb/pool)

bottom-up taxonomy, a user-friendly indexing system intended to make the Web more responsive to end user preferences.[22] Despite any initial urgency or call to action, the transiency of images and texts is concealed by the simultaneous display of their accumulated tags and trails. The images become a meaningful text in their own right; what is evidenced here is not a trail of social actors but rather a quantity of blissfully active readers. This leads me to two related questions. What is revealed in this set of signs and what has escaped transcription?

The King's Cross Station Underground is captured via cell phone camera immediately following the July 7, 2005 bombing. (Photos by Alexander Chadwick, copyright AP/Wide World Photos)

Media Flow and Trauma

E. Ann Kaplan reminds us that an important element in the consideration of trauma is an understanding of one's specific position vis-à-vis an event; in her discussion of trauma, she relates the importance of distinguishing different positions and contexts of encounters with trauma. To this end, we must insert not just notions of biological or kindred attachment (how far genetically we may be removed from those suffering or what form of familial or communal relation we have with those subjects under duress) but also other degrees of directness and indirectness, of which temporal, spatial, and other mappable psychic geographies are a part. And as many of us encounter trauma through the media—or at least encounter many more sites of trauma than we would otherwise be privileged to experience because of a media presence—we also must consider not simply how we access trauma or are exposed to trauma but also its unique aspects as both a real and mediatized phenomenon that may alter the genetics of the event.

Vicarious trauma, as Kaplan suggests, is simply a response, temporally and spatially at least one step removed from the experience of trauma itself. It may be mediated through either centralized modes of production and distribution, or it may migrate through the margins; in either case, it is belatedly induced by some form of exposure (often through images). One of the strongest examples of vicarious trauma appears in Susan Sontag's *On Photography,* in a passage where she considers the quality of feeling evoked by still photos. How does one channel moral outrage at a point where only reflection is possible?

> One's first encounter with the photographic inventory of ultimate horror is a kind of revelation: a negative epiphany. For me, it was photographs of Bergen-Belsen and Dachau which I came across by chance in a bookstore in Santa Monica in July 1945. Nothing I have seen—in pho-tographs or real life—ever cut me as sharply, deeply, instantaneously. Indeed it seems plausible to me to divide my life into two parts, before I saw those photographs (I was twelve) and after, though it was several years before I understood fully what they were about. What good was served by seeing them? They were only photographs—of an event I had scarcely heard of and could do nothing to affect, of suffering I could hardly imagine and could do nothing to relieve.[23]

What interests me about this story is not simply Sontag's revelation about the power of photographs, but also her very narrative. She recalls a chance en-counter in a bookstore, which suggests that just moments before she had been engaged in another act—perhaps meandering, browsing, or reading. Within this chronology, the act of viewing can be understood as an interrup-tion, to the extent that it constructed an abrupt divide in her conscience—an interruption she acknowledges in the abstract (one that bisected her life). But it also constructed a more overt divide in her actions. The narrative has both emotive and physical aspects, which is not surprising, as time, especially in its relation to trauma, is an embodied phenomenon. Yet the contradictory sense of time is also experienced, for an essential dimension of psychological trauma is the breaking up of the unifying thread of temporality; thus, one of the clinical features of trauma is described as dissociation, the effect of being ripped out of time. In lieu of the physical experience of time, space takes on a temporal and affective dimension triggered through an optical relay (in Son-tag's case, the act of looking at the photographs)—space substitutes for the body, especially in the process of recalling the moment of trauma (the book-store is an important aspect of Sontag's experience).

Earlier in her essay, Sontag oversimplifies the concept of flow, as she momentarily turns her attention to another medium: "Photographs may be more memorable than moving images, because they are a neat slice of time, not a flow. Television is a stream of underselected images, each of which cancels its predecessor."[24] While television may have a less-meaningful affective dimension because of its randomness, what I would suggest is that the experience of images of trauma inside televisual flow is less meaningful not because of any negation, but simply because it interrupts other culturally determined signifiers rather than one's own travels. My consideration of trauma is grounded in the terrain of new media where, as Manovich notes, we may encounter a logic of "addition and coexistence."[25] To this end, the concept of cancellation does not seem useful, especially in nonbroadcast data streams, which may be wide and occasionally random but are certainly not an underselected aggregate; deliberation and choice must be considered as fundamental elements in the push and pull of production and reception (especially in a new media landscape, where we are just as likely to contribute to flow as we are to be its recipients).

I also feel it is necessary to complicate Kaplan's own analysis of trauma. She parcels the general field of vicarious trauma into five subfields by offering a series of distinctions structured around the relative perception of an event. Of the five subfields, three merit some revision:

1. Direct experience of trauma (trauma victim)
2. Direct observations of another's trauma (bystander, one step removed)
3. Visually mediated trauma (i.e., moviegoer, viewing trauma on film or other media, two steps removed)[26]

What is the status of the trauma victim who simultaneously witnesses and mediates, making and distributing media while becoming a traumatized subject? And what does it mean to be a bystander, receiving media that relays the traumatized subject's optical point of view? New media frameworks call into question the very nature of visually mediated trauma, a term that otherwise seems to collapse distinctions between media forms, each of which may have different temporalities (some are more proximate to instantaneity), different spatialities (not all screen spaces are equal), different contextual fields (not all flows are the same), and varied degrees of narrative closure (not all texts are complete; some are simply fragments).

At the extreme dissociated end of vicarious trauma, Kaplan situates "empty" empathy, "elicited by images of suffering provided without any context or background knowledge."[27] Yet in new media spaces, context is hard to avoid. Consider a July 2006 clip on YouTube—a fifty-second, low-resolution video recording of several Israeli bombs exploding in Beirut; the brief video is accompanied by the author's explanatory text:

> Listen to the horrifying blasts of Israeli bombs exploding in the Lebanese capital, Beirut. This video brings back haunting memories from the '82 Israeli invasion of Beirut. I was then only 4 years old, but the lasting impact of these blasts has never left me. For those lucky enough to have not experienced a war during their lifetime, it may appear to you that you understand all about it by watching CNN, BBC, or reading the papers. This video is an attempt to give you a more realistic sense of how terrifying a war can be on innocent civilians . . . and kids, just like me, 24 years ago![28]

The author's narrative is followed by a trail of comments and responses, part of YouTube's open architecture—comments that not only respond to the author and the source footage but also drift in other directions as secondary commentators begin to speak back to one another. What begins as a more universalizing appraisal of the horrors of war becomes a tale of two sides in the chorus of responses that follows; and what reads as an intimate and purposeful narrative of retrieval (remembering the 1982 bombings of Beirut, experienced as a child) and abreaction (acting out in the current moment through recording, listening, and writing—or more generally, through exposition) becomes a sign in and of itself. Responding to the initial entry, a June 2008 post reads: "Haha damn straight and plenty more where that came from. You motherfuckers stay on your side of the borders and we won't blow your sorry asses to pieces."[29] Integration is a personal affair, and psychohistory is a tale of individual progressions; so the narrative begins to unravel when it becomes part of a national symbolic. People experience and recover from trauma; nations (as constructs) do not. It is not surprising that personal narratives become less cohesive when they are asked to stand in as expressions of collectivity; to do so, they must be reopened, reexamined, and rewritten. The testimonial becomes a decidedly multivocal affair, subjected to the logic of hypertext and hypermedia. A one-page post becomes a multiple-paged trail of indictments that centers any number of subjects—Israelis, Lebanese, Arabs, Muslims—and engages in both national and personal agenda setting.

The space of new media seems to obfuscate an already-eroding boundary between individual and cultural trauma. By its very nature (as a dynamic text), the networked landscape continuously reframes personal experience and provides its own commodified contextual markers. Beyond the machinations of overt dialogue (such as the inventoried comment cited above), folksonomic tags (descriptive keywords) attach the video and its commentaries to a user-generated list of associations, in this case, "Lebanon, Beirut, Israel, bombs, war, explosion, aggression, Hezbollah, civilians, death." Folksonomies cut across the personal and the social, borrowing and benefiting from both realms. They suggest a potentially democratic inroad into privatized site management, allowing end users to insert missing terms into a site's taxonomic infrastructure. But at the same time, they reflect the work of more broadly held cultural vocabularies, for tags place rather arbitrary limits on meaning; moving images become knowable as text-based systems. A video becomes attached to a series of terms and visual culture must be rigorously categorized if the search engine is to function.

To this end, as trauma is dispersed across new communications channels, we must come to understand the complexity of catastrophe as it registers through multiple positions, not all of which are purely spectatorial or separate from one another. We may at one time or another find ourselves at ground zero, and see our representation (ourselves) translated and watch our experience migrate, or we may only experience vicarious trauma, which may seem less privileged but which merits consideration because it provides an entry point for assessing the work of the apparatus (of distribution and exhibition, for example). Even vicarious experience is not a uniform phenomenon. Our understanding of an event is affected by how we access it, and not all media pathways are created equal. Any data set may be conformed to more than one interface. And the interface, more than simply the product of script and code, is perhaps the most immediate form of context setting.

Mediation is a complex phenomenon in the field of trauma, for media artifacts may occupy more than one position relative to traumatic experience. Developmentally, traumatic affect states are understood in terms of the relational systems in which they take form that play a significant role in tolerance, containment, and modulation. Understood as just such a system, certain media forms may be a critical component of posttraumatic integration. In Chapter 2, I briefly reference three modalities that are used to conceive trauma in the psychoanalytic model: remembrance, repetition, and working through. Interpreting Freud's comments on the connection between past and present, a temporal flux that is critical in psychoanalytic theories of trauma, Linda Belau relates: "The trauma pertaining to an event is less an inherent aspect of the event itself than it is an effect pertaining to the impossibility of integrating the event into a knowledgeable network."[30] The fluctuation is not simply temporal; it is also about a movement between the two poles of knowledge and being. Repetition implies a certain impossibility of integrating trauma into remembrance, while working through as a final and more overreaching view of the process forces us to see the impossibility of integrating trauma at all; we are asked to understand and accept its very nature.[31]

Representations play a significant role in understanding trauma, calling out the very nature of an event as traumatic; on reflection, we see that an image is not able to carry the full weight of an episode or to suture over our psychical wounds. The online cellular archive, one facet of the readily searched database of recent and past events on YouTube, suggests a movement toward integration, but is perhaps only a simulacrum (a distortion of a real process—in this case, of synthesis—that nonetheless stands in as a truth in its own right, despite its questionable authenticity). The flow of responsive comments and essayistic video clips on YouTube gives evidence of working through, but these are just signs of a process and not a measure of any subject's progress toward embodiment or grounding a state of knowing. The fact that these pieces of visible evidence are embedded in a literal network (of things, of other objects) and easily embedded in other contextual frames (in the case of YouTube, a repurposing made possible through Adobe Flash) simply suggests a readier deployment. But what is signified in the ready and rapid circulation of particular artifacts? How do we make sense of a clip's popularity? What meaning should be ascribed to a number of views? We may have an active register of the number of times an object is consumed, but as with any media text, we have very limited knowledge that suggests to what end. The processes of cutting and pasting, embedding and hyperlinking, shooting, dialing, and sending, suggest synthesis at the level of hardware and software—at the interface. But the more important sign of synthesis, of a reembodied subject position, cannot be found online or in a device.

I suggest earlier in this chapter that simultaneity may interfere with posttraumatic integration, collapsing past and present. Images of lived experience may circulate at a speed that naturalizes the screen and may therefore press into our lives quite dramatically. Yet images that may at first spread like wildfire will ultimately find their place in the database, and their transitory nature will shift. An assumed collective experience (at first simply anecdotal) is ultimately given material form, and collectivity itself is made manifest—once thought, now seen, as discussions are mapped out in the Internet of Things. Lodged in the archive, still frames, motion replays, and edited (and editorialized) versions of traumatic events seem firmly integrated. Yet as history literally repeats itself, thanks to the playback controls of the media player or the more generalized openness of the Semantic Web, we become aware of a certain instability—our memories evolve as the narrative continues to be publicly written or as the event's trace simply moves to another domain. In fact, the neurological literature on representation and memory suggests that "representations are best described as emergent phenomena that undergo constant change as processing continues."[32] Online archives serve us well if we do not use them as simple points of investment; instead, we should allow them to open us up to the possibility that traumatic events, by their very definition, cannot be contained by a URL (Uniform Resource Locator). The evolution of the online narrative within the field of trauma might be read as an objective trace of the operation of self.

Survival Tactics

A tagline, stated in the form of a question, from a 2005 *USA Today* column still calls out to me: "In the age of digital and 'delete' are we losing something?"[33] The article cites a statistic from a survey by the International Data Corporation that suggests 23 percent of all images captured by digital cameras are deleted, never getting exported. Social theorist Erving Goffman suggests that individual performance, as a simultaneous presentation both inward and outward, is used to construct identity. In this vein, we might also position a particular performative mode—the photographic act—as an act that includes both taking the photo and circulating it. Despite any apparent and unmitigated excesses of self-expression online, these acts are clearly a controlled working through that reflects a sophisticated understanding of the nature of the medium and its audience. The difficulty we encounter is when particular social fronts get institutionalized and become representations of collective expression. Social behavior in public places is controllable; we have only to look at urban design to understand the relative openness of online space. In the late 1960s, William Whyte launched a multiyear study to observe pedestrian behavior in public settings. As part of the grant-funded Street Life Project, Whyte set up a series of time-lapse cameras that enabled him to describe the substance of urban life in an objective way, and with considerable detail. In his published findings, Whyte suggests: "A good new space builds a new constituency. It stimulates people into new habits—al fresco lunches—and provides new paths to and from work, new places to pause. It does all this very quickly."[34]

As we send our images into public spaces, following YouTube's imperative to "broadcast ourselves," the consciousness that we bring to praxis needs to inform our postpraxis tactics.[35] To put it more simply, now that we have been invited to participate, we might think twice about our actions. We need to consider the unique dimensions of any public forum, as well as the trail of outcomes that will most likely follow our otherwise spatially and temporally bound acts of recording. My goal here has been to call out a series of questions concerning media mobility—about losing control, the allure of technology, and the latent intersections between democracy and technocracy—where social movement rhetoric meets social network rhetoric, and where public welfare is determined by the sum total of our signs on the network. Trauma is a powerful phenomenon that often precludes deliberation and hesitation. Despite the desire to heal, or despite the positive push of the therapeutic impulse, we might pause for a moment to explore rupture itself as a powerful force, a space in which the promise of convergence goes unrealized if only because discourse of any kind seems insufficient. Why do we willfully seal over certain cracks and fissures with an outpouring of words and images? Before we begin to document and narrate, let us pause to explore those moments where speech truly fails us.

4

Intervention and the Kodak Moment

ny discussion of private-to-public media flows inevitably turns to the subject of reality television, a format that promises privileged access to the real. The attention to authenticity is matched by the impulse to mobilize conflict and dramatic development, contouring lived experience to the formal rules of broadcast television. We can see reality television as an industrial projection of life itself, its producers crafting a vision of better living through television by providing a view of things more worthwhile, more interesting. I am not being dismissive of the format, nor is it my intent to establish a hierarchy that privileges the "discourse of sobriety."[1] Some television critics demonize the genre only in the interest of salvaging what they consider the best programs, which they commonly understand as those having the greatest social weight.

The entire history of the form is beyond the scope of this chapter, and I open by admitting that I am turning to a few select images that have recently caught my attention and that I believe are most relevant to my analysis of transience and trauma. I consider reality television with this goal in mind, so I am less concerned with a static definition of the genre and more concerned with the expectations that are brought to the form and what cultural effects may lie in its wake. Reality television is a representational practice that suggests unmitigated access to real people and real situations and, as such, it inherently aligns itself with the perverse thrill of traumatic engagement. In its suggestion of immediacy, reality television thrives on voyeuristic uncertainty, regardless of the particular formal vocabulary at play. It seems readily apparent that reality TV is a site of ideological work, yet the format's close alignment with the real often makes it difficult to discern exactly what is being performed. In her analysis of the slippage between reality and documentary television, Susan Murray notes that these categories are often empty signifiers, with the terms being called out in rather arbitrary ways. Murray suggests that any distinction may not describe a fixed set of textual markers or be bound to any particular content. Instead, these labels reflect an attempt by industry to package and spin a program in a particular way to give the program a frame of reference that might activate certain perceived values. The documentary label is commonly used to suggest that a show is a model of high culture rather than an embodiment of vulgar taste; but even so, any attempt to structure perception can ultimately be undone by the process of reception.[2]

To consider reality television's relationship to trauma, I focus on a program that has trauma at its center; but equally important to my analysis are the residues of trauma that can be found at the program's margins. I am less concerned with positioning this program as a historical artifact and locating its place in a genre. It should be noted, however, that trauma and the therapeutic discourse have always been attached to reality television, if only because trauma is inherently aligned with the real and with temporality; it seems to rise to the surface in a genre that privileges the unfolding of life's chronology. Trauma is found elsewhere on television, and may ground perception in general, framing our experience with looking at television and connected to a certain anxiety that may be bound to perception as a desiring mechanism. In addition, the therapeutic arrangement is a position that the viewer forges with a wide array of programs; it can be produced through texts that are not overtly about trauma and recovery. It is not surprising that such a position can be willfully adopted, as therapeutic relations are nonhierarchical in nature, privileging neither therapist nor patient (or in the case of the television text, neither author nor viewer). For this reason, the therapeutic relation is rather malleable, and in the case of reality television, we find it being woven into quite distinct formulas—from game shows to docusoaps to procedurals.

The difficulty with mapping trauma onto the television narrative is the difference in their arcs; trauma itself is not inherently aligned with the principles of narrative, though it may be approximated and negotiated through a similar act of formal reconstruction. Personal trauma often involves more than one origin story or at least no fixed epicenter, despite the desire to claim one, for locating a center would make reconciliation a much easier task. Private trauma is distinct from national trauma. National trauma is public and is commonly event-based, and it can be reconciled (and managed) by referencing a shared language. Finding no singular flash point, the victim of private trauma recovers the shattering of selfhood as a process; on reflection, the traumatic break is not a break at all, but rather a gradual taking over of its subject, and the language of recovery may not make sense to the casual observer.

The images that seem most poignant and urgent to me are the occasional portraits—childhood photos and home videos—that are part of the narrative arc of each episode of A&E's *Intervention*. The series, now in its ninth season, reveals people in the throes of some of the most severe forms of addiction.[3] Pulling together friends and family, the program depicts the varied struggles of addicts with their personal demons. *Intervention* relies on actual footage of drug use, bodily abuse, or other destructive behaviors to tell its stories, and although it makes liberal use of the confessional address, the show's central narrative device (and recovery strategy) is to prevent each addict from knowing that his or her family and loved ones have been called into the process (although such secrecy is increasingly difficult to maintain with each successive season, as the show continues to become more widely known). Each of the program's protagonists has agreed to be in a documentary about addiction but is not informed of the producers' ultimate goal, which is to lead them to the intervention. Participants are presented with a choice: go into rehabilitation or lose contact with their loved ones. Each friend or family member is asked to call out their bottom line, to identify the form of support they will withdraw if the addict fails to go into treatment at the end of the intervention. The addicts featured on the show receive an offer of a ninety-day treatment plan at one of a number of rehabilitation facilities affiliated with the series. As in real life, not all of the interventions end well. Some addicts have walked out of their interventions and refused to go into treatment; others have agreed to get treatment, only to leave early after violating facility rules, engaging in disruptive behavior, or simply wanting to stop treatment. Some addicts who leave early go to prison or enter another facility to continue treatment, but many do not. All of the episodes end with a series of title screens that form a short narrative; the first few screens discuss the addict's progress since the intervention, and these are followed by a sobriety date (when relevant) and closed by an invitation to find out more about addiction and recovery at the show's official Web site.

The program has been critiqued for its voyeurism, for it seems on the surface to indulge a knee-jerk fascination with watching other people hit rock bottom. But certainly this concern—the public's fascination with the private traumas of others—can be leveled across the genre. Redemptive readings of *Intervention* turn to the program's participants to offer evidence that the show has had a profound and positive effect on their lives; indeed, by involving some of the leading addiction experts in the field (the program has a roster of experienced interventionists), the program consistently provides sound, professional counsel. My position is a bit more nuanced, as I believe the program engages with rather complex terrain, covering trauma, addiction, and recovery; and to its credit, it refuses to engage in such reductivism. This is the program's value. It adopts a formal attitude that seems clearly aligned with its subject matter; by doing so, it sheds light on the aesthetic choices that seem to govern the television industry. Without being an empty exercise in self-reflexivity, the show calls out the often overlooked role of form as a structuring agent. It seems an important lesson in genre coding. The recovery narrative is always tentative and never completely over. An addict is always in recovery and is acutely aware of his or her personal timeline; the trauma narrative yields to a recovery narrative that becomes a new, healthier origin story. But an addict can always relapse, and his or her sobriety date can always be revised or completely erased. As a media scholar, what I want to discuss is the significant absence of closure that surrounds *Intervention,* which I believe is the program's greatest use-value. While the program certainly operates more intimately and purposefully, reaching out to those who might also be victims of addiction, beyond its role as a talking cure, the program functions as an important lesson in narrative construction. Both operations are valuable.

Better Living through Television

Television programs are often explicit problem solvers; there is a broad range of self-help programs across the broadcast spectrum, tackling everything from home improvement to lifestyle management. Of course, such programs are often ratings bonanzas, as therapy in all of its manifestations and permutations can be deployed as a strategy of engagement. There is a certain power to the open text that the therapeutic relation produces, and its discursive strategies seem to overcome the technological limits of one-way communication. Therapy engages in relational transactions rather than fixed hierarchies; participants are given the ability to constantly reassert their centrality and to claim the discourse as their own, even when they are listening to the confessions of others. The goal is to enable participants to see themselves as both the target of and responsible agent for their own cure.[4] Power is a dynamic force in psychotherapeutic practice, and participants are envisioned as agents who might regulate their own behavior; in this manner, patients can choose to assume positions of authority despite the presence of competing professional voices. In the case of television, it is within this discursive context that the public is willing—and is invited—to participate. The therapeutic transaction provides the grounds for understanding the appeal that counseling programs, talk programs, docusoaps, and related reality fare hold for viewers, and also the readiness with which individuals are willing to confess personal problems to the mass television audience.

The relation between the individual and traumatic experience becomes more complex when we understand the therapeutic process as a means through which individuals are encouraged to problematize (and shape) their own conduct. The patient brings his or her thoughts to the surface, only to subject those thoughts to a historically situated discursive practice. History provides certain conditions of possibility that determine how individuals recognize, reflect on, and transform themselves.[5] And television can become bound to this transaction, imposing yet another series of limits. Mimi White pushes quite far in pointing out the impact of television on therapeutic discourse, proposing that "contemporary deployments of therapeutic and confessional discourse produced through the television apparatus modify and reconfigure the very nature of therapy and confession as practices for producing social and individual identities and knowledge."[6]

How has television reconstituted the therapeutic exchange? To answer this question, I look backward. *Queen for a Day* is an early manifestation of the therapeutic discourse on television. Born at a moment when television was defining its social function as a mediator between the family and the economy, the program and the medium in general tried to suggest ways to resolve the conflict between consumer desires (that were flagrantly individualistic) and familial needs (that were collective and universal). The television industry promoted consumption as a healthy domestic enterprise, and addressed the American family as a uniformly knowable body. Premiering on radio in the forties as *Queen for Today,* the program moved to local television in 1948, broadcasting live in Los Angeles before being picked up by NBC in 1956. Hosted by Jack Bailey, the general format pitted four female contestants against each other; each had a tale of woe, and each made a personal request that might make her life circumstance more tolerable. After the women told their stories, the studio audience registered its vote for the most beleaguered woman, with the popular vote tallied by an applause meter. The winner was showered with a range of sponsor-provided gifts, but also received the request that was at the heart of her story. These requests ranged from washing machines (one housewife wanted to earn extra income doing laundry to help support her family) to specialty beds (this particular contestant had a brother who had been disabled by gunshot). One of the more unusual pleas came from a woman who simply wanted a hole cut through the ceiling of her two-story home; her hope was that the hole, as a makeshift air duct, might allow heat to rise to the upstairs bedrooms to keep her children warm at night.

Queen for a Day showed women in crisis actively relaying their potential to resolve unique familial problems, while its advertisers in their own way sought to give these women the tools to resolve a whole host of other (manufactured and generic) familial problems. The program was truly act-based, breaking from its confessionals to pitch products and stage fashion shows. The program aired these processes side by side and, in fact, integrated them with Bailey's help; as the emcee, he was naturally charged with narrative continuity, binding the program's segments by talking across them.

On reflection, a certain tension seems to develop in the program between what contestants claim as real, experienced needs and what the advertisers claim as more authentic, immediate needs; the constructed needs relayed by the program's advertisers and sponsors nevertheless reflect a contemporary familial arrangement and are quite explicitly staged inside the home. Pitching Peter Paul candy miniatures, announcer Gene Baker relates: "When the crowd congregates at your house or when the children charge home after play, there are only two things to do: look out or be prepared." Likewise, in a pretaped spot for Rinse Away shampoo, a fictional housewife proclaims: "It's my job to see this family has clean healthy hair and scalp." Here, dandruff is positioned as a deep-rooted social problem, and Rinse Away is the easy fix.

Throughout *Queen for a Day*'s run, the basic requests of its contestants seem to exceed the abilities of the industry. Or perhaps they are simply too specific to be useful to advertisers. Consider the push in ratings discourse and audience studies to broader demographic categories and more generalized consumer needs that define mass culture. The women speak in terms of responsible consumption, relating their actual needs. That their needs often go unanswered and that they have the type of needs they do points to a social problem of poverty, unemployment, inner-city violence, and the lack of health care. These issues are eclipsed or sealed over by the problem/solution arc of the sponsor-supported narrative, and the program audience seems rather complicit, or simply disempowered, as they respond in only the most measured of ways to this tragic popularity contest. Yet the rift the program exposes between actual and constructed need is rather positive in that it points to the ability of individuals to recognize themselves as citizens first and consumers second. The television industry is ill-equipped to answer their pleas or to indulge in a more prolonged and potentially productive therapeutic relation. The list of unanswered social concerns speaks to quite a different problem—an institutional failure, a failure inside television.

There are, of course, other curious moments that follow the lead of *Queen for a Day,* most of which are equally dissatisfying attempts at serious therapeutic engagement. The brief series *Road to Reality* ran on ABC from the fall of 1960 to the spring of 1961. The series aired alongside *Queen for a Day* (which had moved from NBC) during its run, and was responsible for bringing psychoanalysis to daytime television. Each episode opened with announcer Joel Crager explaining:

You are about to see and hear the reenactment of sessions of group psychoanalysis which actually took place and were recorded. The men and women know each other only by first names. Their parts, and that of the psychoanalyst, are played by actors. The actual people involved have consented to this portrayal. Names have been changed to protect their identities. What they say may sometimes embarrass or even shock you. But only by speaking frankly can they help themselves and each other and perhaps also find the road to reality.

A useful complement to its partner program, *Road to Reality* teased out some of the underlying social tensions of the day, perhaps to let *Queen for a Day* continue its more fantastic project.

Queen for a Day marks the birth of a long legacy of therapeutic television, a drive that truly coalesces in the 1980s with the rise of counseling shows—programs that might be understood as a hybrid subgenre of reality programs and talk shows, airing social and personal concerns and speaking through them. The therapeutic formula has been reinvigorated through television documentaries in subsequent decades with the therapeutic moment becoming part of an editorial fabric that is subjected to the logic of a narrative fiction (moving from character development to denouement). But what is the contemporary cultural impetus for reinvestigating trauma?

The Culture of Trauma

Trauma reflects a general movement from event to story in which episodes—national or familial—are given form, considered, and contoured; we move from incident to meaning and from the irrational to the rational. The production of narrative is generally a constructive, organizing affair. But the narratives vary, not just in terms of their foundational events but also in terms of their trajectories. In his critical examination of the 1995 Oklahoma City bombing, Edward Linenthal identifies three distinct narrative responses to traumatic events: progressive, redemptive, and toxic.[7] These responses are not necessarily contradictory, as they are motivated by slightly different impulses and grounded by unique ethical queries. The progressive narrative moves forward from the event and is focused on building something positive out of tragedy; such a narrative is transformative in that it reflects a desire to build new healing communities that might extend the bonds of kinship and caring. However progressive, the narrative seeks to lessen the blow and bring fear and anxiety down to manageable levels. The progressive narrative is about lessons learned; it is a tale of rebirth. The redemptive narrative moves in the opposite direction, responding to a crisis by returning to convention. There is nothing new here; this is an act of translation rather than transformation, an attempt to use the crisis situation as evidence in support of an already-held belief system. This form of recovery is theological to its core. What progressive and redemptive narratives share is an insistence on making sense, on reestablishing coherence in life's larger narrative. Conversely, the toxic narrative does not allow such coherence; its effects linger, and it prevents life from ever returning to a pre-event state. It is a messy narrative that interferes with other spheres of existence, refusing to let the tragedy fall to the background. It intermingles with other negative influences that surround the individual. In the case of the Oklahoma City federal building catastrophe, Linenthal writes: "It is a story of an unfinished bombing, one that still reaches out to claim people through suicide, to shatter families through divorce, substance abuse, and the corrosive effects of profound and seemingly endless grief."[8]

The toxic narrative is useful in considering the relative value of TV therapy, for trauma is about excess; it speaks to failed containment. And the toxic story line refuses to go away, though it may be buried for the moment. In this way, the televisual reenactment of trauma (and the therapeutic deliberation) seems quite desperate; it demands closure and seems decidedly free of contaminants. Trauma is, of course, timeless at the same time that it is historically grounded. We find trauma in every decade, experienced both culturally and generationally. Very often, it originates within the family circle. Families are fluid and migratory—they evolve. But they also respond anxiously to the culturally pervasive notions of the familial, which are rigid and impossibly fixed. Within this terrain, trauma and addiction are intimately connected; emotional and psychological pain often can lead to addictive behavior, while addiction in turn can produce even greater distress. Victims of trauma and addiction may find themselves caught up in an endless cycle of destructive behaviors that only intensify the initial experience of trauma and push with ever-greater force against the entire family framework. And amid this turmoil, we are so focused on the destructive power of addiction that we may ignore the possibility that the family itself is the formative agent of trauma. The home can be a toxic environment.

The Birth of Trauma

Focusing on the family and holding the home under a microscope, *Intervention* makes rather liberal use of the family photo album. Every episode plays through a nostalgic photomontage in search of an origin story that grounds the addictive persona before navigating toward the final meeting with friends and family. Located fairly early in each addict's story, it is through the family photo album that friends and relatives begin the search for the addict's traumatic break. Most often, the parent narrates the addict's backstory, recounting the moment at which the normal child veered off course and began the downward, self-abusive spiral that birthed the current-day addict. The audio track is synched with what stands in as visual evidence—a montage of still images culled from family photo albums, and an occasional video fragment pulled from the family archive. This happenstance synchronicity prompts the viewer to scrutinize each image for signs of breakage, engaging the reader in the "where's Waldo" task of locating sign and symptom. The camera zooms in and out of photos, pulling us in and pushing us back out, prompting us to search for clues and then moving back to context, separating the subject momentarily and then situating the subject back into its familial frame.[9] A brief excerpt from the synopsis of "Sara" (Season 1, Episode 5, April 2005) is indicative of this orientation: "At 24, Sara had everything she ever wanted in her sleepy Minnesota town. She had a fairy-tale wedding in Hawaii, a beautiful baby girl, a house, three cars, and even competed in beauty pageants. Then, it all abruptly ended in divorce."

In "Salina and Troy" (Season 2, Episode 18, January 2006), the on-camera confession of Salina's mother leads us into the familiar photomontage. Asking and recounting, her mother relates: "What made her turn at this point, I don't know. But this isn't what was supposed to happen to my daughter at 24." As the background music opens on the second audio track and the voice-on becomes a voice-over, the montage proceeds, first with baby pictures, then with family photos, then with school portraits, holiday photos, and photos with friends. The Ken Burns effect (a zoom in or zoom out on a photo still, often combined with a panning movement) opens each image up to increasing scrutiny, changing our proximity and mobilizing an otherwise static image. And Salina's mother continues: "When she was a baby she just looked like a cute little doll, so I just started calling her dolly . . . When she was a small child, we were pretty strict with her. Her dad was pretty strict with her. . . . Salina made a poor choice and left school with her cousin. Someone was showing a gun and the gun went off and Salina's cousin was shot right in front of her. Salina was devastated." Intertitles push causality further, relating: "By 15, Salina was purging six to seven times a day. That same year, she witnessed the death of her cousin." The combined forces of strict parenting, peer pressure (Salina confesses her teenage years "sucked"; as a Hispanic minority at her school, she felt the proportions of her body did not match those of the girls around her), and death are posited as a series of sequential ground zeros for her bulimia, and the individual tale of displacement is posited

Stills from the family photo album frame the subject of A&E's Intervention.

as a larger morality play, urging us to reread our own family photos, searching for signs of trauma.

Migratory Patterns

One of the leading titles in each episode of *Intervention* inflects the program with cultural weight, and at the same time moves from the statistical to the anecdotal: "Millions of Americans struggle with addiction. Most need help to stop. These are two of their stories."[10] This movement is also one from the national to the local and from a broadly public crisis to one understood as the sum total of individual, private case histories.[11] The naming of each subject follows a similar binary. Salina is positioned as "The Nanny. The Bulimic." Far from static poles of identity, these categories are literally morphed together in title form, mirroring the goals of the intervention—unifying the split subject, yet simultaneously making the subject knowable to us through a series of otherwise fixed categories of normality and its opposite.[12]

Each episode's arc closes postintervention, moving the subject into treatment and, in some cases, pushing further along the timeline to recount the subject's success or failure (read in terms of completing treatment and staying clean and sober). The outcome can be read back temporally against the program's airdate, leaving the lingering question as to the subject's more current state. While the intervention itself is the climactic moment of the narrative arc, the denouement, found in the movement to what most closely approximates the current day, yields the greatest dramatic punch. The final minutes of each episode either affirm or deny the process (the use-value of the intervention as a moment in an addict's life). And these minutes also reveal whether the evidentiary trace found somewhere in the montage-effect of childhood can be dismissed as a site of misrecognition. As an equally subtle form of signification, the evidence either affirms or denies the possibility of mitigation much later on in life, a possibility that returns the photo to a safer order because it potentially detaches any lingering aura of a psychic break that might otherwise remain attached to the image. The damage has been contained and the photo can be returned to the family album, no longer a phantom limb of a traumatic subject. In a similar fashion, the intervention at the heart of the show seems more about the needs of friends and family, which are less about cure and more about closure—a terminal point for grief and mourning, yet another sealed referential vessel with its own rituals (most notable the reading of first-person letters or testimonials drafted specifically for the occasion). Perhaps I am being too severe in my assessment, for the intervention serves a dual purpose, moving both the addict and the family forward; this is a doubly therapeutic relation that often locates other destructive agents in the room. While the show's full narrative may speak to causality, the intervention intentionally focuses on the addiction. People go into rehab because of their addictions, not because of their traumas, though the rehabilitative environment allows them to address their traumas in order to provide a long-term recuperative strategy.

The range of addictions covered by *Intervention*, defined both by substance (heroin, crystal meth, morphine, crack, alcohol, Vicodin) and behavior (gambling, shopping, raging, binging, purging, cutting, huffing) is as varied as the individuals profiled in the show's nine seasons. Yet just as addiction itself, which suggests excess at its very core, is reduced to a formulaic narrative trajectory (which is what we expect of any episodic television drama), so too are its subjects reduced to a shared vernacular, firmly grounded in the familial and its stable of representations. And I do not mean this in the limited sense of their relative sobriety or their physical location, but more in the sense of fixing exactly where they are signified in the body of the story, in the episode's narrative geography. As I try to stage my own intervention with a series of representations, it seems the honorific portraits littered throughout the series are destined to take on their inverse function as repressive instruments or tools in the assignment of typology (either criminal or pathological), always positing the individual as addict—pre- or postaddiction, but always in relation to the term. This is the only point of entry, at least for the viewer, who is not invested in the family album and only able to position the addict as one in a million. This is not a liberatory gesture; it does not suggest an escape from the repressive function of the familial gaze. As the localized family (the circle of biological kinship) fades from view, the national family appears on the horizon.

Yet *Intervention* succeeds when it pauses to explore the darker side of the American family. As the program moved into its fourth season, it began to probe more deeply, as if looking for direct evidence of how early trauma (in the form of abuse or family dysfunction, either as an isolated incident or a prolonged event) can lead to addiction. In doing so, the program started to more fully address its speaking subjects and to think more concretely about narrative ownership.

Tressa's tale (Season 4, Episode 56, January 2008) recounts her Christian upbringing on a farm in rural Nebraska. Her mother recalls: "You could always count on Tressa to do the hard jobs on the farm. Anything that was backbreaking, she could handle it. She pulled more than her weight. She pulled part of your weight." Tressa's sister, Rachel, continues the story: "My dad always did want a boy. And when Tr . . . I don't think they intentionally . . . you know." And Tressa's father, Jim, begins to fill in the blanks, but creates gaps of his own: "Tressa's as close to a boy . . . I don't know how to say this. I don't think I've ever looked at Tressa as a son. I just looked at her as a very strong capable girl." The story struggles for narrative cohesion, and the silences speak volumes. And as the family's words fade, the montage of Tressa's meteoric rise in the world of professional track and field leads to a personal confession of anxiety and despair: "Despite the whole glory and being so successful, I didn't let anyone know a feeling of loneliness kind of overtook me. My life consisted of my job. I was a workaholic . . . athletics. And I just had ignored who I was and what I needed as a human being." An intertitle carries this series of prompts to what seems rather striking (though perhaps obvious) closure: "At 22, Tressa was introduced to the gay club scene in Nebraska." And what follows is a series of personal images, not found in the family photo album or among her parents' home movies, that shows Tressa away from the public eye, outside of the scrutiny of her family, and in the company of other women.

This particular episode is very good about examining the family and attending to its dysfunction, as it calls out the homophobia that may have sent Tressa into self-destructive isolation. In this case, Candy Finnigan, Tressa's interventionist, relates: "We've all made mistakes." Tressa's father is not able to discuss or accept Tressa's sexuality, and uses Christianity as his rule book. At the same time, his early confession speaks to a certain sense of guilt, as Jim ties together gender confusion (that he may have caused, by wishing for a son and treating Tressa like a boy) and sexual orientation in a rather knowing (if erroneous) way. His linking of gender and sexuality is even more complicated, as he reads both through theology and subjects both to the same repressive agency. This is a very complex formation that is momentarily addressed but never unraveled.

Equally complex is the story of Charles (Season 5, Episode 62, July 2008), a homeless heroin addict. Early in the episode, his half sister, Lindsey, reveals: "I've always known why he uses. He can't handle the memories." As she makes her statement, the tale turns from one of promise to one of tragedy, and the photomontage takes on a different tone. Recounting the sexual abuse that both he and his brother suffered, Charles furthers his own story by referring to his father: "He said it was normal. That's what every dad does with his son." As he speaks, the camera zooms in on a photo of a young Charles with his surfboard, as if looking for clues, prying, getting more intimate with its subject. Like many stories of molestation, the trauma did not manifest itself until later in life, so from a narrative perspective, Charles's story feels fragmented and seems to lack causality, if only because the timeline is interrupted, with the addiction quite delayed from the site of trauma. In this instance, however, the timeline restores itself, folding back on itself and using Charles as a vehicle to connect the dots that unite the past and the present. The power of this gesture is that it restores Charles as a narrative agent; it gives agency to a subject who has otherwise given up. The gesture parallels the purpose of the intervention itself, as well as the therapeutic act, which is to restore Charles's agency. Here, form, function, and use neatly and productively align; not simply an empty rhetorical strategy (more than coy self-reflexivity), the show uses form as a practical tool, following the goals of the therapeutic impulse. Elsewhere, this gesture is repeated. From the fleeting privacy of a bathroom in a fast-food restaurant, as Charles lifts his shirt to inject heroin, his microphone pack comes into view and the wiring that runs up his torso is exposed. In this moment, the show's technology rather explicitly rubs up against its subject in what is a powerful yet purely casual reveal. The camera operator looks on from a low angle, as Charles injects himself and pauses momentarily to glance down into the camera. In *Intervention,* there is no applause meter and no prize. We are left wondering about the intent of such an open, drug-induced gaze. We are also left with a rather muddy assessment of Charles's victim status—subjected to abuse, yet abusing substances; aware of the camera, yet clearly attendant to other concerns; losing his veins, but still desperate to find them. The conflicted status of the whole affair (from production to reception) seems to mirror the uneasy locus of addiction.[13]

Recovery

Intervention seems committed to such quandaries and consistently occupies a moral gray zone; yet in doing so, the program is able to speak back to the genre. Exploitation is a charge too readily leveled at reality fare; it is too reductive. It refuses to acknowledge the nuances, the difficulties, and the differences within the format. Instead, we need to take the discomfort factor head-on and understand why such a claim is put forward. What do we deem too raw, too personal, and too emotional? What knowledges do we deem inappropriate?

I return to my discussion in Chapter 1 of missing children and my suggestion that we need to pull back crisis rhetoric in order to come to true insight. The same holds true when we consider the seamless integration of confessional discourse and the concomitant attention to therapeutic engagement within the spaces of reality television. The confessional is quite malleable; it is a rhetorical trope that needs to be scrutinized, for it can speak to our cultural attitudes about trauma. We find it in both the game show and the television documentary: in the former, it is shaped into an open and participatory exercise; in the latter, it is safely embedded in a self-contained text. While, as Mimi White has suggested, participating as the confessional subject became part of the therapeutic ethos that followed the onslaught of reality dramas in the late 1980s, certainly not all confessional spaces are created equal.[14] How many housewives aspire to be featured on *Intervention?*

I turn to *Intervention* in a book that traverses both older and newer media forms because one of the most important aspects of the show is its online supplement. The series Web site includes video follow-ups with many of the program's subjects. The subjects reflect on their addictions, their interventions, and their foundational traumas. These brief videos privilege single-camera direct address; each follow-up is structured around the confessional interview, centering the subject and allowing his or her knowledge and voice to contour the use of establishing cutaways that always seem to respond to (rather than direct) the subject's narration. This truly becomes their story, an individual story, not a more conventional discursive construction. The three-to five-minute clips allow the subject to speak about the intervention and reflect on the process; taken together, these segments form a subtle reveal that illuminates the original program. It is important to see the addict stepping outside of the addictive frame, and it is significant that such a gesture occurs online, isolated from the sensationalizing efforts of ratings-driven narrative. The goal of the intervention is, after all, to return the addict to a state of normalcy, and the online updates provide a slow fade, allowing the quiet and uncelebrated return of the subject to society (without forcefully reclaiming the family as a necessary signpost of normality). Many of the subjects discuss their episodes (most reflect on the insight they have gained from seeing themselves on-screen) and consider how far they have come since their show's initial broadcast. The causes of their addictions are not the main story here; rather, the focus is on movement through (and an analysis of) their behaviors. Perhaps this is for the better; by focusing on the present, each subject returns the familial to the private realm. The cameras are slowly but deliberately retired from each case.

In her follow-up, Lauren, a recovering heroin addict (featured in Season 2, Episode 34, December 2006), relates: "Every time I see it, I'm in a different place, and I'm further from that day." Lauren is speaking to other addicts, relating a perspective, a series of experiences, and a number of concerns that only the addict would understand. She beams about the positive feedback she has received. Audrey, also a recovering heroin addict (featured in Season 2, Episode 15, January 2006), reflects on the experience of seeing herself and admits: "The image of me nodding off in the bathroom against the mirror is burned into my memory. I totally admit that I used to glamorize heroin use and heroin addiction. But I didn't know that that was happening to me when I was high. I didn't know that that's what I looked like when I was getting high. After I saw that, it completely disgusts me. To think of using again, to imagine using again . . . the image has saved my life."

Articulating the authorizing power of the confession, Michel Foucault suggests that the act "produces intrinsic modifications in the person who articulates it: it exonerates, redeems, and purifies him; it unburdens him of his wrongs, liberates him, and promises him salvation."[15] The ritual unfolds within a power relationship, for, as Foucault continues: "One does not confess without the presence (or virtual presence) of a partner who is not simply the interlocutor but the authority who requires the confession, prescribes and appreciates it, and intervenes in order to judge, punish, forgive, console, and reconcile."[16] Rather than masking and naturalizing this power relation, *Intervention* reveals it simply by shifting the interlocutor. The center of authority changes in this transmedia enterprise without necessarily privileging the audience. Following through with the tactics of therapeutic practice, the act of interlocution ultimately turns back on the subject who, if successful, becomes capable of self-regulation. While such an authorizing gesture may seem prescriptive, and may demand that the addict return to a socially sanctioned model of normalcy, it ultimately redeems the demonized individual. I do not believe that *Intervention* can be dismissed as yet another incarnation of television's co-optation of neoliberalism; the program is not an empty call to citizenship, though it may indeed seem to be outsourcing the therapeutic exchange to its cast of interventionists.[17] I argue that the program outlines the process to further the process; it reveals more than it conceals.[18] Thomas Elsaesser reminds us: "Remembering, giving testimony, and bearing witness can be tokens of a fight not only against forgetfulness, but also against history."[19] Addicts do exist. Teenagers do go astray. Families can be dysfunctional. While our fears may be manufactured, their traumas are certainly not. *Intervention* takes the only tactic possible with vocalizing trauma; it engages with narrative. But rather than letting the ideological work of convention take hold, the program sets its sights much higher and aims to bring us to a much more productive understanding of crisis rhetoric.

5

The Architectures of Cyberdating

The nature of things, their coexistence, the way in which they are linked together and communicate is nothing other than their resemblance. And that resemblance is visible only in the network of signs that crosses the world from one end to the other.

MICHEL FOUCAULT, *THE ORDER OF THINGS*

In the previous chapters, I have identified a number of distinct drives that motivate the use of personal images, urging us to send them out into various public domains. We use them as devices of memory and recovery, as agents that can serve these restorative impulses. But, on occasion, we use our images to fulfill a different desire as we forge a forward-looking narrative. In a move that seems counter to fear and paranoia, many of us have thrown caution to the wind and joined online social networks with no decided aim other than to find old acquaintances and double our connectedness to those who are already a part of our daily lives. But others of us have done so much more purposefully, turning to cyberspace to become romantically (or simply sexually) entangled. Technophobia has given way to technophilia, and even though common generational distinctions still seem to inform the relative appeal of new technologies, for every cautionary tale of a rape in cyberspace there is a recuperative tale of kinship found and life's promise fulfilled.

Socialization has been altered dramatically since the introduction of networked communication and, with it, traditional notions of family and locality no longer seem to dominate the formation of our private lives. No longer bound by these conventions, our personal attachments have become individualized, freed from the moorings of such outmoded contextual (and place-bound) constraints.[1] With the aid of print- and Web-based dating services (both commercial and noncommercial), we have been able to make contact with potential partners in ways that complicate traditional notions of locale and even bodily copresence.[2] Therefore, it is not surprising that information technologies (the combined resources of computing and communications) and the Internet in particular have long since exceeded their initial status as tools of workplace productivity and have become increasingly important in leisurely pursuits (which might nevertheless still be understood as productive), helping us create and mediate our romantic attachments, and hastening our evolution into efficient desiring machines.

Technologies always have played a significant role in interpersonal relations, even when they have not been designed to do so. One of the first commercial computers, the UNIVAC, became a staple of popular entertainment in the 1950s; host Art Linkletter began using the machine to match couples during the 1956 season of the NBC variety show *People Are Funny*. Video dating services emerged in the mid-1970s, taking the camcorder revolution in a distinct direction. And the rise of networked personal computing birthed new arrangements in the collective gaming environments of the earliest MUDs (multiuser dungeons) that proliferated in the eighties, the socially oriented MOOs (object-oriented MUDs) and text-based BBSes (bulletin board systems) of the nineties, and the dedicated online dating services that began to emerge by the middle of that decade with the widespread use of the Internet.

The most obvious reason for turning to the matter of online dating in a volume on transience is to chart new patterns of flow and to follow personal images as they are sent along yet another pathway. But there is also the matter of psychological depth; my goal throughout this volume has been to find transience objectified, but also to define it as a more deeply entrenched phenomenon that is attached to the human psyche. That these pathways exist is fairly obvious; the number of dedicated online dating sites exploded in the first few years of the twenty-first century, introducing genres and subgenres of online engagement. More than an industrial push, however, the proliferation of these spaces seemed to suggest a psychic need, perhaps as a response to a perceived absence of opportunities for interaction off-line. And, despite the attempts of an industry to isolate desire, to channel it within particular fixed commercial venues and house it in specific Internet architectures (an effort formalized with the introduction of subscription-based online dating sites in the mid-1990s), other forums soon took center stage. As early as 2004, online social networks began to erode any fixed sense of where dating might and should occur, and Internet porn sites began to reconfigure their own architectures, adding file-sharing components that could connect users to each other. These new, less hierarchical arrangements allowed participants to connect with each other in more dynamic (and oftentimes free) ways, and redefined long-standing commercial sites that had been designed to bring individuals together through rather fixed patterns of interaction.

Desire became a messy affair. But the responsiveness, the malleability of online Internet architectures reflects the very nature of our needs (and here I purposefully refrain from speaking of need as simple consumerism). Unlike earlier print-based models that invoked both spatiality and temporality (one sent letters across a fixed geography), Internet dating is characterized by a seamless movement between reading descriptions, writing responses, and exchanging messages that invokes proximity and immediacy and binds to-gether rather distinct forms of information handling.[3] The online exchange clearly collapses regionality, as distinct locations (cities, states, and countries) come together under one domain name; and the lag of this new communica-tive relay remains anxiously open-ended, perpetually teasing our imaginations.

In such open terrain, looking is a privileged and powerful affair; we can survey (and be surveyed by) multiple others with a single glance. This is not a pure optical relay; faced with the uncertainty of how we might be read, we take measures to manage our impressions as we move online, following some of the same tactics we use in managing our off-line social lives. But we also deploy a number of unique cues that form part of the ever-expanding tool set of online communication. Profiles, personality and compatibility testing, digi-tal photographs, digital voice recordings, Web cameras, real-time chat capa-bilities, e-mail, and Instant Messaging are teamed up in an effort to help overcome the so-called restricted cues of online information gathering.[4] Taken together, these tools reduce the hyperpersonal nature of online dating.[5] Each artifact serves as a corrective measure; though these distinct elements com-bine to create a more detailed portrait, they also provide a series of checks and balances. At the same time, as we peruse these additional fields, we also begin to prolong our engagement; perhaps these tools promote more authen-tic forms of communication, slowing down the fleeting glance.

Reminding us that "it's okay to look," Match.com began running advertise-ments with the provocative tagline at the end of December 2006, rebranding its print and television ads and its online banners.[6] Earlier in the month, Jim Safka, the company's former CEO, gave readers an opportunity to look be-hind the scenes of the campaign's Los Angeles–based production. He posted photos on his ongoing MatchCEO Blogspot page, and invited readers to en-gage in a dialogue about the new ads. Not everyone was pleased with the ef-fort. In the months that followed, people weighed in with their responses, some of which were decidedly negative. In May 2007, one reader commented:

> Will you please end this campaign? IT'S DESTROYING OUR GENERA-
> TION! It's NOT okay to look! You're advertising that it is okay for hus-
> bands and wives to take their eyes off one another and view their
> "possibilities." You're advertising that it is okay for young teenagers

(females especially) to log on, make an account, and look for a partner (someone who could be twice her age). You're advertising that promiscuity is okay! You're advertising adultery! Why? Why must you kill our generation and condemn us for death? Why? We will stand up, stand up against the impure, stand up for the One who gives us Eternal life, we will stand up against anything and everything that does not honor our Lord! So please, will you stop this advertising campaign? It's DE-STROYING OUR GENERATION![7]

The following month, another reader posted a similar derogatory remark:

My husband and I don't like the ad campaign. My husband and I saw it for the first time a few weeks ago and then again earlier this week. He and I both agreed that the phrase "it's okay to look" seems to target married people. I mean, if you're not married, then it being "okay to look" on what should be a dating site for singles is obvious, isn't it?[8]

Looking is apparently a multivalent act; while Match.com encourages the activity, not everyone seems to agree. That we need to be told it's okay does, in fact, suggest that we are being invited to indulge in a certain guilty fixation, and the fixation is not simply about viewing other people but also about going online to do so, activating the mirrored forces of exhibitionism and voyeurism.

Match.com's redesigned banner showcases a number of abbreviated portraits, framing each of its subjects with an iris effect—a simulated peephole; the sitter's username is written in script, imprinted as a personal signature that nevertheless reveals neither name nor surname. One such ad features a young man in a casual pin-striped suit, seated on a vintage Schwinn bicycle; these signs of stylish geekiness are matched by his username (BeamMeDown2) and his introductory tagline ("I'm willing to give Earth girls a shot."). These tidy, professionally produced black-and-white tableaux, devoid of location markers and populated only by the occasional planned and determined prop, read as carefully constructed and publicly secure points of investment. They are like and not like the profile photos on the general site; they are beautiful approximations of direct communication. Taken together, they function as a whimsical narrative shorthand (replete with personal quips) for the site itself.

Vision cannot be reduced to a single mode of perception; though an ocular process, it invokes a power relation that calls out the role of the singular observer in an entire history of looking.[9] While online dating presents us with a new way of looking (partly invoked by a new interface—that of the data-

In its December 2006 advertising campaign, Match.com tells singles that "it's okay to look." (http://www.match.com)

base), a new place to look, and a new category of images, it is difficult to let go of the old ways of seeing and the ideological investments attached to such modes of perception. Kevin Robins suggests: "Rather than privileging 'new' against 'old' images, we might think about them all—all those that are still active, at least—in their contemporaneity."[10] This is what I suggested in my reading of photographs of missing children as I drew out the persistence of a particular disciplinary method and the persistent return of particular narratives that authorize containment (mechanisms of fear production). While we are presented with new imaging technologies, we are also offered new ways of organizing the visual field. But such new patterns, structures, and forms of organization may find opposition in the cultures and traditions (the social contexts) that ground them. The digital age, as with any significant evolutionary period, necessitates looking forward and backward; it warrants a dual attention, an understanding of both continuities and discontinuities. Safka's regular blog posts intend to help current and prospective members negotiate this divide between past and present; the conversation is designed to help people become more comfortable with the service, and the dialogue fosters a sense of engagement and camaraderie. Safka establishes a participatory relationship with his consumers, talking to them about ad campaigns and interface revisions and listening to their replies, sometimes acting on their feedback in an effort to win their consent and to position Match.com as an empathetic partner that might enable them to secure a similarly healthy investment in a life partner.

The self-described vision of Match.com's parent company, IAC/Inter-ActiveCorp, "is to harness the power of interactivity to make daily life easier and more productive for people all over the world."[11] There seem to be two oppositional trajectories or impulses embedded in this business model. The push to converge is represented by those IAC ventures that bring people together (including Match.com, Ticketmaster, Evite, and Expedia) and the company's investment in the consolidating enterprise of interactive commerce, while its opposite, the push to diversify, is found in the outward flow of global capital, where technological convergence is being deployed toward a globalizing end.

But the convergence narrative I want to consider here is not about technology but about identity. Do dating sites articulate a generalized push toward a singular pole of identity? As I turn to consider the contemporary architectures that frame personal advertisement photography on the Internet, my aim is to examine the popular, critical, and institutional discourses that attempt to position personal advertisement sites as contemporary manifestations of community; these readings commonly suggest that online personal ads signal the death of community, but they occasionally celebrate the birth of new forms of community. How can these sites be understood as both dystopic and utopic formations? Perhaps what these sites expose are more fundamental questions and indices of community and its evolving parameters. My goal, in part, is to address the physical—in this case, technological—mechanisms that have caused anxieties around notions of community; the blog roll cited earlier indicates a fear that the call to unite online may have a destabilizing effect, impacting already-existing social relations. However, I want to avoid a model of technological determinism that suggests that new technologies themselves have changed our communities; what they have done is modify our "sense" of community. The question here is how we perceive what the technology is "doing." Linda Singer writes of community as a culturally overdetermined term, an elastic referent.[12] It is the term's very elasticity that makes it extremely powerful; the term is an authorizing signifier, ready to be differentially deployed (attached to an agenda), yet always linked to an economy of discourse that simultaneously invokes inclusion and exclusion. Likewise, photography itself is a discursive construct. As Allan Sekula notes: "The discourse that surrounds photography speaks paradoxically of discipline and freedom, of rigorous truths and unleashed pleasures."[13] There is clearly a paradox at work here, and my goal is to explore its politics. What are the particular forces that try to move the pendulum to one side or the other, toward truth or pleasure?[14] As we send images of ourselves into cyberspace, asking them to take on a specific function, they can be readily pulled back out and asked to work in the service of a decidedly different narrative. Like the child's photo that serves as a lingering signifier of fear (through abduction) or the relative's photo that serves as a lingering signifier of terrorism (through catastrophe), our own images, willfully or not, can be asked to serve as lingering signifiers of community.

Reading the Body

Internet dating is constructed around the presentation of biographical narratives that provide individuals with an avenue through which they can reflect on and create a discourse about who they are and what they want from a relationship or a partner. Self-descriptions provide an important starting point from which others decide whether to enter into communication; and despite the amount of reflection that goes into their production, the claim is always one of authenticity (and immediacy). The claim operates in two ways—in the manner that the profile embodies its subject and the way it objectifies the subject's desire. The question of a profile's authenticity often hinges on how honestly it portrays its subject; but the question might also be answered by considering the quality of the response. Do the respondents match the subject's desire? This more significant question reveals to what degree desire can be approximated in a text-bound system. While photographs are an instrumental component of personal advertisement sites, they are not the only component. The question is how to privilege them. How much power should be given to photographic evidence? Where does the photograph fit in the signifying relay of any personal ad? At some level, the image seems the most important cue in online dating sites, perhaps because we place so much value on the visual register in our everyday lives—making assessments about people, reading them through their visages and their physical bodies. But the ad space takes away part of the physical body; it removes demeanor, presence, and comportment, and leaves only a static entity. And the ad space offers individuals as thumbnails or thumbnail collages. The image is easily scanned; as part of a hypertext that we might quickly scroll through, images seem well aligned with the speed of our glance, the rapid trailblazing of Internet surfing where there is so much to see. And when the search result offers up hundreds of similar individuals (and tells us exactly how many are to be found and exactly how far we have moved through our reading list), time seems to be of the essence; we need to economize, and images help us to do so.

But images are not entirely open signifiers, despite our desire to fixate on them. They do not exhibit true semiotic freedom. They are contained by the

structuring tendencies of photographic practice, formal conventions that
are historically and culturally situated. And at the same time, we should not
overlook that as readers we too are contained and situated. The practices of
representation may be ideologically inflected, giving symbolic weight to material practice; but as subjects, we are also historically and culturally situated.
As we foreground the forces that are exerted on photography, shaping it as a
discursive practice, we should not lose sight of the forces that are exerted on
our very subjectivity. On the one hand, as Sekula notes, we need to understand that representational practices give form to other discursive constructions; they can be central to ideologies of family, nature, sexuality, history,
and governance.[15] Visibility is a powerful tool that is often used to define
these terms, to offer up evidence. On the other hand, we need to understand
that these same ideologies structure our attitude toward photography. This
seems to be an inescapable loop that ultimately naturalizes our practices of
seeing and secures us as bourgeois subjects. New media forms may enable these
traditional ideologies, practices, and subject positions, but only with a certain
renegotiation that involves both new technologies (digital imaging in an interactive, scripted interface) and new forms of textuality (that nevertheless still
invoke traditional forms of composition—for instance, understanding how to
conjoin text and image). Yet this negotiation does not always work. Beyond
simply exploring new ontologies (distinctions between, for instance, analog
and digital photography), we might ask more meaningful questions. How do
we reconcile the bourgeois subject in the face of the desire for community?
What tension is evoked in the desire to know, as we approach a dating profile
from a place of certainty? To what extent do personal advertisement sites
present an affront to subjectivity? While many profile markers are individually authored (for example, the relatively open character space of the free-
form narrative), others are selected from a menu of offerings; in all, these
work as a form of *de facto* autobiography, the goal being self-description.

In its current iteration, the Match.com profile interface includes menu-
based responses to a long list of self-identifying attributes. Filling in the general category "about me," participants are asked to complete multiple-choice
fields for a number of personal markers, among them: relationships, have kids,
want kids, ethnicity, body type, height, religion, smoke, drink, hair, eyes, sports
and exercise, exercise habits, interests, education, occupation, income, languages, politics, sign, pets I have, and pets I like. In turn, responding to the
header "about my date," the site asks participants to specify the responses they
seek in a match (allowing the Match.com search engine to rate results in
terms of a percentage of equivalence). Responding to recent trends in folksonomic tagging and allowing participants to refine how they may be known
in a term-based search, Match.com also endorses the inclusion of Match-

words, which reference the subject and the subject's varied interests (professional, personal, political, social, and cultural) and commodity fetishes; these terms also allow respondents to collate profiles that feature similar key terms as they seek out individuals with common interests and sensibilities. Here, the guiding principles of word selection function as yet another layer of individuation, providing a more nuanced trace of the respondent's psychology (one that might be understood by sympathetic others). Beyond these abbreviated term-based signposts, Match.com also allows its participants to narrate themselves more elaborately under the profile heading "in my own words," and, of course, follows through with the promise to flesh out each of its members by featuring a profile photo album.

The desire to know, in the context of online dating sites, is manifest as an attempt to ground disembodied subjects; there is a strong push toward embodiment, a process that in modern society has been achieved through a range of techniques that include visual classification (photographic portraiture and fingerprinting), and other tactics such as genetic mapping (which still has a visual register) and the assignment of unique identification numbers.[16] However, as Celia Lury points out: "Having a (recognisable) body has historically not been sufficient to define an individual. Continuity of *consciousness* and *memory* are also necessary for a person to claim separate status as an individual."[17] Consciousness and memory are not produced by an accumulation of signifiers; rather, they are the products of narrative. As we approach the personal ad, we may add up the formal cues and the site's specific forms of data, but we do so in order to construct a different type of portrait. Beyond the literal image found on the page, we create a projection by narrativizing the subject, or pulling the subject out of its immediate context and repurposing it.[18] We do this despite the fact that the image is already once removed from its original context; it is simply a photographic projection of its author (this is what Lury refers to as "outcontextualization," a process discussed in Chapter 1).[19] Differentiation, drawing distinctions between subjects in our list of results, is accomplished only by indifferentiation, by taking their assets and subjecting them to an algorithm. The aspects of self that are socially determined are mapped alongside aspects of self that are biologically determined, and these variables are leveled, taken out of context, and fed into the database.[20] The subject is truly objectified—even subjective markers become objective factors. Individuals are rewritten as units of analysis that site designers can manipulate and users can analyze.[21] Aware of these processes, we try to work within these guidelines; we take pictures of ourselves knowing the paths they will take on their way to being inscribed in the site, or we repurpose (and edit) pictures taken for other occasions and carefully attempt to reinscribe them, as we try to massage the data to mirror what we perceive to be our likeness. Perhaps as an attempt at self-narration, many online daters include multiple images, showing themselves in varied contexts (at work, at play, with family, and with pets) and from varied perspectives, as a storyboard of sorts, creating a bare-bones plotline that also yields a greater assurance of authentic communication (more representations suggest a more detailed inflection). These images produce a virtual slide show and a closer approximation of movement, giving the body greater contour. It is indeed a frustrating process for many online daters, as they attempt to actively rewrite themselves as units to be analyzed, and try to hold steadfastly on to some trait of personality in the process. The goal is to delimit possibilities, to develop as close an approximation of ourselves as possible, to present our unique selves even as we unmoor our photos and send them on their way into the collective space of the gallery. To our dismay, the process is never precise.

Toward a Science of the Subject

On reflection, we may see that even the most scientific of processes yields a degree of imprecision. Working at the end of the nineteenth century, the French criminologist and anthropologist Alphonse Bertillon developed an anthropometric system that was adopted by the Paris police force. The system identified individuals by a series of measurements, recording the contours and shape formations of the head and body, as well as individual markings such as tattoos and scars, and arriving at a formula that made this data refer to a unique individual. The data was then recorded on a file card, conjoined to front and profile photos of the subject, and filed away for later retrieval after being rigorously cross-indexed. Though not a perfect system, as it was labor-intensive and the measurement process itself prone to error, the goal was to develop a "speaking portrait," and to this end, the methodical analysis was written in a common vernacular.[22] Extending these investigative tactics, which were measures of individuals, Edmond Bayle, then head of the Department of Judicial Identity in Paris, employed the departments of physics, chemistry, and biology to aid in criminal detecting. Under Bayle's guidance, the Paris police began examining crime scenes with equally intense scrutiny and attaching the suspect to location. Without tracing the entire historical trajectory of scientific practices, it should suffice to say that there are contradictory impulses at work in the varied deployments of photography throughout the nineteenth and twentieth centuries—both in honorific practices and in those attached to Enlightenment rhetoric (getting to know the body). What the history reveals is that the techniques for reading the body consistently yielded both egalitarian and authoritarian results—knowing the body and controlling the body.[23] What we see in this history is both threat and promise. But which result is which? Before turning to discuss Bertillon, I was commenting on the lack of precision in inscription, considering what does not translate as we put our square selves into the round holes of script. Following through with this metaphor, I want to explore the bits of subjectivity that do not fit and position the individual in relation to the community. My aim is to connect theory to praxis. Reflecting on both Bertillon's foundational methods and his own nascent procedures, Edmond Bayle proposes: "Truth lies always between theory which moves too fast, and routine which moves too slowly."[24]

Desire in the Database

Most online dating sites follow a conventional operating scheme; the photographic image is part of a standardized template, an image box placed alongside textual data that is inherently more quantifiable (that is to say, it can be categorized) than the photograph it elucidates. While many advertisers take snapshots of themselves specifically with the intent to attach these to their profiles (this is quite explicitly the role of Web cameras as they are linked to computercentric space), personal advertisement sites are also populated with a wide array of photographic artifacts, including family and vacation photos and occasional portraits (such as event photos). Most advertisers attempt to mask or crop secondary subjects such as partners, friends, or children, often producing phantom limbs that protrude from the borders of the frame. As occasional portraits and group photographs find new life in this particular cyber venture, they cannot shrug their profilmic residues; as advertisers frame or reframe themselves for public display, they often provide clues to their habits, tastes, leisure-time pursuits, and familial leanings. The images in any one album may be produced by a range of authors and, in every case other than a self-portrait, they implicitly document previous relationships between photographer and subject.

In the case of both the unique and appropriated photos, the image is made public for private consideration. And in both cases, image selection, cropping, retouching, and/or manufacture are performed for an assumed audience. The most readily consumed advertisements contain particular details that are at once unique and personal and at the same time familiar and somewhat universal (marketing according to type). Here is a form of self-regulation, an act of self-surveillance that is performed with the hope of emitting a localizable sign, a referent familiar and easily categorized yet still imbued with the cult of personality, registering simultaneous sameness and difference. While the primary goal of personal advertisement photography is to reveal physiognomy, circulated images may contain contextual markers that implicate the sitter. At the same time, these photographs are part of a multimedia text that situates

them alongside a number of textual and iconic markers that work as interpretive mechanisms, pushing the reading of the photograph in nuanced
directions.

Yet menus rather than images often mark the reader's first encounter with
an online dating site. One of the most common and practical features of online dating sites is their deployment of search engines. While members can
browse through posted advertisements, the search engine provides a productive narrowing of their focus. Most sites allow a laundry list of search
criteria. Beyond simple physiognomic markers such as age, height, and eye
color, Yahoo! Personals lists personality type, love style, body, have kids, want
kids, education, employment, profession, smokes, income, drinks, living, social, TV, speaks, religion, services, political, humor, interests, and sign among
a range of attributes. "Body" itself is a loaded term, and although the choices
are somewhat expansive in the interest of precision, they are not scientific:
slim, slender, average, athletic, fit, thick, a few extra pounds, large, and volup-
tuous. Felt, but not determined (we may interpret the physical contours of
our bodies in a manner that belies somatic experience), members apply body
type in a rather subjective manner, but one that is nevertheless culturally
overdetermined and therefore understood as a rigid signifier (to the extent
that profilers often call each other out on their incorrect use of terms). To
ascribe "personality type" involves a similar negotiation: explorer, idealist,
leader, traditionalist, individualist, rebel, giver, creator, champion, protector,
equalizer, and observer. These self-assigned choices ultimately invoke too
much of the self, once again producing an overdetermined subject that, despite
the number of labels, still reads like an unknown quantity. After all, self-
evaluation can only play a limited role in mutual attraction.

Yet, as Yahoo! formulates degrees of attraction, it shapes the most elusive
of markers into a known quantity, collapsing biological and cultural referents
(including television). As members move through their respective checklists
and set the search engine in motion, the results come back as quantified af-
finities. Those profiles with the highest overall fit are listed first, and their
value is signaled through the site's unique iconography—a rating system of
hearts, with five hearts indicating the highest degree of likeness. Of course,
privileging likeness seems to be a productive gesture, but it is also self-
affirming, eliminating certain degrees of not knowing and not wanting. It
produces a grouping structured around likeness. While site users are actively
working through their desire, activity (as opposed to passivity) does not necessarily suggest a progressive movement beyond ideology, nor does it inherently
yield a critique of the very bourgeois subject position that is being acted out
and drawn out by the interface.

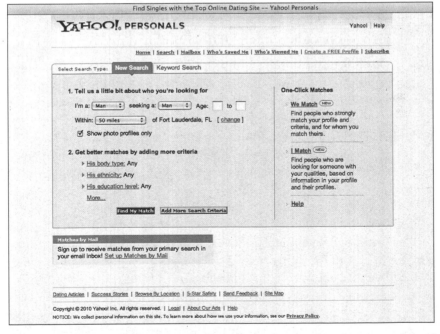

Yahoo! Personals follows the menu-based structure of most online dating portals, and channels desire through a search engine. The site was rebranded and redesigned in May 2010, when the company began outsourcing its dating service to IAC's Match .com. (http://personals.yahoo.com, accessed January 20, 2010; site now discontinued)

As Miriam Hansen notes, the process is found more generally in the theorizations and articulations of the culture industry: "Horkheimer and Adorno ascribe the effectivity of mass-cultural scripts of identity not simply to the viewers' manipulation as passive consumers, but rather to their very solicitation as experts, as active readers. The identification *with* the stereotype is advanced by the appeal to a particular type of knowledge or skill predicated on repetition: the identification *of* a familiar face, gesture or narrative convention takes the place of genuine cognition."[25] Hansen suggests that the ideological effect of what Adorno and Horkheimer refer to as "mass-cultural hieroglyphics" (the visual images of the culture industry) is one that prevents human beings from changing. While the suggestion is more purposefully about not differentiating between true acts of self and those called out from above, I argue that this quandary is also apparent in the field of online dating, where the call to sameness is supported (and, in fact, promoted) by site architecture.[26] The repetition is about seeing oneself in others, a quest made all the more powerful in the realm of explicit desire.

The effect is much the same on most dating sites. Match.com allows searches by city as well as by keyword. The basic search on Match.com specifies zip code, age, and gender (with sexuality collapsed under the correlative gendering of searcher and subject); detailed searches allow greater specificity and include a number of variables within such general categories as appearance, background/values, and lifestyle. The last term is not used here as a marker of sexual orientation, but rather refers to such facets as diet and exercise, employment and income, and living situation and family status. In the domain of Match.com, a checklist of turn-ons—which run the gamut from body piercing to meteorological fantasies—approximates desire, but any overt reference to sexual play is avoided. Searches may be framed by a geographic radius, and the search process climaxes with the mapping of photographic evidence onto the database.

While some personal advertisement sites position dating as their central purpose, many have a more ambiguous design. However, the latter are still containers for particular outpourings of identity, and their subdivisions are still driven by both the architecture of site engines and those desiring engines attached to particular formations of identity; subcultures still have labels. But at the same time, the classifications used on sites designed to meet the needs of more-focused interest groups often escape generalized cultural decoding. These sites often engage in productive semiotic complexity, and their unique signs and gestures cannot be universally accessed. In line with the work of the subculture, we may find users experimenting with language and rejecting certain existing linguistic practices. Though site architectures provide structure, they are not unilaterally prescriptive.

The organizing schema of sites that are more focused (those designed for subdivisions of the general dating pool—or, for lack of a better term, "special-interest groups") is often reflected in their domain names; yet, in these sites, the central organizing principle may leave a space for more subtly inflected uses and audiences. To counter any assumption about the uniformity of gay male desire, we need only to look at the enormous diversity among sites that cater to gay men. Sites such as BigMuscle.com foreground muscularity as a privileged attribute of the male body.[27] Within this domain, the homosocial and the homosexual intermingle, with the site populated largely by gay men, but inclusive of a voyeurism and exchange that willfully embraces straight men or simply assumes erotic and sexual play without needing to address sexual orientation. Moreover, the desires that are expressed range from mutual admiration to those of a more explicitly sexual nature. The site architecture is very responsive to the community's needs. At BigMuscle.com, a "free online community for adult males who enjoy fitness," profilers may develop buddy links (displaying thumbnails of profilers who are friends, admirers, workout partners, sex buddies, or relationship partners) and they also may list site profiles that they have viewed and like for one reason or another. Within this domain, profilers and end users may be looking for any number of connection types, including one-time sexual encounters, extended sexual encounters without commitment, sexual encounters outside of already-established committed (and perhaps open) relationships, long-term relationships, friendships, activity partners, and chat buddies, or they may simply be voyeurs or "pic collectors" (browsing sites and collecting pictures to add to their database of fantasy photos).

Manhunt.net, though deemed largely a network for casual sex, encourages its users to "love, lust, chat," and its unique profile markers give members a heads-up as to "when" ("Right Now!" or "Ask Me") and "where" ("Anywhere," "In Public," "At Your Place," or "At My Place").[28] As a site that openly embraces cruising, "status" (in this domain, understood as HIV status) is a profile attribute and users can see who is currently online (a common feature on social-networking sites that takes on added significance in the hunt for a quick hookup). Set to a techno beat, the site's Flash introduction asks: "What are you looking for?" and pushes the fantasy further by prompting: "College jocks, Latin papis, Hairy daddies, Muscle men, Bi-curious, Young and hung, Black guys, Boy next door, Total tops, Hungry bottoms, Thugs." Evoking early text-based bulletin board systems, the introduction's stylized DOS-prompt conjures up a long history of Net-assisted encounters.

In the spaces of Manhunt.net, profile descriptions are succinct, speaking rather directly to each member's specific sexual interests and using a vocabulary not found on more generic sites. One member writes: "love men to men

BigMuscle.com features search terms that match the interests of its membership. (http://www.bigmuscle.com)

Manhunt.net playfully draws in its clientele with a rather overt come-on, and playing to the uniqueness (and abundance) of desire suggests there is "someone for everyone." (http://www.manhunt.net)

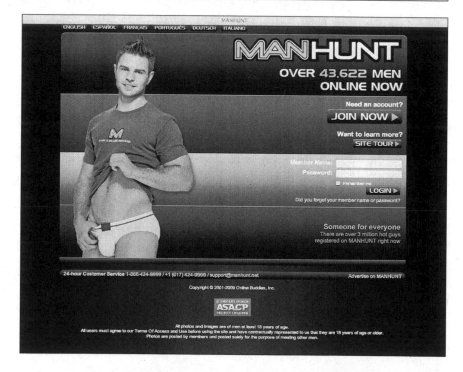

hot sex. if want to chat open priv pic. if i don't reply, we r not comparable, dont take it personal. we r here to have fun, and lots of it. very vers. if we click . . . love to fuck and get fucked, also have my cock serviced. Depending on the chemistry sometimes more. Not into queens or barbies. Some hair is ok, shaved head and goatee football build manly bodies A+. glory holes are fun too. Cannot host. sorry, no pics, no reply." The shorthand is quite purposeful and lends itself to a quick read, a gesture that seems to reflect the urgency and speed of anonymous encounters.

On Gay.com, profiles sit alongside more traditional tabloid fare; in fact, the site reads like a community magazine and is positioned as a general-purpose informational portal for its readership. Gay.com hosts personal ads as well as conventional featured sections that cover news, health, business, entertainment, travel, style, and other related fare. Though not a literary magazine per se, it promotes a different type of informed readership because it locates desire and knowledge side by side. Dating is simply one of many channels on the site. And cities are not coded simply as lists of men profiled within them, but also as lists of local attractions and events (found in the site's various city guides).[29]

Among these sites, there are clearly multiple forms of desire at work, and the participants themselves may be operating with desire in a constant state of flux; it is counterproductive to quantify and fix these mechanisms. Therefore, I use the term "dating" rather loosely in this chapter, for individuals produce, read, and respond to personal advertisement sites for a wide range of reasons; for instance, some participants are looking for relationships, others are looking for casual sexual encounters, and still others are simply browsing sites as voyeurs without the intent to respond to a profile. Most sites allow advertisers to specify their goals and motives.

The status of personal advertisement sites has been complicated by the emergence of social networks, which not only provide new arenas for meeting but also redefine the expected outcomes of online social engagement in what are much more open-ended arenas; these postindustrial architectures can cater to the varying needs of the membership. Some members use Facebook and MySpace to connect with friends and family, others to hook up, to date, to file share; the use-value is seemingly limitless. In response, even more-focused sites find themselves receptive to multitasking. XTube, an Internet porn site launched in 2006, is an adult video–hosting service that allows users to share adult content (trading on the YouTube moniker of personal broadcasting), to consume commercial content, share photos, post profiles, and send Instant Messages. Beyond the rather open admission that XTube can be used by its gay clientele to "find a hot stud to fuck in your city," the site welcomes other uses.

Likewise, Dudesnude.com, which launched in 2002, features streaming amateur and professional video clips, as well as profiles; while largely a free portal for content sharing, the site also includes an adult video store with pay-per-minute, streaming, and downloadable movies. Dudesnude.com does not advertise itself as a dating site, but a more-detailed profile search can locate men looking for relationships in a particular city; yet such a focused search offers up members' photos as a general list of thumbnails and keeps their motives buried in their narratives. In this way, the site seems to foreground casual browsing rather than more purposeful connecting.[30] Indeed, the site's search engine, which privileges "physical type" and "content type" is designed as an inventory for the site's images rather than a filter for aspects of sociability.[31]

Desire and Community

As sites of social interaction, these arenas are commonly interpreted as new forms of community, and are consequently attached to particular anxieties in popular discourse that simultaneously decry these new places of engagement as the death of purer forms of the term. Internet engagements are often understood as new social relations built on the ruins of community itself. "Community" is, in fact, a catchphrase deployed by these sites.

Match.com refers to itself as a "diverse, global community" and suggests: "We're a real community—an overused, but accurate term—of men and women who respect each other and are looking for relationships. We're as diverse as America itself, even though our members tend to be college-educated professionals."[32] Posting Polaroid snapshots of its various service teams, the site binds its workers to its customers, formally bridging the gap between corporation and consumer. Match.com provides several predefined subcommunities within its system: gay.match.com, lesbian.match.com, and senior.match.com. In this manner, Match.com caters to a wide range of individuals, but can be used to outline subcommunities of subscribers/participants through preestablished affinity groups or by deploying a search engine in a way that engages such groups.

Despite its open invitation, Match.com defines success (as evidenced in its posted success stories) primarily in terms of long-term monogamous heterosexual coupling, with marriage as the ultimate goal. Searching beyond the top menu story categories of marriage, engagement, and relationship by adding the keyword "gay" brings me to five testimonials, two of which use the term not in reference to the matched couple, but as an offhand contextual remark. One heterosexual woman comments, "I figured all the good ones had to be taken or were gay or something," while another recounts the moment her last boyfriend came out to her. The lesbian success stories on Match.com are even fewer; on my last visit, I found only one. These gay and lesbian success stories are not readily visible on the site; they are difficult to discern, to locate, and to group together. One has to actively search deeper into the site's hierarchy to find them.

On the most broad-reaching gay dating sites, the need to differentiate a form of queer identity is balanced by the need to find a shared vocabulary to express that identity, to locate a subcommunity of a shared sensibility; in the best-case scenario, the imagined community manifests itself as an actual viewing community, and readily definable production techniques (that are not invisible but can be easily read by a viewer) promote a bond between producer and viewer. The impulse to describe a bounded community—to locate, for example, queer culture—is not simply an imposed ideal. It seems responsive to general challenges in the cultural field, where gay men often look for community, and physical signs play an important role in visibility as objective markers of a more felt quality of acceptance, belonging, and pride. Yet the reverse impulse to deterritorialize or defy categorical distinctions (to question body boundaries, body types, and other forms of communal attachment—even moving outside of the gay ghetto or not identifying as part of the "club scene") does not signify so clearly online. It is hard to deterritorialize neat categorical distinctions when the interface demands a choice between a limited number of categories of being, and when sexual orientation (among other culturally-charged variables) is foregrounded as a primary and distinct asset in menu-driven interaction. Complex identity formations are undone at each level of a forked file structure (where each file system object is governed by metadata), both in the primary organization of raw data and in the secondary delivery of raw data through the graphical user interface.

The cyberdating sites discussed here may not be communities per se, but only signifiers of that potential, perhaps activated, perhaps not. It is tempting to label these sites as community because their members often can be literally displayed as a group and, at the very least, there is an understanding that other advertisements exist, even if only one at a time can be displayed. Match .com displays the reader's selected advertisement alongside a list of other similarly matched ones, and quantifies the current display as one out of a finite number of pages of matches, a list that is the product of a search that may generate too large or too small a result, and can be accordingly refined. The inhabitants of the searcher's particular subdivision of this online arena of advertisements can grow quickly or diminish. It may be tempting to refer to the searcher's results as a personalized community or to his or her resultant circle of communicants as a community, but the participants themselves do not necessarily constitute such an arrangement. Community is not found *in* them but *among* them. In *The Inoperative Community*, Jean-Luc Nancy suggests that community is not a place but a passage, and commonality does not inherently lead to any significant act of sharing; in fact, the work of capital is antithetical to community, for it can only privilege the general characteristics of its products (which define its institutional identity) and can only dwell in inauthentic forms of community.[33]

The dating sites considered here might be pathways to community, but the larger institutional narrative is an obstacle to such an arrangement; not only does the narrative shape the discourse within but it also repurposes the actions of its users. The search engines quantify, sort, and display textual data, while the images are quantified and sorted by the searcher, positioned as acceptable or unacceptable, saved or discarded, printed, downloaded, deleted and/or simply skipped over. The user's internal search engine is driven by typology and by an assumed potential for sharing. This engine is fueled by desire, driven by the brain's capacity to categorize and concretize. The drive to type involves categorizing others but also categorizing oneself, as well as positioning oneself in relation to others.

These sites themselves are not communities. As the product of work and works in progress, they are evidence of *potential* communities, the remains of once-active communities, or the intercepted broadcasts of communications taking place elsewhere and between others. These are transmissions that have been sent, are being sent, or are simultaneously in limbo in an inert state. In some cases, they are transmissions that are never received, or are received and never returned, remaining one-way, unrealized communicative pathways. By their very nature, these sites impede a reading of the existence of community; their use-value remains hidden. How and to what end people consume the profiles they view is unobservable.

Advertisers have varied motivations for posting to personal advertisement sites and end users have equally varied motivations; moreover, each participant's motivation may be in flux, shifting over time and with each encounter. To complicate any effort to perform a singular read, sites are consumed and interacted with in ways that may exceed their official purpose. The profile guidelines for Match.com place specific restrictions on advertising for multiple sexual partners or additional sexual partners, while the site's statement of purpose welcomes "all single adults seeking one-to-one relationships ranging from companionship to friendship, romance to marriage."[34] Soliciting for a relationship that is primarily sexual in nature is not allowed, and sexual innuendo or discussion is regulated by the site's profile guidelines; however, outside of performing a close read of explicit solicitations with unregulated language, it is unlikely that Match.com has been able to unilaterally prevent censurable relations.

Discourses about the demise of community are grounded in a reading of specific objects, which ultimately concludes that there is no residue of community to be found in them; therefore, community must have been lost. Discourses about the perversity of particular forms of desire are grounded in a reading of specific objects as well, in which generalized bodies are attached to specific practices. But desire exceeds a practice-status in the same way that community exceeds an object-status.

Yet the institutional discourse about (and the architectural rendering of) real bodies invokes their physicality in only limited ways, promoting only the most safely consumable desires. But the Internet is not simply about disembodiment, and Internet dating sites are not simply about a certain type of object choice. People are meeting online and having sex off-line. While Match.com suggests "it's okay to look," the missing part of this imperative—its negative complement—is "but it's not okay to touch." The double entendre has lost its double. The come-on is about tempting us to visit the site, but it does not take us to its foregone conclusion. The anger expressed in the feedback cited at the head of this chapter suggests that readers are filling in the blanks. Unfortunately, their attempts to regulate desire hide the more important negation found in Match.com's rhetoric. However, in the same way that we cannot find community online and must inevitably accept the site as a passage and look for community elsewhere, we should also consider that despite not seeing more playful (and sexual) engagements online, the more significant actions and perhaps ruptures are in those performative acts that are off-line, where, freed from the visible field, they can exceed our speculative (and linguistic) limits. I am not referring to online identity play; rather, my reference is to "real" sexual activity—points where the rubber hits the road, so to speak. It is here that we must look (despite how obscene that suggestion may be) to understand how limiting Match.com's play really is and, after all of this prescription, how willfully end users are acting out.

Desire by Any Other Name

The shifting attachments in cyberspace suggest a far more active engagement with code and convention on the part of the end users of personal advertisement sites; the hegemonic push, however, is in the rapid manner that site designers themselves identify the permutations of identity and successfully reduce them to a series of menu options, replacing the specificity of identity with the specificity of the interface. Visible and nuanced subcultural codes are replaced by the invisible binaries of script; self-definition is performed by using a template and identity is articulated by recourse to a generating engine.

It is common to move from one personal advertisement domain to another and find many of the same participants; often, the names change but the faces remain the same. Members in any given site begin to recognize each other, may observe each other's status without communicating, may watch each other's profiles evolve (and see them go off- and online as the individuals partner up and break up), and may at some point in this chronology decide to engage in a dialogue; some online exchanges only begin after a lengthy period of studied engagement. Watching the neighborhood evolve, members become aware when new individuals join the group. And policing the neighborhood themselves, members may exchange feedback with each other, either online or off-line, about each other's behaviors; it is common to encounter familiar faces from the database in off-line spaces, especially in more tightly knit or geographically bound communal environments. While it is easy to identify the rules of conduct that govern online dating sites, as most have rather extensive community guidelines on their policy pages, it is more difficult to locate those moments when end users are policing each other. Of course, most sites have a method for anonymously reporting policy violations, but the more meaningful injury occurs as end users talk to each other, weighing in on each other's social capital. In many cases of false advertising, users talk to each other about the wrongful appropriation of photos (posting misleading or altogether false pictures). Governance emanates from both the top and the bottom of these Internet architectures, and these arenas are more productively understood as communities in these periods of action. While policing is commonly understood as a negative act, it produces more obvious traces of the work of community as it visualizes context setting.

Multiplicity does not always suggest duplicity. Within the confines of a single domain, one may find participants that go by more than one name; of course, this form of multiplicity is also easily found outside of personal advertisement sites, as it is a mainstay of even the most traditional online ventures. America Online (AOL) allows subscribers to create multiple screen names, pitching the feature as a way to separate personal messages from work-related correspondence, to assign a name to each online activity or each online family member (with the ability to differentiate access privileges across the family). Yet in a localizable space, naming also imbues the body with meaning, calling out such defining features as geographic location, age, race, ethnicity, body type, sexual position, or fetish. The subculture becomes a community by developing, sharing, and participating in its own naming strategies, and the architectures of cyberspace interfere with community only as they begin to map sharing onto a fixed interface. Sites such as Match.com regulate naming conventions much more closely, restricting such obscenities; usernames speak less about desire and more about being, and are built around more commonplace pursuits (hobbies) and workaday interests (careers).

Clearly, the interface and terms of use may function normatively as a naturalized grammatical construct, in part by allowing and disallowing. And the

site itself as a database functions as a cultural form subject to an equally insidious hegemonic predisposition. The database as a general construct offers
a particular model of the world and of human experience, and despite the
variability of potential interfaces, the tendency toward branching-type interactivity (menu-based movement) that presents the user with finite choices,
sending him or her along an ever-narrowing pathway, seems to overtly channel and delimit desire.

Restoring the Frame

In his 1995 essay, "Domestic Photography and Digital Culture," Don Slater
claims that: "Snapshot photography—images taken by ourselves of ourselves,
the self-representation of everyday life—has barely any place at the new
electronic hearth."[35] While his judgment is reserved, framed by an understanding that the digital domestic snapshot had perhaps not yet entered its
heyday, that "private images" had "not yet entered the datastream of either telecommunications or convergence," Slater is not blind, of course, to the unrealized potential of a medium that had, at the moment of his writing, only
reached a state of advanced hobbyism.[36] To this end, Slater expresses a sense
of loss; what he fears most is not the technological transformation of photographic practice, but rather the continuing erosion of authentic personal experience. The history of photography speaks to the more general (and ongoing)
domestication and commodification of everyday life. Private photography
yielded first to family photography (a commercially-codified application of
the apparatus), and is now yielding to self-conscious public performance.
Centralized and convergent media practices have, in fact, recontoured photography, but they pose a greater threat to personal identity and agency.

Cyberdating has been discussed in popular discourse as yet another har-
binger of the disappearance of community, sign and symptom of increased
privatization, cause and effect of distancing and alienation, the doublespeak
and double bind of Internet technology itself. Weaving a cautionary tale of
cyber-romance, a February 2001 *Newsweek* story by Brad Stone is framed by
the week's cover header, positioning the header for Stone's story below the
header for its international-focus column on Osama bin Laden. In this manner, "Dating Online" is linked with "Global Terror." As one of many notable
moments of dramatic intertextuality, this particular issue of *Newsweek* frames
the cyberdating article with stories that weave a much grander cautionary
tale. Taken together, the issue's discussion of AOL Time Warner's monopoly
on domestic digital technologies, the testing of angiogenesis inhibitors on human subjects, the effect of hard soda advertising on teens, genetic mapping,
and Internet privacy contributes to a general thread of paranoia writ large in

the magazine. Herein we are given a literal (or at least "literary") manifestation of an attack on subjectivity being staged on several fronts.

In a June 1999 column on cyberspace and community published in *The Nation*, Andrew L. Shapiro echoes popular distaste for a particular aspect of computer-mediated communications, reading online experiences as less satisfying than real-world engagements, and less meaningful than even the most immediate technological antecedents—television and radio. He laments: "Ultimately, online associations tend to splinter into narrower and narrower factions. They also don't have the sticking power of physical communities."[37] Citing media critic David Shaw, Shapiro suggests that as television and radio draw us away from direct interaction, these particular media at least provide "a kind of social glue, a common cultural reference point in our polyglot, increasingly multicultural society," while "online experiences rarely provide this glue."[38] Shapiro's concern is the weakening of local community building by the increase in social networks that are both more distant (less geographically immediate) and perhaps less permanent.

It is worthwhile, of course, to concretize the importance of local community building, of focusing on the local as a key tool in democracy and social activism. We should not lose sight of the vitality of localism in political action, nor should we privilege the national or the global at the expense of the local. But certainly all forms of computer-mediated dialogue are not analogous, and in reaching out beyond local interests, we may in fact discover what is missing in our own neighborhood.

Perhaps this is a point of investment of cyberdating services that cast the net over a wider geographic and demographic nexus than ever may have been singularly possible. In addition, the variables deployed in the arena of cyberdating and the specificity of search engines seem to give form to Shapiro's insight about the splintering of online associations into narrower factions. But I suggest that we can put a positive spin on narrowcasting.

The Self-Portrait and the Imag(in)ing of Desire

In her examination of emergent social meanings in computer-mediated communication, Nancy Baym privileges those moments in which users "creatively exploit the systems' features in order to play with new forms of expressive communication, to explore possible public identities, to create otherwise unlikely relationships, and to create behavioral norms."[39] She suggests: "When, and if, these emergent features develop into stable group-specific understandings, the group gains the potential to be imagined as a community."[40] A sense of (localized) community emerges from a set of stable social meanings.

As I have already stated, among the images that litter online dating sites are both occasional portraits (photos taken for a previous purpose, only to be posted later on the site) and photos more likely taken for the sole purpose of posting on the site. Of this latter group, the most explicit evidence of offering the image for a particular audience is the self-portrait of the sitter with a camera. A number of images posted on adult personals sites are of the sitter holding a digital camera up to his face, usually photographed in the act of recording the image, undoubtedly standing in front of a mirror to read position and framing. The sitter may be holding the camera in front of him to conceal his face or he may be doing so unconsciously, which is the naive habitual gesture one assumes when taking a photograph.

The self-portrait with camera, as one signpost among many in this particular landscape, provides evidence of work in both its content and form; such self-portraits can be found on most Internet dating sites. This particular form of portraiture shows production and embodies production; hence, it is the end result of the performance it displays. This is not a camcorder (or rather, digital camera) revolution. These image makers are not video vigilantes; nevertheless, this display of self, of technology, and of production (literally revealing the process and the apparatus) manages to take us beyond simply "being in common." The photographic presentation can take us beyond a reductive reading that sees the other as a collection of familiar physiognomic signifiers; in this respect, this form of self-portraiture may take us further than many other images of self, literally embodying a higher form of sharing. But this is simply a display of sharing, not sharing itself, despite the fact that these images display their authenticity (in that they capture the moment of actualization by embedding the technology within, and in that they evoke the real or imagined narrative of offering oneself for consumption). These images embody the performative mode of documentary practice articulated by Bill Nichols; these autobiographical artifacts embroil their subjects in history.[41] Nevertheless, this group of images reveals a collection and not necessarily a community of producers. The textual markers that surround these images perform a standard function of containment, providing a narrative that can be only partly scripted by the image's producer. It is otherwise conformed to a site-specific template. The impulse to share is reduced to the site's drive to quantify sameness and difference, to quantify the degree of being in common.

But communication and community are not undone by these sites, nor have they been destroyed by this limited index of a new cultural arrangement; rather, these sites provide needed terrain for the unworking that is the essence of community.[42] These domains yield evidence of the necessity for interfering with narrative. They point to the potential for the interruption of myth. Perhaps

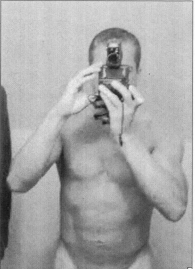

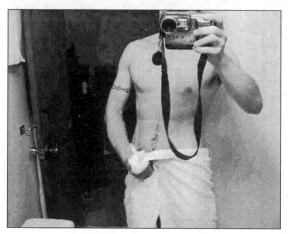

The self-portrait of the sitter with a camera is a common signpost in the landscape of personal advertisement photography, and suggests a keen awareness of being on display. (Photos by anonymous, http://www.bigmuscle.com)

the anxiety in popular discourse is centered on the ill-conceived quest to locate something that by its very definition exists without a locus.

My exploration of the "sitter with camera" subgenre of self-portraiture is not without its limits, for the conventions of this photographic practice may vary across demographic categories. My samples are drawn from the postings of gay men (which is why I have used masculine pronouns); as such, my cursory study does not examine the variability, if any, across the lines of (for example) gender and sexuality with regard to gestures of self-representation. Access to technology and strategies for deploying technology also may vary across demographic groupings. As I locate the limits of my initial foray into the architectures of these Internet sites, I also note that Nancy's theory of community has its limits, so a critique of an apparent poststructuralist synthesis needs to happen here as well. For it is posited that community in the concrete may be differentially accessible across such demographic indices as age, race, ethnicity, class, gender, and sexuality; differentially motivated; and called out for with differing urgency. My aim, however, has been to locate the restrictions that are often placed on the utterance of community. Regardless of the elasticity of the term, its ability to be appropriated and directed as an authorizing force for a particular interest group is compromised (for better or worse) as it is mediated. The author/producer of the utterance is often not the author/owner of the vehicle through which the utterance is passed. In the case of my analysis, the appeal to community must pass through a number of mediating architectures. The appeal encounters the Internet as a metamediating agency with distinct authored/owned subdivisions—the hardware and software of computer-mediated communications, as well as the addresses and territories of sites themselves. This is not a cautionary tale of the limits of community, but rather a shift in attention. We should not be concerned with the relative rise or fall of community, nor should we blame technology itself for community's present proximity to a presumed past state of grace. Rather, we should shift our attention to the authorizing institutional forces that satisfy our more significant yearning for communion by offering up a trademark of community. At the same time, we should be aware that community, even when divorced from explicit institutional mandates, can still act as an exclusionary appeal. Images can be subject to an array of institutional imperatives, but people too subject even the most personal images to their own ideologically inflected gazes, telling each other how and when it's okay to look.

6

The Social Fabric of Images

*However richly endowed we may be, we always lack something, and
the best among us feel our own inadequacy. This is why we seek in our
friends those qualities we lack, because in uniting with them we share
in some way in their nature, feeling ourselves then less incomplete. In
this way, small groups of friends grow up in which each individual
plays a role in keeping with his character, in which a veritable
exchange of services occurs. The one protects, the other consoles; one
advises, the other executes, and it is this distribution of functions or, to
use the common expression, this division of labour, that determines
these relations of friendships.*

EMILE DURKHEIM, *THE DIVISION OF LABOR IN SOCIETY*

More interesting than the entrance of the Google trademark into the lexicon is the manner in which its active form—"googling"—bridges two distinct activities: looking for and looking at. The term is a se-mantic and structural neighbor to another voyeuristic term—"ogling." As the search engine pulls together several customizable menu-based channels (that include the Web, images, maps, news, and shopping), we can quickly move across media forms, spaces, and activities without ever changing the initial terms of our search; such movement creates a rather absurd hybrid text, with a web of term-based intertextuality that is nevertheless grounded in the logic of an algorithm.[1] This arrangement, this fluid logic, leads me to a final case study in transience; in this last chapter I turn to consider the role of images in online social networks. Understanding why we look and why we use images can be a complicated affair, as the Internet caters to a wide range of drives. At the same time, the most commonly used interfaces urge us to keep our options open; designed to produce a state of hyperactive hypertextuality, they encourage us to change our minds and our motives with reckless abandon.

Patterned after our interactions with generic search engines, social-networking sites reflect a similar obsession with looking (even when looking may simply be equated with reading, in those networks that privilege text over image), framed by equally complex motives; here, too, the role of the image is not so straightforward. Online social networks have proliferated since the beginning of the twenty-first century, with the players shifting as each moves in and out of favor with the bloggerati, and with corporate buyouts constantly tweaking their mission statements; Friendster, MySpace, and Facebook (and, most recently, Twitter) have all taken turns as the favored social nexus, and there are certainly other arrangements on the horizon. Despite the apparent variety, these sites share the basic attributes of hypertext and hypermedia, translating social relationships into standard nodes and ties (or links). Even YouTube functions as a social network of sorts; with video as its primary participatory gesture, the site's poster frames produce a form of horizontal comradeship that lets everyone know what everyone else is watching.

In the preceding chapters, I consider cases where images circulate with some degree of explicit intent, and where context setting activates a quantifiable number of narrative propositions. Yet images do not always enter cyberspace with such clear motives or under such focused contexts. Often, the most we can claim about transient images is that they play a general role in articulating sociability. Like most generalizations, such a claim warrants closer scrutiny, for it is probably masking a more complicated relay. Something beyond a pure identity politic is being expressed in online social networks; when individuals already know each other, their shared images are not usefully understood as tools of self-description. And when images circulate in more anonymous frameworks, they may speak about something other than their authors.

In social networks, the individual actors function as nodes, and their ties are a hypermediated approximation of the relationships between them. Such networks are commonly used to measure each actor's social capital, though the links are structured around a wide variety of both objective and subjective markers—sometimes knowledge, attitude, or a material artifact (such as a photo or video clip). Oftentimes the material artifact is imbued with a nonmaterial value that speaks to the actor's position in the fabric of the network, but on occasion, the matter of value is a bit vaguer and perhaps too personalized to assess. Within the network, ties (relationships) are often more meaningful than any material object, and they commonly suggest shared values between nodes, which can be understood as a form of evolving kinship as the social actors become more complexly interwoven.

Contemporary online social networks give form to the metaphor of togetherness, and they also remind us that postindustrial societies, like their industrial precursors, feature a reduced dependence on traditional kinship. Network analysis, or social network theory, focuses not on the attributes of individuals but on their generalized position in the network—the emphasis is on the relationships between people rather than the characteristics of individuals.[2] The approach rightly complicates the notion of individual agency, as the ability for any person to succeed depends, in part, on the structure of the network; discursive agency is mitigated by the network's script, interface, organization, and frame. Social network theory allows us to evaluate the importance of social capital, to study the inflection of the networked position of any node, and to understand the place of each node in the resource fork (a measure of the individual's ability to contribute to and draw from the network's goods and services).[3] Within this framework, the image is important not simply for what it represents, but for the relationships that it supports among actors in the network.

One way that the social utility of the network may be broached is to consider the degree to which local knowledge continues to supplant the authoritarian metanarrative assumed to be part of the general drift of postindustrial society (where rationality and efficiency reign supreme and technology is used toward a globalizing end). Identity management takes a range of forms, and the sheer number of online social networks, each with its own focus, utilities, and interface, is a testament to how varied narrative discourse has become. These networks reveal the complexity of self-expression within a database structure.

Online social networks also forge their own forms of social capital, creating internal systems of exchange. Facebook, for example, encourages users to collaborate in interactive games, to send limited-edition virtual gifts, and to trade applications; the network's applications commonly indulge rather trivial pursuits and seem to work as icebreakers, giving members more to talk about and fostering greater interdependence among them. Facebook also provides its own profile markers; members can select from a wide assortment of posters and other bric-a-brac to decorate their virtual hangouts. Each social network has its own productivity suite designed to keep users involved in the network, but these tools also reorient self-definition and collectivity as they place more emphasis on the commodities trade. Facebook's user-generated quizzes function as a social quizzing system. Participants refine their Internet identities in a process akin to outsourced identification; as they follow a series of inquisitive prompts, such as "Which TV Mom Are You?" Facebook users willfully send their profile data through a number of distinct filters that situate them as socially knowable objects of popular culture. The proliferation of time-sucking commodities is not surprising, given that these privatized networking arenas function much like traditional broadcast networks; they compete for viewers, all in the name of ratings and advertising revenue.

Six Degrees of Stanley Milgram

In a 1967 experiment funded by the Harvard Council on Social Relations, American sociologist Stanley Milgram devised a study to test one of the principal theories of social connectivity, more commonly referred to as "six degrees of separation." Milgram's small-world experiment was designed as an empirical tool to measure what can be more formally understood as the average path lengths of social networks. Milgram's contributions to social psychology extend beyond his research on interconnectivity. In the early 1960s, Milgram began a series of experiments on obedience, and from his work developed a theory of agency. His theory suggests that individual conscience can operate in two distinct states: an autonomous state in which behaviors are seen as self-directed, and an agentic state in which people see themselves as agents of others. We learn to function in these two states from an early age, as we respond first to parental authority and then to a host of other individuals similarly positioned above us in the social hierarchy—members of various institutions.

Although an examination of agency may seem worlds apart from an analysis of small-world phenomenon, Milgram's studies share more than simply a method (generally contained under the rubric of quantitative social science research); and my participation in an array of contemporary social-networking sites has prompted me to consider what may be a more meaningful connection. As subjects on the social network contribute to its viability, do they become agents of authority, taking up the task of maintaining the network and assuring its well-being? After all, many cultural critics and journalists argue that online networks are merely "pseudocommunities." They are understood as impersonal and inauthentic, tools of mass communication that are at once everywhere yet nowhere—entirely undirected (perceived as not being goal-oriented in any conventional or practical sense).[4] While I question this particular assessment of the genuineness of online interaction, such a dismissive read begs an inquisitive reply. If the individuals on the social network are not doing anything (critics commonly suggest that participants should be doing something else, rather than simply wasting time), what exactly are they doing there? Coming to terms with this prompt, and rethinking what was an initially dismissive posture, journalists are beginning to take social networks more seriously. Responding to efforts at coordinated cyberactivism—such as the protests launched against the Iranian government following the nation's June 2009 presidential election (protests that moved from the streets of Tehran to the walls of Facebook and the feeds of Twitter, as citizens rallied to publicly decry what they believed were fraudulent election results that reinstated

Mahmoud Ahmadinejad)—journalists, media companies, and governments are retooling their narratives about the promises and pitfalls of Web 2.0 and harnessed collective intelligence.[5] Public and professional opinions are still in a state of flux, as individuals and institutions grapple with what is a rather abbreviated history of contemporary social network formations.

Though certainly not the first interface built on a foundation of online social engagements, Friendster reenergized social networking when it was launched in March 2003 (after being posted in beta mode the previous year) by founder and CEO Jonathan Abrams. Abrams had previously worked as a software engineer at Netscape and Nortel and began his work on community bookmarking with the founding of HotLinks. Launched in 1999, the HotLinks Guide functioned as a public bookmarking service, aggregating the favorite Web sites of its users and producing a shareable directory of reviewed URLs.

Friendster first gained popularity because of its sense of exclusivity. Its users were initially concentrated in the tech-savvy cities of San Francisco, Los Angeles, and New York, areas either in proximity to Silicon Valley or populated by a young urban demographic. But the network grew rapidly by word of mouth and through e-mail invitations; new users often discovered the network only by receiving an invite from a current community member. Friendster was originally developed as a matchmaking service, introducing people to one another through a database of interconnecting social networks (in which friends are linked to one another, as well as secondarily networked to outward-branching peer groups of mutual associations). Abrams designed Friendster as a social tool for meeting people that one might actually encounter in real life (finding overlooked congruence), or for migrating preexisting real-life connections online; however, the site quickly took on other functions, responding to the unique needs and desires of its members who seemed to be massaging the system, often engaging in less-determined and more playful acts. Friendster did not spawn the new social revolution; other ventures such as SixDegrees.com (which lasted from 1997 to 2001) and Ryze.com (which launched in 2001) charted similar terrain; SixDegrees.com failed, partly because of its open-ended and vaguely defined purpose. In a 1999 interview, Andrew Bein, the general manager of the site, claimed: "We're more a 'real' community than a virtual community because you build your circle with real life contacts—the people you know in real life."[6] Yet the suggestion that SixDegrees would give form to already-existing social networks made the site somewhat stagnant; there was little to be gained from simply migrating real-life contacts to the virtual realm in the absence of any definitive goal. Ryze.com took a more focused approach, and dedicated itself to business networking.

Friendster was the top online social-networking site until mid-2004 (according to Nielsen Online, which measures page views), when it was overtaken by MySpace, which had launched in August 2003. Newer entrants in the field include Facebook, which launched in February 2004, and Twitter, which emerged in March 2006. Each service tackles a slightly different niche or feature set, with Facebook initially targeting college students (since its inception, the network has branched out to include all age groups) and Twitter foregrounding the microblog, short instant messages, and mobile texts that circulate within the service's variously circumscribed social circles, answering the site's tagline, "What are your friends doing?"

Each Friendster profile is associated with other profiles on the network, and the list of associates is displayed as part of each affiliated member's profile. Profiles contain the usual statistics associated with dating, including such personal information as gender, age, sex, relationship status, sexual preference, zodiac sign, geographic location, and occupation, as well as personal interests and cultural attitudes and tastes (running the gamut from lists of favorite books and movies to music and TV shows). The site also allows users to post responses to more open-ended narrative prompts—such as "about me" and "who I want to meet"—as well as post photos to enhance their biographies. Adding to the textual density, Friendster also fosters the inclusion of testimonials and comments, and embeds thumbnails of networked friends in each user's profile, a narrative shorthand that provides an immediate snapshot of the individual's place in the network. While some participants use Friendster as a self-directed dating service (in contrast to more formally situated networks such as Match.com), the site's architecture accommodates a range of other functions, and many members engage in more than one pursuit within the network. Some surf for lost friends, an activity made possible through the site's search engine, while others use it as a substitute for a stand-alone e-mail client, to keep in touch with current contacts; some use the service to find out about local happenings, while others participate with less direction. Many social-networking sites also have become multimedia players, integrating music, video, and games, while adopting and enriching many of Friendster's core functions.

Faking IT: The Pleasure of Misrepresentation

While most of the transactions on Friendster have caused little fanfare, there is one moment in the network's history that merits closer analysis. The Fakester revolution, which broke out in 2003, is an inspired moment, and perhaps one of the most inventive uses of the system, exploiting its potential to rethink the spirit and tactics of both identity and affiliation. Fakesters were virtual guerrillas, Friendster participants whose fake profiles signaled not a knowable individual but rather a more iconic marker (commonly a cultural signpost or collectively understood identity); they thrived for quite some time, as these ardent fans and users of Friendster actively attempted to create anarchy in the online network. These Fakesters purposefully and perhaps playfully violated the site's user agreement by creating fictional characters as profiles instead of, or in addition to, their "real" profiles. The profilers portrayed themselves as everything from inanimate objects or geographic locations to celebrities or historical events. My limited archive of Fakester profiles houses a surreal cast: Bud Light, Flowbee, Home Depot, Hoover Dam, Internet, Joan Collins, Log Lady, Miami, Mommie Dearest, and Toothbrush. As Fakester interventions began to proliferate, many Friendster users competed to link to as many of them as possible, interweaving the fictional characters of Fakesters into their social hubs, binding Fakesters ever more tightly into the fabric of the total network.

Despite the public photo policies that prohibit the posting of photos that contain animals, pets, children, cartoons, comics, celebrities, nudity, artwork, and copyrighted images, the network is littered with image violations. And despite the posted content prohibitions that restrict, among other things, information that the profiler knows is false, the network is also littered with content violations. Fakesters are less bound to the more evidentiary notions of productivity espoused by the site and more invested in anarchic play, a surrogate social experience in which phony identities create a community of secondary revision, of attachments that are evidentiary but built on concealment. Identity is explicitly performed yet not vocalized as such.

As Fakesters gathered first on the Friendster bulletin board, prompted by attempts to purge their profiles from the system, and then in a Yahoo! Groups board titled FriendsterRevolution, they began crafting their manifesto, speaking to identity, free speech, and the public nature of online engagement and community formation. Roy Batty, one of the leaders of the revolution, penned the group's manifesto, whimsically but forcefully defending the rights of the people against what was termed a "Fakester genocide":

> We hold these truths to be self-evident, that all fakesters and real people are created equal, that they are endowed by their Creator with certain unalienable Rights, that among these are Life, Liberty and the pursuit of Happiness.
>
> We believe that Friendster's genocide of fakesters is the suicide of Friendster. It is the fakesters, this explosion of creativity, that differ-

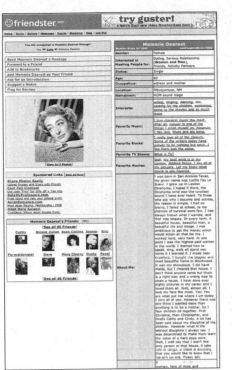

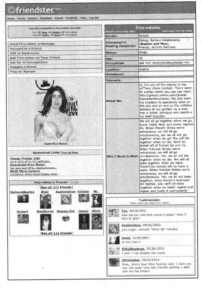

As Friendster founder Jonathan Abrams began purging the site of Fakesters, they responded in turn by cloning his profile. (http://www .friendster.com)

One of many Fakester performances on Friendster. (http://www.friendster.com)

entiates Friendster from all other boring networking/dating sites. This genocide must end!

 For the support of this Declaration, with a firm reliance on the protection of divine Providence, we mutually pledge to each other our Lives, our Fortunes and our sacred Honor. LONG LIVE THE FAKESTER REVOLUTION![7]

In an open letter to the Friendster management team and the membership, the Fakester collective proclaimed:

> The corporate masters at Friendster should be thrilled that they have such a vibrant online community as they now have on their hands. What they forget is that a living community, by definition, has a life of its own.
>
> There are many of us here who play at being an alter-ego, and take the guises of celebrities or fictional characters, and are typically known as "Fakesters." It is true that we appropriate imagery in

theoretical violation of both the Friendster user agreement and copyright law. However, I believe both recent legal developments and legal precedent are on our side.[8]

Citing parody and fair use, the Fakester collective defended its infringement and, in a return to community standards, made the claim that "the community is defined by the individuals who comprise it, not simply by the people who mixed the cement for its sidewalk."[9]

The local press took notice; Roy Batty was interviewed by the *SF Weekly* in August 2003, in a column titled "Attack of the Smartasses." Mirroring a long history of critical discourse on identity politics, Batty proclaimed: "Identity is provisional. It's fluid."[10] *Salon* published a similar article, "Faking Out Friendster," drawing attention both to Abrams's plight, as he upheld his conviction that "fake profiles really defeat the whole point of Friendster," and to the function of Fakester interventions as both humor and pointed social critique.[11]

The apparent tension here is brought about as the physical and the social are being mapped onto one another. The assumptions bound together concern not only an assessment of the relative utility of this deployment of the technology but also an assessment of representations (the physical matter of photos) and an assessment of what is being represented (the content of photos). By extension, this conflict also concerns what lies outside the representations—the varied forms of textual inscription (the textual markers). And beyond image and text, what seems of central concern here, in light of the codes of conduct (which are about individuals and their actions), is the persona that articulates the relationship between text and image. What is the proximity between the persona and the profile? Can the profile be used as a gauge of a unique sensibility, or is it a more oblique sign of a creative impulse? This final matter for assessment, the consideration of what lies outside these representations, connects the immediate subject to larger questions of inscription. The aura of photos themselves, one of the most privileged elements of the Fakester performance (by virtue of their density as signifiers) has become an infinitely malleable proposition. Indeed, the Fakester performance exceeds a series of images; it cannot be located precisely in the photographs themselves. The type of performance most notable here is the diffusion of one's identity across the network—evidenced, yet not contained, by the photographic trace. Performance permeates the membrane; for example, testimonials provide yet another occasion to perform outside of one's own profile—to display one's personal style and authorial trace across multiple others. Identities commingle in this discursive system, and all claims to authenticity are put on hold for a moment.

The Fakester revolution provides an occasion to reflect on (and act out) the liberatory prospects of online identity management, and to reconsider the utopic and dystopic discourses of online identity politics of early cyber theory. But what are the stakes of identity as pure performance in the Fakester exchange? What is being expressed through multiple identity pathways can no longer be reduced to different character facets, nor can such activity be neatly regrounded in a body that is the sum of its parts. Writing about early communal formations in cyberspace, Allucquère Rosanne Stone relates that participants in virtual communities are involved in participatory social practices in which their actions, and the actions of readers, have consequences.[12] In this network of engagement, Stone suggests: "The boundaries between the social and the natural and between biology and technology are beginning to take on the generous permeability that characterizes communal space."[13] Fakester role play invoked potentially useful boundary crossings, and made all too obvious the general rules of embodiment in cyberspace—or suggested there are no rules. While it is tempting to label the participants as a subculture, engaged in a creative public performance, it is more useful to consider these actions as evoking a kind of culture or attitude toward the site itself. It would be counterproductive to try to gather up the participants and position them as a definable group; and such an act would be difficult, as the profiles are simply a trace and have little biographical determinacy. It would be almost impossible to determine, from an observational standpoint, how many people and who exactly were involved, and quite likely what started as a limited impulse became a more widespread tactic as participants encountered the odd artifacts of the Fakester revolution. At the same time, faking it is a more generalizable strategy, and those involved do not necessarily see themselves as hackers; many participants in social networks regularly mix fact with fiction. These participants play with their identities in a more self-involved fashion, constructing multiple profiles to play out multiple selves, limiting the aspects of self that might be shared with any particular social group.

Regulatory Bodies

The networked identity is complex. Its composition may be planned, but the performance itself is always grounded in a specific context; the context may shift over time, but it is fixed from moment to moment by an act of interpretation attached to a reader in the here and now. As participants familiarize themselves with the network's contours and its circulation, they become more adept in the construction of their online selves, but there is still no guarantee that they will construct a stable persona. At the same time, however, participants in any network may act collectively, working together to establish norms and to create the contextual frameworks through which meaning is read. As I relate in Chapter 5, participants in social networks are confronted with certain static architectures—the database logic of sites such as Friendster mandates that every profile has the same layout, though users are allowed a certain degree of freedom as they act out within the profile frame. Confronted with categories that allow a finite range of responses, participants also have the freedom to choose their own photos and craft their own self-descriptions; these are the most obvious performance spaces on the site. Over time, however, as more users join the network and more friends interconnect, even these spaces are brought in line with the limits of certain cultural norms; participants may start to think more thoroughly about the resonances of their images.

Yet as a corporate venture, Friendster is not a space where participants control the discourse and manage the norms. Behaviors may be tested and acted out, but the environment remains a space subject to privately controlled commercial imperatives. As with most publicly occupied yet privately owned spaces, the owner sets guidelines for acceptable practice, and these are manifest through both the formal rules of conduct and the formal (grammatical) rules of the interface. Ultimately, site architecture establishes certain constraints, felt though not heard. And site management removes any infringing material that may slip through the cracks. Indeed, following the onslaught of Fakester interventions, Abrams began to purge the site of phony profiles, a tactic that was difficult to bring to a halt because users simply activated new Hotmail accounts and resubscribed to the system under new network IDs. Some Fakesters responded by cloning Abrams's profile, tweaking its details and taking creative liberties with its images; Abrams's face was attached to a number of other bodies, regularly clipped and composited. Other Fakesters could be found on Fallen, an online memorial for those kicked off the site.

Despite the end of the Fakester revolution, the Friendster network still has become an ever-more-complicated hypertextual array; the boom in membership has naturally diversified the social networks that are represented, but these spheres of affiliation have inevitably become more concentric as they crowd into the same space. As a result, participants often find themselves existing within and moving across multiple social groups, negotiating boundaries and confronting occasional contradictions. This is often experienced as the difficulty of keeping a separation between one's personal and professional lives, even as members try to ignore certain communities and reject certain affiliations. My own circle of friends includes colleagues, students, family members, and personal acquaintances; and what one group of friends may assume I am revealing, another may simply take at face value (having *a priori* knowledge of my personal affairs). The manner that I am read is complicated by the manner in which my friends actively and openly hail me in my profile; their comments speak volumes, and their own profiles are an integral part of my context. My performance is complicated by my inability to control the performances of others who occupy my space; because Friendster maps multiple social contexts into a single performance space, it does not allow any nuanced or controlled negotiation of what might otherwise be displayed as separate aspects of the self; it visualizes and collapses discrete positions.

As participants construct themselves on Friendster, they must negotiate the site's code, which is an integral part of the social architecture. Lawrence Lessig has made clear that code is a part of the regulatory process, though it is differentially applied; he suggests that some Internet architectures make behavior more regulable, while others make behavior less regulable.[14] By acting out, we adopt an aggressive stance to claims for, and the operation of a certain determinism (most notably biological, but secondarily one grounded in the assumed stasis of identity) that lends itself to policing. But the body cannot simply return with a vengeance, for with that return comes the dominance of physiognomic systems. Though we take as self-evident the idea that theory is a process, we often forget the evolutionary nature of representational practice; focusing too much on ontological considerations, we fail to situate the medium—be it photography or the information network.

As digital social networks expand, the way that community may be constructed through them also changes, a fact most readily observed by surveying the shift in the ranks among Friendster, MySpace, and Facebook; the swing in ratings (with Facebook now the dominant player) reflects in part each venture's relative attention to research and development, which might best be approximated by studying the functionality of their evolving application suites and the responsiveness of their interfaces. The interface must be inviting and easy to navigate, as well as customizable or responsive to user demand, while the network's applications must deliver viable user data to advertisers. Yet, while it may seem that a large-scale social network can no longer manifest community (as corporate ventures, they are subject to the standard measures of productivity and viability and must produce consumer relations that are knowable and quantifiable), or simply loses the quality of its connections (a quality felt both literally, as servers become clogged with traffic, and figuratively, as the growing number of affiliations places increasing demands on our time, and as nuanced conversations yield to the exchange of commodities), even those networks that are too large to be easily mapped may be spaces in which smaller communities still exist, operating underneath the radar.

The relations that are articulated in contemporary social networks are not easily aligned with the utopic conceptions of community sketched out by Howard Rheingold. Reflecting on the conversations he carried out in the mid-1980s on the WELL (Whole Earth 'Lectronic Link), Rheingold positions computer-mediated social groups as productive social tools, where even idle chat can be considered productive context setting, as it serves to tease out the varied strong and weak tie affiliations within the network. Such affiliations undoubtedly still exist in modern-day social networks (which can indeed function as social utilities). As one of the more self-evident examples, consider the work of MobileActive, a global network of activists and campaigners using mobile phones and online social networks for civic action and public engagement; the organization positions SMS (short-message services) as a critical tool for e-advocacy, given the high rates of mobile phone penetration throughout the world (a rate that surpasses Internet access). The group's work highlights the possibility for thinking differently about code and network. Pointing to the vitality of mobile technologies, the organization details a few of the more instrumental uses of cellular phones and distributes user-friendly strategy guides, drawing from case studies. Engaged with commercial technologies, yet putting them to informed use, the organization understands how important it is to infiltrate open networks; following well-proven models of integration, MobileActive has a Flickr tag that pulls public photos with a MobileActive badge into its own taxonomy within the ancillary photo-sharing site. In effect, it pulls its activist streams together, promoting the collective within multiple frameworks—some central and visible, others more marginal and dispersed. And similarly, the organization promotes Twitter as a powerful tool for knowledge transfer, social organization, and collective action.

Yet as many contemporary networked spaces are populated mostly by people who already know each other, the social contracts are commonly much more casual, following the social norms already established outside the network (rather than being forged within the network) and with only the most publicly viable pronouncements being exchanged. Indeed, Facebook continues to become a far less dialogic space. It is instead punctuated by enunciations; the application window reads as a discontinuous array of conversational fragments, as temporal filters displace contextual ones (time-based organization reigns supreme, privileging brevity and instantaneity over depth and continuity). And perhaps Facebook's ascendance has much to do with the popular anxieties that circulate around identity play. The Fakester revolution was built on the commonplace practice of turning Friendster into an arena for accumulating social capital; participants prided themselves in the number and types of new friends they could collect, mixing together known and unknown acquaintances. Facebook, conversely, encourages participants to simply formalize and organize their existing social relations, even as it reconnects long-lost friends and acquaintances; the rubric is an address book (and living scrapbook) of sorts. As such, Facebook can forego context setting, and completely disassociates itself from the anxiety of experimental social relations. Nonetheless, as individual identities settle into place, the network can become an important arena for larger battles, even if these are momentary directives. As strong tie relations settle (those long-standing connections among friends, family members, colleagues, and other institutional affiliates), weak tie relations may take center stage, furthering social cohesion and inspiring more pronounced civic action; these newfound relations can expand the networked community's focus without inducing the strain of ego conflict.[15] Outside immediate circles of acquaintance, psychological discord is less likely to appear; at the outer reaches of interconnectedness, personality is less likely to interfere with goal setting. Strong tie relations establish confidence and create trust, while weak tie relations are instrumental to cohesion as they constitute the very fabric of the local network.

As mentioned earlier, social media can provide a significant challenge to state media control, as evidenced by the public response to the June 12 presidential election in Iran. The user group "100 Million Facebook Members for Democracy in Iran" went live six days after the election, and as its statement of intent proclaims: "Though most of us are regular folks, some very important people from the world of politics, entertainment, arts, business and journalism have joined our group."[16] This Facebook group is a repository of sorts that gives form to the assorted blog posts that began appearing on Facebook and Twitter in response to the election. The decenteredness of Twitter, a service that can channel multiple points of origin (including mobile phones and Web browsers) to multiple outlets makes it resilient to censorship, as communications can migrate; their power lies in their transience, and in their namesaked ability to be "retweeted" (the act of rebroadcasting a message). Even as President Mahmoud Ahmadinejad began limiting Internet access and communications in Iran, these varied forms of social media (as utilities), tethered to a number of localized production tools (including mobile phones and portable consumer-grade cameras), provided a means for Iranians to circumvent local media restrictions. Twitter and Facebook were used to send pictures and messages both inside and outside the country, reaching the world in real time, as events unfolded; and as an important component of organizing, end users tweeted about their tactics, as the Iranian government began to block the flow of public information, interfering with access to mobile networks, the Internet, and satellite broadcasting, while also restricting access to foreign and domestic journalists. Citizens turned to the technologies of Web 2.0 to fill

The Facebook user group "100 Million Facebook Members for Democracy in Iran" was formed as a gathering point to disseminate information, circumvent local media restrictions, and foster civic participation. (http://www.facebook.com/group.php?gid=105160039272)

the journalistic void, counter the spread of government disinformation, organize activists, and mobilize the diaspora, as information flowed (and was reframed) across handheld devices and desktop interfaces.

I Network, Therefore I Am

While text and image coexist in the social network, the relations of these sign systems are varied. They may operate in tandem (text may be applied as a commentary to an image) or they may simply sit side by side. More often than not, conversational threads are perfunctorily illustrated by the profile thumbnails of their participants (a less purposeful positioning of the autobiographical trace), while images sit in their own albums or are called forth to narrate the subject without the benefit of captions. Some conversations are bound to the production of images (as participants post still or moving images in order to prompt discussion), while others are simply textual exchanges, and in the case of Facebook, often produced by the site's prompt to let others know "what's up."[17]

Within these systems of exchange, text and image provide participants with several ready-made possibilities for the ongoing objectification of their unfolding experiences.[18] As we share, participating in the ebb and flow of conversational exchange, adding text and photos, initiating or responding to discursive threads, or posting appropriated leads, our lives are both approximated through a trail of signifiers and punctuated by them (as we pause to log on and contribute). While we are more or less continuously engaged in hermeneutic or interpretive activity in our day-to-day routines, these meaning-making practices are largely overlooked or dismissed as inconsequential, perhaps because they are so common.[19] Yet these actions, often channeled through linguistic signifiers (both words and images), and in the case of the social network embedded in an interface, form a significant part of our understanding of the social environment. Reality can be understood as a social construct and, as Peter Berger and Thomas Luckmann suggest in their sociology of knowledge (a rigorous analysis of the process of construction): "Because of its capacity to transcend the 'here and now,' language bridges different zones within the reality of everyday life and integrates them into a meaningful whole. . . . This transcending and integrating power of language is retained when I am not actually conversing with another. Through linguistic objectification, even when 'talking to myself' in solitary thought, an entire world can be appresented to me at any moment."[20]

In the same way that sign systems organize the world for us and perform an integrative function, we must also consider the manner in which we use sign systems in dramaturgically prudent ways to selectively present ourselves within the world (a tactic sociologist Erving Goffman refers to as "impression management"). We relive our own ambitions and vulnerabilities through the interpersonal other; we are self-reflective and we adjust, not simply in the interest of self-knowledge and growth but also with the willful intent of maintaining the community of which we are a part and which defines us.[21] This didactic model governs our interactions in the absence of any immediate feedback; though our posts are not always met by replies, in the social network, we anticipate the feedback of our peers and model our entries accordingly, based on a history of experience. From this viewpoint, knowledge is not only a social, historically rooted product but is also an ongoing social process; we learn to participate with our communal peers in the collective interpretation of the world.

The insecurity that haunts the human condition has proven a boon to the postindustrial forms of the contemporary culture industry. If, as Zygmunt Bauman suggests, "the *spiritus movens* of consumer activity is not a set of articulated, let alone fixed, needs, but *desire*—a much more volatile and ephemeral, evasive and capricious, and essentially non-referential phenomenon," then it is no wonder that the social network can plug itself in all too readily to meet the anxieties that surround the human condition.[22] The very malleability of the network interface makes it a rather welcoming vessel that can conform to and contain our desires: "The fragility and precariousness endemic to the pleasure-and-distraction-seeking life has been reclassified from major threats to the stability of social order into its chief support. Modernity discovered that the volatility of condition which results in the perpetual insecurity of actors may be made into the most reliable of pattern-maintaining factors."[23]

Our transiency betrays us. The life of the organism—of the online social network—as an objectified trace of agency and society, is a salve to the transient nature of our lives as individuals. The online narrative, fragmented and unsustained, fortifies, in an opposing fashion, the egocentrism that grounds our apparently holistic understanding of everyday life. The selective experience of instability—the here and now of our networked exchanges—allows a peaceful return to the sustained experience of the individual ego. Fracture has its place in contemporary capitalism. Life may be unstable and fleeting, but the networked organism is even more so. As individuals, we find refuge in biography, in the subjectivization and individualization of the world around us.[24] Social networks are part of a generalized turn to a cocreative model of production; yet they also may be understood as a collaborative commodity fetish. The network, though a relatively open and democratic arena (to the extent that it is user-dependent), still objectifies its labor and produces its participants as commodities. The pleasures of the network mask the pains of alienated labor capital that govern our everyday lives. But before I wax too pessimistic, let me suggest that although the social network may have been birthed from an escapist fantasy of attachment, as willfully hypermediated subjects we have, over the past few decades, become sophisticated archivists, and are now rather adept at playing with the processes of signification that might situate and individualize us. Our actions in the network may seem readily quantifiable, but in the context of what is a living social entity (by its very nature, the network is in flux and discontinuous—it is being constantly renegotiated), each expressive act exceeds its object status to become an index of subjective meanings.

Transience and Mobility

As articulated in Chapter 5, personal advertisement profiles provide the most conventional cues for seeing collaborative identity play at work, as they are typically composed only of tried-and-true signifiers—text and image arranged in what has become a rather normative layout despite the nuanced strategies taken on by various sites, as individuals learn the narrative shorthand of self-objectification. Though their grammatical signage is more porous, photo-sharing sites also provide a forum to read the machinations of a similar identity politic. Foregrounding image over text, often simply using text as an ancillary marker and revealing the producer only through secondary links, photo sites still function as a performance space. And though to the casual observer, any set of postings may seem like a loose thread devoid of a clearly inflected authorial presence (for that matter, a visit may start and end with an image and never lead to the author), closer inspection may reveal a narrative through line (a deliberate plot that exceeds the pure chronological outline of story), an arena with a focused point of inquiry, or at the very least, provide a trace of a unique subject position (however constructed—the point here is not to argue about authenticity).

I turn to the subject of mobility. Though the term is commonly used in reference to transport, I am using it to refer to another form of movement. Mobility suggests migration, and in particular, it can help to articulate the more intimate boundary crossings that are forged by new technologies. However, I am not using the term simply as a metaphor, for new technologies can create very real changes in our cultural identities. There is an inherent conflict between the nonontological status of technology and the ontology of being, where our openness and dynamism, though instrumental to the development and application of new technologies, can nonetheless lead to a certain degree of artifice. We transform the world and our social relations through technology, and we come to understand these new relations as natural. I am not suggesting that technology is an obstacle to self-identity or a threat to the real (which is another essentialist narrative), but it can change what we demand of each other and what we expect from our interactions. At the same time, though technology is essentially a situation conditioned by our being, we often naturalize the position that it occupies in our lives.[25]

To highlight the connection between subject and object, consider the technological origins of the moblog. Simply put, mobile blogging is a form of online publishing done from a camera-enabled mobile device.[26] The mobile Web log is a product of the social software movement and the telecommunications industry. Looking more closely reveals that the histories of cellular imaging and Web-based personal publishing often overlap; even in its infancy, mobile media began to reshape the formally flat environment of the personal home page, making it over into a rich autobiographical foray and a forum for hosting multimedia content. Beyond basic Web-based page construction, the formal structure of blogs emerged with newly available publishing tools that enabled users to journal through their Web browsers, fostering a diaristic mode, as entries were dropped into a chronological chain; stasis gave way to a malleable structure that added a time and date stamp to each new post. Several popular account-based blogging services were launched in the late 1990s, including Open Diary, LiveJournal, and Blogger. Moblogs have added to the textual density of earlier text-driven blogs, taking such easy-to-use publishing tools and shaping them into powerful mobile communication engines, layering the ability to look on to the ability to speak; we can now speak through location as we post from our cell phones.[27] Even without taking pictures, mobile users leave a rich trail of data, but those largely overlooked traces have evolved into complex metanarratives riddled with intentionality. Here, narrative is constructed around a database of nodal fragments, and the syntax of time and space stands as a cursory trace of the author's own developing subjectivity. The images of the moblog are collapsed signs of a more elaborate personal geography, as they reveal the author's movement through the terrain and elicit presence (as past, present, or both, as the images linger in the online gallery). Beyond the personal stories embedded in these chronologies, these histories also reflect an ongoing investment in using media for social self-organization, as new tools to decentralize communication and reinvigorate active citizenship, a concept forcefully developed in Howard Rheingold's *Smart Mobs*.

Autobiography also can be used as a signpost of civil disobedience and at the same time connect individuals to the sociopolitical register. As smart mobs (self-structuring forms of social organization) gather around evolving communication technologies, they manufacture lived experiences that mark yet exceed the technobiographic subject. While these applied forms of collective intelligence do not always involve image making—they are often shaped by text-based systems on cell phones or computers—mobile imaging technologies (such as cell phone cameras and Web cameras) are commonly used to develop alternative media flows that may speak back to broadcast media or simply document and contour the group's self-representation. Again, the deployment of personal images in response to recent political unrest in Iran provides a poignant example of the possible attachment of individuals to the social register, and the powerful recontouring of nascent information pathways. Among the numerous video posts hosted on the Facebook group for "Democracy in Iran" are several brief records of the funeral of Sohrab Arabi, an Iranian teenager who disappeared during a June 15 protest march that began in Tehran's Enghelab Square.[28] Within this framework, Arabi's body (and the bodies of those that bear witness, many with cameras in hand) becomes a purposeful barometer of the political climate; it is difficult to read his body otherwise. While this gesture suggests that the individual has once again been situated to serve the nation, as a personal narrative gives way to a public narrative, the arc here is different from the one sketched out in Chapter 3, where I suggested individual trauma is regularly made over into national trauma. Here, network analysis must consider the intentionality of this repository, birthed out of circumstance, a circumstance that echoes through all of the objects contained within, however diverse (in addition to housing raw-form biographical video records, the group also houses more poetically constructed vignettes). The overarching mission of this member group and its participants (living or dead) is, in part, to manufacture a series of consensual relations among its embedded artifacts—to speak publicly and directly about the nation. Unlike the vagaries of terror, a term whose very openness is a key to its power, the bodies contained in this narrative of civil disobedience speak to more direct, visible, and linkable causations (one can assume, for instance, that Arabi's goals match the goals of the collective). As the connective threads of this social network have direct corollaries in the nation at large, the use of metaphor is less prevalent. And though the goals of the group are not fixed (they may evolve) and are subject to the same disruptions and tangential inflections that impact any open network (as varied members narrate and spin their own stories), the principles of membership that structure Facebook proper (one must join to participate) and the principles of the group (structured around an organizing theme) foster the production of what is, for the most part, a more cohesive master narrative controlled by those within it. Weak ties are not necessarily casual ties; they can be very strong, as they maintain the integrity of the network and can bind together in direct ways what otherwise would be individual media fragments. The volume of harmonious weak tie relations conceals any irreconcilable tensions within the network and expands the limited frameworks of the personal media within it.[29] First person singular ideally yields to first personal plural (a movement from "I" to "we") as text, image, and interface form a common ground for collective action. Your footage and your contribution become part of my experience; in this scenario, collective memory should not be misunderstood as a repressive cultural memory, for here it is not a blockage but rather a powerfully transformative aid (as distinct from the forms of erasure under trauma discussed in Chapter 2). Image and interface continue to function as instruments as long as they produce dialogic action (as opposed to groupthink); but one may still assume, based on previous lessons in activism, that at some point any agency will be undone, and these tools will simply become dead objects in a static archive. Classic smart mobs gather and swarm at a terrestrial nexus; communication is dispersed while individuals are aggregated in a balanced movement forged by mobile communications and pervasive computing.[30]

Cooperative work migrates beyond technologized nonspace to produce civic action. Too often, however, the promises of agency remain lodged in the social network.

Open and Closed Networks

Just as readily as the openness of new modes of communication is lost to new standards, such openness also yields to new industries. Blogging is not simply a personal affair; it is also big business. When it first launched in 2002, Text-America.com, one of the originators of the moblog, offered a free site that mobile phone users could use to post and share digital snapshots of their daily lives via the Internet; however, this free service was merely the armature of a research and development platform for the Rancho Santa Fe start-up, whose long-term business strategy was targeting the private sector with its propriety software. Even in its nascent state, the cellular imaginary in part has been the product of venture capital.

The long-term business model of TextAmerica was to target any company or organization that could benefit from quick access to images shot in the field that might assist in critical business decisions. For example, emergency medical technicians could use camera phones to send pictures to waiting doctors, and real estate brokers could relay site photos to clients. Forecasting the company's future, Chief Executive Officer Chris Hoar suggested: "There is potential anywhere there are people and projects that can be helped by having images immediately available. The key is making it simple."[31] The commercial applications would be similar to the personal moblog platform, but adapted to the needs of a specific industry, allowing Hoar's company to expand into vertical markets with its proprietary multimedia publishing platform. Yet despite the company's early success, and its subsequent announcement that it would be transitioning to a commercial-only site in mid-2006, TextAmerica.com posted the following notice of termination in 2007:

> Upon our dismay, despite our best efforts to provide the most comprehensive and versatile moblogging platform in the world, maintenance costs have far exceeded budgeted expenses to such an extremity, the financial burden of continuing service is too high for us to bear in 2008. In result, effective December 1, 2007, TextAmerica will cease to provide moblog services to both individual and commercial users. TextAmerica users have until November 30, 2007 to access existing moblogs and remove and/or archive moblog images. TextAmerica domains will no longer be accessible after December 1, 2007.[32]

Of course, one blog's cancellation is another blog's gain, and TextAmerica's earliest advocates began fleeing the site when the movement to a subscription-based service was first announced. Users quickly voiced their disdain for TextAmerica on the site itself, and then on other blogs such as BoingBoing, while also referring each other to the competing photo-management service Flickr, which launched in February 2004; some migrated their images to a rather specific address on Flickr, "exTAmerica," a group for TextAmerica émigrés. The exTAmerica account still features an introduction to the group's purpose:

> From the fallout of a large community uprising at the semi-popular moblogging website, came a whole new community: exTAmerica. It was originally founded as a safe haven for those that felt like TA let them down, by fundamentally changing how the site was going to work. This never came though, and since, exTAmerica has changed as a whole. It's now a community built upon an idea, that something can live past its means.
>
> It's been a while since any of our members have been on TextAmerica, and now exTAmerica stands as its own community. The name originally came out of a hatred for what TextAmerica had done, but has now fallen into its own right: Ex-TextAmericans. That's what we are here. En masse, we moved to a different place, and we started a new community. We're here to stay.[33]

Here was a community built around disenfranchisement, a group born out of a newly developed shared sense of purpose that may have run its practical course, but nevertheless still was being upheld as the group's *raison d'être*. The group's origin story is displayed as a persistent reminder of venture capital run amok.

Flickr, though a more open conduit, is not an independent venture. Acquired by Yahoo! in 2005, Flickr was one of the first sites to recognize itself as much more than a hosting service for personal photo albums. Developed by Ludicorp, a Vancouver-based company, the site includes what have been described in popular reviews as post-Friendster social-networking tools. Most notable within the Flickr environment are user-friendly image-tagging codes that yield what can be termed a folksonomic matrix. Folksonomy, a term credited to information architect Thomas Vander Wal, refers to the collaborative and seemingly unsophisticated way that information can be categorized in a bottom-up fashion on the Web, as end users mark various Web-bound artifacts with terms crafted from their own vocabularies. Vander Wal explains: "It's very much people tagging information so that they can come back to it themselves or so that others with the same vocabulary can find it."[34] Instead of using a centralized form of classification, users are encouraged to develop their own organizational systems, built from personally-selected keywords. Folksonomic practices are critical to the development of a Semantic Web (a more responsive World Wide Web that can attach meaning to information); as a collective act, the process adds more vocabulary for describing data, making it less tidy but perhaps more useful. Such metadata can be used to fine-tune the precision of search engine retrieval lists, yet it can also be used to more playful ends, yielding an exquisite corpse, a surreal assemblage of oddly associated artifacts, following a rule path to a surprising effect.

In this manner, what once was described as simple photo management can now be understood more readily as social networking—at the level of the text (built into data encryption and not simply read out of the artifact). Flickr cofounders Stewart Butterfield and Catarina Fake suggest that the ability to comment and add descriptive tags is a crucial part of the service because it gives members a sense that they are part of something social. Users can tag each other's photos and map them out of their original photo streams into a concentric network of other associated texts. In this manner, Flickr is not simply a passive archive, a massive collection of digital photographs from individuals all over the world, but rather it is an activated aggregate of images linked together by user-to-user relationships like "friends and family" or interest groups, and by content-based associations like keyword tags and collections. The success of the site lies in the fact that it links every entity—be it a person, a photograph, a date, or a comment—to dozens or hundreds of other entities based on those relationships. Members can easily jump from one picture or person to another, following articulated yet dynamic (member-generated) links; this exploration gets them more enmeshed in the fabric of the apparent community. Vander Wal suggests that Flickr's power is in its implementation of a narrow folksonomy that is performed in a rather limited manner, with only a few people (all of them members) assigning tags to each object; the tags compensate for their limited address by the directness of their association, making them useful for getting back to the object, but perhaps less useful (from an empirical perspective) for identifying emergent vocabularies.[35] Folksonomies help people find objects and retain their pathways, and the upended (taxonomic) structure suggests a democratic arrangement that is antithetical to centralized site governance. Folksonomies depend on our participation, and though they produce trails of differing practices, they also depend on a shared vocabulary (among the readership). Flickr provides a tool that adds metadata to files that have no inherent search properties; it creates a taxonomy for media files that have no innate textual limits. As it frames and reframes its images, the process of tagging seems to steadfastly eliminate

The Flickr photostream can be represented as a chronological thumbnail collage or viewed as a slideshow. (Photos by Katy Robinson, http://www.flickr.com/photos/ pinkishkaty)

The personal Flickr photostream opens up to subdivided albums and photo sets; each image can be tagged, attaching it to others with a shared vocabulary. (Photos by Katy Robinson, http://www.flickr.com/photos/pinkishkaty)

Flickr reveals its folksonomic matrix by posting the site's most popular tags. (http://www.flickr.com)

any vestige of Barthes's *punctum* (the emotional bond between spectator and image that is unique, direct, and beyond words). The addition of terminology interrupts the pensive gaze, concretizes an otherwise accidental discovery, and confuses the image's visual narrative. Tagging suggests an interpretive pathway. But what are the broader social implications of folksonomies? In many ways, they privilege the *studium* (the linguistic dimension of the image that corresponds with convention), if we consider that any folksonomy is inherently derived from a greater cultural consciousness that suggests terms and modes of identification.

In his casual review of Flickr and photo sharing in the *Village Voice*, columnist Julian Dibbell remarks:

Time was, when some drunk guy in a bar challenged you to elucidate the relationship of photographic technology and the reification of personal experience under the conditions of 21st-century global capitalism, gosh, you couldn't even get started without plowing through a stack of books by Walter Benjamin, Susan Sontag, and assorted other pointy-heads. Nowadays you just tell him to go take a look at flickr. com, the classy little photo-sharing site all the bloggerati are uploading their visuals to. Or better yet, you whip out your camera phone, snap a shot of the guy, key in a caption, e-mail it to your Flickr account, and tell him to go take a look in a few hours, after friends and strangers from around the world have marked up the image with comments on his haircut, his waist size, and the phenomenology of digital media.[36]

Yet despite the seeming interconnectedness of the feedback suggested in Dibbell's example, comments bound to a particular image and body (that of the drunk guy), these texts, these annotated images on Flickr are not necessarily successfully bound by a metanarrative. And when an apparent binding narrative can be constructed, there may remain an ideological tension that threatens to unhinge the system and produce an exploded form of seriality. The serial narrative is grounded by an organizing ideological project and is dependent on an aggregate of concrete elements to develop its central characters and themes. Yet the more the text embraces narrative complexity and movement, the more it is forced to contend with its inability to completely seal the cracks within the assemblage as it struggles to produce a narrative.[37] In the case of photo sharing, as the image traverses space, it picks up any number of cues that may interrupt the causal chain; in Chapter 3, I liken this process to an old-fashioned game of telephone, where it is impossible to control the narrative thread and difficult to secure meaning. Consider, for example, any image in Flickr's London Bomb Blasts Community (an archive discussed in Chapter 3), a group with a membership of more than four hundred people, and a collection of more than one thousand items. Though we may start on a page with a thumbnail collage of images tied to the 2005 incident, each image also opens up to its author's own photo stream; and these individual streams commonly include a range of entirely unique narrative threads, cataloged in distinctly themed albums, borne from other temporally and spatially determined events. Personal and public albums commingle and the psychological register shifts. At the same time, the thumbnail collage itself evolves as new images are added to the pool, linking an event-based chronology to a new chronology of memorializing, posting, and networking. This system of cross-referencing and subdividing is too dense to fully visualize or contain within a cohesive narrative rubric; Flickr's evocation of the "stream" (with the site's conception of the photo stream) suggests fluid association and migration. While we might understand the folksonomy as an attempt to produce a new linguistic system that is grounded in local and individualized practices and counter to the hegemonic push of technocracy (though dependent on technologically mediated practices), the very nature of the system as open and democratic is also its undoing. Chaos always lurks on the margins.

Autobiography and Technosexuality: "Tag, You're IT"

As already suggested, the transient image works as a tool for autobiographical discourse, as it replicates subjectivity and aligns the lived context with the apparatus of production. Yet the mobile producer enmeshed in the network has moved beyond personal photographic practice to using networked space as a self-referential public sign. The technosexual fucks the network (this is not rape, for the network is receptive by design), ejaculating signs, creating a form of pornography aligned with his or her desire (this is not always an act of conscious exhibitionism); and the reader is complicit, or at least responsive, marking the bodies that he or she encounters and attaching them to other desiring mechanisms (while this is not always an act of conscious voyeurism or complementary exhibitionism).[38] Though distinct in their narrative actions, both tales are equally productive. The reader is engaged in a form of writing that is not simply about access and interpretation but also about scripting (a graphical engagement with programming language that does not impact the application's core code), as the reader may deploy a number of tools to pull the image from its photo stream and blaze a new authorial trail through the database (or simply add to the image's textual depth by tagging or commenting). Photo-sharing sites such as Flickr express nostalgia for conventional modes of photographic presentation that let readers look at slide shows or albums, or print photo books, which are all forms of narrative fixity or containment. But they also allow readers to extend a preestablished autobiographical arc; on Flickr, tags can produce norms of their own, as users often form groups around tags and purposefully take pictures to extend the tag's associated archive, making the metadata more meaningful. Likewise, in social networks such as Facebook, users can reference each other's photos and weave them into their own autobiographical frames by both tagging and commenting on them.

Yet several questions remain unanswered. What does the social network do? What kind of work does it perform? Is the social network best understood by calculating the social capital of its individual actors? Though it may be read as a social aggregate based on the empirical observation of the sum of its tags, clearly it is multitasking and has multiple goals. But can all of these be contained under the nomenclature of one ideological project? Is the technosexual simply a narcissist, a depoliticized virtual graffiti artist tagging objects in cyberspace? Is he or she acting out or being acted upon by metadata? Clearly, we need to do more than annotate our existence; we also need to be vested in understanding what it means to live a hyperexamined life. The general critical assumptions that currently govern social media suggest that (in its most positive incarnation) it is capable of increasing and improving civic participation. What does the social network accomplish?

Following what was then the journalistic tendency to simply dismiss the work of the social network (perhaps because journalists were still in denial about the developing crisis in the newspaper industry), in an October 2007 *New York Times* op-ed column, contributor Alice Mathias notes: "Facebook did not become popular because it was a functional tool—after all, most college students live in close quarters with the majority of their Facebook friends and have no need for social networking. Instead, we log into the Web site because it's entertaining to watch a constantly evolving narrative starring the other people in the library."[39] Mathias does not identify any ground for productive civic engagement in the spaces of Facebook; her reading privileges passivity over activity, and leisure over labor.

In an April 2006 *Newsweek* article on social-computing start-ups, authors Steven Levy and Brad Stone lead their critical overview of MySpace with the statement: "It's not an audience, it's a community."[40] And turning to Flickr, they note: "What was once the digital equivalent of a shoebox became a vibrant community built around photos and a vast collaborative effort to produce an infinite scrapbook."[41] The repeated reference to community makes the term lose its force. If collective intelligence is indeed being harnessed here, to what end? Collaboration suggests a common goal, but within the social network we often find individuals expressing their own goals. The code aggregates, pulling items together under a folksonomy, but the goals often disaggregate, pushing things apart as a response to individual motives. Pierre Lévy suggests that collective intelligence is a mobilizing ideal for information technology that is attached to the fusion of intellectual energies, a sharing of experience though the widespread exchange of knowledge, a process meant to help both the individual and the group. While collective intelligence is being industrialized, its industrial products are also being utilized by collectivities themselves. As he attends to this symbiotic arrangement, Lévy cautions: "Although new communications technologies enable human groups to function as intelligent collectives, they do not automatically determine them. The defense of exclusive power, institutional rigidity, and mental and cultural inertia can obviously result in social uses for new technologies that are far less positive on the basis of humanist criteria."[42] As cyberspace continues to be territorialized and its infrastructure becomes more firmly enveloped in an industrial program, the social movements that fueled the growth of the Internet are being further effaced; what is left is simply their movement rhetoric.

Reviewing Iran's election crisis and reflecting on the utility of social networks, in a July 2009 position paper published by the conservative think tank, the Heritage Foundation, author James Jay Carafano concludes:

> The Iran protests may or may not prove to be a model for sweeping political change and activism in the new century. The lessons of the crisis do illustrate, however, the challenges of operating in a Web 2.0—enabled world. The lessons also suggest that Washington is not ready for prime time. The U.S. government needs to focus more on the professional development of its workforce, the role and responsibilities of federal agencies for turning Web 2.0 into Government 2.0, and implementing more robust public-private partnerships.[43]

"To every action there is always opposed an equal reaction."[44] Every push toward democratization, every productive opening up of the limits of information exchange is met by an equal push toward prescription, toward shoring up policy. The products of civic action and citizen journalism are not always understood as tools for burgeoning activism; from a legislative standpoint, they are scrutinized like clues at a crime scene, as governments seek to seal over any residual cracks in their information infrastructures. Perhaps social networks always have been microcosms for thinking strategically about (national) security, governance, and commerce; the democratization of information does not invariably lead to the democratization of government.

The emergent Living Web suggests a return to self-organization, a process that can be understood as technosocial, yet the degree to which cyberspace will remain open to exploration remains to be seen. Collective intelligence may be at the heart of contemporary communal formations on the Web, but it is also central to the commercial development of the Semantic Web (Web 2.0). Sites such as eBay and Amazon depend on the collective activity of their users, evolving in response to their browsing, purchasing, and commenting; the empirical analysis of user engagement yields lucrative data. This is not to suggest that collective intelligence has collapsed under the weight of capitalism alone; for it seems that social media frames engender mass communication but do not inherently produce a new public sphere, regardless of whether or not an economic imperative is pushing the medium. But the outcomes of the social network provide some useful lessons in understanding to what degree individuality is compromised by the general computational codes and filters of social media forms, or to what degree these codes can be massaged.

It is clear that social networks have been colonized; that they are for-profit ventures is signaled powerfully by Rupert Murdoch's (News Corporation) acquisition of MySpace in 2005, and Google's acquisition of YouTube in 2006. Google's press release speaks clearly about the company's motives:

> The acquisition combines one of the largest and fastest growing online video entertainment communities with Google's expertise in organizing information and creating new models for advertising on the Internet. The combined companies will focus on providing a better, more comprehensive experience for users interested in uploading, watching and sharing videos, and will offer new opportunities for professional content owners to distribute their work to reach a vast new audience.[45]

Each venture seeks to position itself as the premiere lifestyle portal—as a centerpiece for digital media delivery, as a necessary plug-in for life in the digital age. YouTube has evolved into an online archive; the digital clearinghouse is an invaluable resource, and the company's embed technology is a practical tool that has made content universally accessible. YouTube is a popular place to go, to watch content, and to find references. What the Web is to the library (impacting the way people conduct research), YouTube is now to the Web itself, organizing its contents, collating media from other sites, and consolidating the discursive formations of many distinct industries, disciplines, and enterprises. But YouTube is not simply an archive or a digital library; it is also a social network, establishing communities through its visual artifacts.

Herbert Marcuse warns: "In advanced capitalism, technical rationality is embodied, in spite of its irrational use, in the productive apparatus."[46] He cautions about the loss of viable space for transcending historical practice.[47] Perhaps this serves as a reminder that despite our awareness that the technological imaginary cannot be equated with technological necessity, we still carry certain preconceptions about productivity, about use-value, unaware that our sense of utility may be structured by habitus. The determinations that govern the social network may not be strictly technological or economic, but they do in fact exist; they have simply been channeled into more general formations about the technological imaginary, that now second nature, now naturalized, are speedily being used to argue for the particular form that the network may take.

Most contemporary theorizing of social networks recounts a history of work that first emerged in the 1980s, when the basic characteristics of contemporary social networks were introduced on bare-bones computer-mediated systems. These networks have been understood rightly as computer-supported cooperative work environments emphasizing the interdependence of virtual space and off-line space, and the particular purpose of the online environment, which allowed for sharing and organizing information, collaboratively authoring new content, maintaining relations among members, and facilitating direct communication. By comparison, today's social networks are understood as having significantly less functionality and focusing on communication but not supporting as diverse a task set; collaborative authoring has been displaced by collaborative feedback sets, and comments have replaced actions. But other functionalities still exist. Sharing, for instance, takes other forms, such as the cooperative seeding of BitTorrent clients (collective file swapping, mapped across several users and their respective Internet service providers); yet many of these uses are met by resistance.[48] And, as already indicated, the true potential of networked communication is realized on occasion; in such moments, the repository (the archive of civil unrest) functions as an ancillary to action rather than as a surrogate for it. Here, the technobiographic subject returns with a vengeance and refuses to stop becoming.

While online autobiographical practice may seem like an open venture, there are a number of parameters that govern the speech act—some technological, others economic and social. Each of these parameters takes on a linguistic function. There may not be a singular industrial imperative, a singular push toward a normative grammar; rather there is a complex interplay that starts from both the bottom and the top, in which users themselves may also be shaping the flow of traffic, determining the rules of representation and the codes of conduct. My goal in this chapter has been to draw attention to these varied levels of contouring. My project has been made all the more difficult because personal photographs and home videos are not simply uploaded into an archive; rather, they are asked to join a network that by its very definition is a social space, but one that eludes any singular form of sociality. For this reason, it is almost impossible to determine every way that the autobiographical project may signify because the community is by its very nature elusive—not found in the nodes, but at their edges. The moblogger (and the social networker) is an agent engaged in what Pierre Bourdieu terms practical reasoning; the image maker is goal directed and understands the climate of the social network. Positively, we may note that the network as a socializing institution might enable rather than limit the user's practical abilities; negatively, we may note the channeling of the social network and the establishment of microcommunities that obscure the larger industrial forces at play—forces that govern the totality of the network.

The Final Frame

In *Time* magazine's lengthy end-of-year spread on the YouTube generation (December 2006), columnist Lev Grossman leads his article "Power to the People" with a provocation and an invitation: "You control the media now, and the world will never be the same. Meet the citizens of the new digital democracy."[49] Though a number of high-profile investors are rallying for dominance, competing to become the central conduit to the digital lifestyle, as *Time* surveys the various actors driving the decentralized media revolution, its reporting keeps centering YouTube as the place to see these things, and the moniker has now become firmly stuck to a generational sensibility. Despite "our" ability to control the media, we are gathered under a particular rubric. But the phrase "YouTube generation" is used quite loosely to describe an age group that has grown up online, so to speak, experiencing and obsessing over networked communication at an early age. The phrase also gets woven into a cautionary narrative about the role of autobiography—about revealing too much and seeing too much online. The fear that networked social spaces will pervert young subjectivities is perpetuated through almost every media outlet. We see it expressed on television, where it is narrativized in almost every genre (from hard news to talk shows to fictional series), and we see it expressed on the Internet itself (Mydeathspace.com is a well-publicized MySpace graveyard, an archival site of obituaries for former MySpace members).

Autobiography seems to get reframed wherever it goes. But beyond these new object positions are new subject positions; reading communities themselves are being impacted by convergence and its explicitly industrial corollary—vertical integration. The limits we may see imposed on contemporary autobiographical practices, at least those looking to migrate online, do not stem from an industrial discourse about the mode of production, about how to shoot and edit, but rather from a discourse that orchestrates the network, shaping the mode of distribution and the context of reception. Beyond the editing application window and the local desktop interface, we need to consider the interface of the social network as an institutional product that speaks to our desire, has a spatial politics, and encourages particular forms of socialization.

Picture taking and the storytelling logic that molds photo albums are structured by certain premises about communication that cut across the essential organizing logic of interpersonal discourse and the more overtly commercial imperatives of industrial design. Yet these are not separate spheres of action. Both discourses are goal-oriented constructs, shaped by a broad range of cultural determinations; and in return, they also drive the culture. These discrete forms of advertising (of self and other) converge in the social network; they are made obvious in spaces such as YouTube, MySpace, Facebook, Twitter, and

Flickr, where personal artifacts and autobiographical musings compete for space with product advertisements, and where work and leisure often intertwine (as amorphous productivity). Yet the closed arc of commercial development—the problem and solution attached to product and sale, or research, design, and implementation—does not neatly align with the open arc of the online image blog or video blog. Despite any attempt to read a narrative arc, many image diaries feel much more fractured, though they emerge from a unified subject. Individuals may correspond with each other through photographs, showing each other what they have been up to (a form of telling, of narration), but the backstory is only filled in by knowing the subject. In this process, two or more complicit individuals willfully bind the narrative. Yet even willful complicity can become a speculative enterprise.

In August 2006, Google launched a beta mode of its Image Labeler, a feature that shapes the company's image search capabilities into a game. By teaming up random participants online, Google's goal is to improve the quality of its search engine. Over a two-minute period, paired players view the same set of images and create tags that describe the images they see; they continue to do so until their responses match. As they match, they move on to the next image, and they are awarded points for the degree of specificity in their matched tags. After the time expires, players can review the full set of images they have seen and the Web sites where those images were found, and they also can review their partner's tags. Players are given no way to communicate, other than knowing when they match or by indicating to each other their desire to pass on an image. The purpose of the Google Image Labeler is to layer human mapping onto algorithmic context mapping; by storing more information about the image, Google stores more possible avenues of discovering the image in response to any user's search. The folksonomy becomes a taxonomy, and the local dialect becomes subject to more totalizing sanctions. Will it or will it not become part of a search rule and enter the common (coded) vernacular? As I play through Google, the most interesting moments are in the endgame, when I add up the clues and attempt to build psychological profiles out of other people's tags; at the same time, the reward system frustrates me during the game, as I see the seconds tick away while my semiotic attachments fail to line up with my partner's readings. I desperately want to find consensus; I want to think like my partner. There is something decidedly hegemonic and Pavlovian about this Rorschach test.

My aim in this volume has not been to fix the complex chain of variables, of indirect learning, that shapes our understanding and our actual practice of image production, distribution, and exhibition. Transience draws our attention elsewhere, and what is more fascinating to me is watching meaning shift. The object's original fixity (and the producer's foundational subject position), while important, is not the end of the story. Yet despite this movement, this flux, there still seems to be a fundamental belief that we can glue these narratives together—that our endless reading of images yields some form of progress, a continuity brought about by the insistent impulses of an integrated subjectivity and a desire to believe in development. Implicit in this act of binding is the ideological notion that our passage through time will lead to something; it will develop our knowledge, secure our well-being, strengthen our social bonds, increase our social status, and perhaps help us realize material gain. Yet progress is not a necessary state of affairs, and we seem to be opening up to this possibility as we embrace new forms of interactivity and accept the tangents that are implied by navigating the Web and the new grammatical constructs that such activity produces. These possibilities are being realized in the private sphere as well, with the development of new personalized archiving applications (domestic forms of data management) that allow us to rapidly reterritorialize our own digital image archives. Though these processes seem orderly, they are in fact introducing the possibility of semantic variance and chaos, reminding us of the arbitrary nature of sign systems.[50]

While the discourse on community has expanded significantly since the origins of social theory, there seems to be a rather persistent return to earlier pronouncements, repeated efforts that theorize the present through archetypal conceptions of the past, grounding contemporary notions of community in terms of a nostalgic longing for a paradise lost. Contemporary communities, capable of transcending the modernist grid, partaking in what Fredric Jameson refers to as schizo-space (having a privileged cognitive dimension), come into being through the act of narrativizing a shared sense of history and place. Michel de Certeau comments on this phenomenon with the metaphor of group storytelling. Mourning the loss of the traveler, de Certeau suggests that the map in its current flattened geographical form is disengaged from the dimensional itineraries that were the condition of its possibility. Mapping marks a movement from description (and the actual experience of the terrain) to prescription; the mechanics of drafting produce a stagnant concretization of travel—not even a souvenir, but simply a grid. The representation of movement fosters inertia, allowing us to move without warranting any dialogue about the process. De Certeau's concern is made manifest in contemporary navigation programs, such as Google Maps or the grander Google Earth, as well as dashboard global positioning systems; these are all variations on a database, commonly used only as mechanisms for getting somewhere. Travel has become politicized only in its very depoliticization, in its reduction of the neighborhood to a coordinate, which may seem inherently practical, but which is nevertheless a value-laden transcription. Holding on to the political utility of storytelling, de Certeau suggests:

It "describes," to be sure. But "every description is more than a fixation,"
it is a "culturally creative act." It even has distributive power and performative force (it does what it says) when an ensemble of circumstances is brought together. Then it founds spaces. Reciprocally, where
stories are disappearing (or else are being reduced to museographical
objects), there is a loss of space: deprived of narrations (as one sees it
happen in both the city and the countryside), the group or the individual regresses toward the disquieting, fatalistic experience of a form-
less, indistinct, and nocturnal totality. By considering the role of stories in delimitation, one can see that the primary function is to *authorize*
the establishment, displacement or transcendence of limits, and as a
consequence, to set in opposition, within the closed field of discourse, two movements that intersect (setting and transgressing limits) in such a way as to make the story a sort of "crossword" decoding
stencil (a dynamic partitioning of space) whose essential narrative
figures seem to be the *frontier* and the *bridge*.[51]

Of course, contemporary communities do not simply narrate themselves into
being. As Edward Soja suggests, we must understand them in terms of macro-
and microgeographies, situating what might be misunderstood as autonomous
communities (the micro) within a larger context (the macro); the connection
between micro and macro is not simply an interpretive trick, a product of critical theory, nor is it simply a matter of willful positioning, choosing a place in
the rank order. Instead, communities are strategically linked through a conflu-
ence of both internal and external forces into what is ultimately a complex but
decipherable order. This is not merely structuralism at work, though an informed cultural analysis may illuminate the structuring tendencies, revealing
the forces (and parties) at play and the myriad ways that communities are assigned categories based on their assumed or visible attributes. Soja reminds
us: "We must be insistently aware of how space can be made to hide consequences from us, how relations of power and discipline are inscribed into the
apparently innocent spatiality of social life, how human geographies become
filled with politics and ideology."[52] We must not lose space to the illusion of
opaqueness, where space seems undialectical and devoid of social origins, or
to the illusion of transparency, where space is dematerialized, understood simply as a mental construct.[53]

While *Transient Images* opened with a discussion of images, leading with
two citations from Roland Barthes and Susan Sontag, my goal has been to move
beyond any study of images to consider the architectures in which they are
embedded. We have a tendency to get too close to our images; the goal always
seems to be to throw the frame out of focus, to lose it to our peripheral vision.

But as I have argued throughout this manuscript, we need to pay equal attention to the image frame. More than simply a materialist exercise, the frame is part of a purposeful social practice, operating within a particular mode of production; its function is to organize space. While we may draw out generalizations from our observations of what is contained in the archive, we need to be equally attentive to the formal properties of the archive itself, as a legislating structure. It is not enough to speak of its aura; we must also understand its status as a commodity, especially if our goal is to understand its transformational potential and to translate our ideas and our identities into actions. Otherwise, we risk becoming relics lodged in the archive, empty placeholders for other people's tags.

Notes

Throughout this book, where a URL is identified as "site now revised," the URL is func-tional but might not reflect the original Web site content. Where a URL is identified as "site now discontinued," the URL no longer exists or is not functional. Access dates are only used in these identified cases. In some instances, an institutional home page has been substituted as a general reference to a revised or discontinued secondary page.

INTRODUCTION

1. John Urry, *The Tourist Gaze*, 2nd ed. (London: Sage Publications, 2002), 2.

2. Homi K. Bhabha, *The Location of Culture* (New York: Routledge, 1994), 55.

3. Paul John Eakin, "Foreword," in Philippe Lejeune, *On Autobiography*, trans. Katherine Leary, ed. Paul John Eakin (Minneapolis: University of Minnesota Press, 1989), xvii.

4. Jonathan Culler, *Framing the Sign: Criticism and Its Institutions* (Norman: University of Oklahoma Press, 1988), 162.

5. Marshall McLuhan, *Understanding Media: The Extensions of Man* (Cambridge, MA: MIT Press, 1994), 197.

6. Hans Magnus Enzensberger substitutes the term "culture industry" with the concept of the consciousness industry to more fully examine the sociological and political consequences of industrial control and mediation; pushing further than Theodor Adorno and Max Horkheimer, Enzensberger considers the impact of commerce on the human psyche. See Hans Magnus Enzensberger, *The Consciousness Industry: On Literature, Politics and the Media* (New York: Seabury Press, 1974).

7. In the mid-1880s, George Eastman had already begun to expand his business into the amateur market, and he had reduced the complex process of picture taking into several easily explained steps.

8. Douglas Collins, *The Story of Kodak* (New York: Harry N. Abrams, 1990), 156.

9. Sarah Kennel, "Quick, Casual, Modern," in *The Art of the American Snapshot, 1888–1978: From the Collection of Robert E. Jackson*, ed. Sarah Greenough and Diane Waggoner (Washington, DC: National Gallery of Art, 2007), 89.

10. Polaroid reversed its position in January 2010, when it unveiled a prototype for the PIC 1000, a redesigned OneStep camera. Yet after its announcement at the

Consumer Electronics Show, the company switched gears and began production on the more compact Polaroid 300 instant camera.

11. Roland Barthes, *Camera Lucida: Reflections on Photography,* trans. Richard Howard (New York: Noonday Press, 1981), 26–27.

12. Ibid., 45.

13. Ibid., 9. Barthes adds a caveat to his outright dismissal of Polaroid, allowing those occasions "when a great photographer is involved." Interestingly enough, certain editions of *Camera Lucida* include a Polaroid frontispiece—a 1979 color image by Daniel Boudinet—that is never mentioned in the text. The photo is from a sequence, *Fragments d'un Labyrinthe,* which traces the changing light entering through the windows of the artist's apartment.

14. Susan Sontag, *On Photography* (New York: Anchor Books, 1990), 7.

15. Pierre Bourdieu, *Photography: A Middle-Brow Art,* trans. Shaun Whiteside (Stanford, CA: Stanford University Press, 1990), 19.

16. Ibid., 27.

17. Joseph Grigely, *Textualterity: Art, Theory, and Textual Criticism* (Ann Arbor: University of Michigan Press, 1995), 71.

18. Jonathan Crary, *Techniques of the Observer: On Vision and Modernity in the Nineteenth Century* (Cambridge, MA: MIT Press, 1990), 13.

19. Ibid., 13–14.

20. Philippe Lejeune, *On Autobiography,* trans. Katherine Leary, ed. Paul John Eakin (Minneapolis: University of Minnesota Press, 1989), 109.

21. Ibid.

22. Edmund Leach, "On Certain Unconsidered Aspects of Double Descent Systems," *Man* 62, no. 214 (September 1962): 133.

23. Michel Foucault, *The Order of Things: An Archaeology of the Human Sciences* (New York: Vintage Books, 1970), xxiv.

CHAPTER 1: "HAVE YOU SEEN THIS CHILD?"

1. Michael Curtin suggests we may readily quantify the televisual and extratelevisual factors that produced the network documentary boom of the early 1960s. At the same time that the networks were repairing their public image and competing for favor in the public arena, their respective news divisions were being made over by portable field technology, and their mission statements were being refashioned by the Federal Communications Commission. Yet, as Curtin continues, an equally pressing (and often overlooked) critical pursuit would be to understand the ideological work performed by the genre at the time, at a moment in U.S. history when network, political, and corporate interests formed a unique alliance that channeled the threat of Communism. For a more detailed analysis, see Michael Curtin, *Redeeming the Wasteland: Television Documentary and Cold War Politics* (New Brunswick, NJ: Rutgers University Press, 1995).

2. Though the concept of individuation is used in a number of fields, my use runs counter to the conventional psychological application that (following the work of Carl Jung) describes the process of becoming aware of one's self, of discovering one's true, inner self. My emphasis is on the constitution of the individual always in relation to the

collective, which highlights the possibility of what Michel Foucault suggests is a disciplinary society.

3. Talk TV is a literal manifestation of a paranoid attempt to work through trauma and produce coherence; it is a technocentric traumatic negotiation of its own kind (that utilizes fear), though it is fundamentally a move toward integration fueled by industry. At the same time, the ebb and flow of talk television produces a paranoid supertext that is at risk of falling apart at any moment. It is unstable, and needs to be constantly fortified; this may explain why talk television hosts constantly return to those sensational topics that most closely approximate a threat to our subjectivity.

4. Celia Lury, *Prosthetic Culture: Photography, Memory and Identity* (New York: Routledge, 1998), 19.

5. Kenneth Paradis, *Sex, Paranoia, and Modern Masculinity* (Albany: State University of New York Press, 2007), 23.

6. National Center for Missing and Exploited Children and Canon U.S.A., "How Parents Can Use Digital Imaging to Protect Children," *Canon4Kids* (2007), http://www.usa.canon.com/html/ciw/AboutCanon/canon4kids_parents.html.

7. DIGIKIDS, "Franchise Information," *DIGIKIDS Franchise Information* (2007), http://www.digikids-id.com/franchise.htm.

8. Barry Glassner, *The Culture of Fear: Why Americans Are Afraid of the Wrong Things* (New York: Basic Books, 1999), xxviii.

9. Ibid., xxiii.

10. Tom Baker and Jonathan Simon, "Toward a Sociology of Insurance and Risk," in *Embracing Risk: The Changing Culture of Insurance and Responsibility*, ed. Tom Baker and Jonathan Simon (Chicago: University of Chicago Press, 2002), 28.

11. François Ewald, "Two Infinities of Risk," in *The Politics of Everyday Fear*, ed. Brian Massumi (Minneapolis: University of Minnesota Press, 1993), 221–222.

12. Michel Foucault, *The Birth of the Clinic: An Archaeology of Medical Perception*, trans. A. M. Sheridan Smith (New York: Vintage Books, 1973), 23.

13. Ibid., 25.

14. Ewald, "Two Infinities of Risk," 224.

15. Ibid., 225.

16. Ibid., 224–225.

17. Ibid., 227.

18. Joel Best, "Missing Children, Misleading Statistics," *Public Interest* 92 (Summer 1988): 90.

19. These claims are made on quite a few Web sites, often without any reference to their origin, or with merely a casual reference to a more official source such as the NCMEC, the Federal Bureau of Investigation National Crime Information Center (NCIC), or the U.S. Department of Justice. These claims represent, at best, a very loose extrapolation of gathered data, yet they are often completely outdated or unverifiable. For example, the statistic on the rate of increase in missing children since 1982 is drawn from an FBI file report published in January 2001, that includes both juveniles and adults; and the three-hour murder rule is pulled from a 1997 study conducted by the Washington State Attorney General's office. Without providing an exhaustive list, the following three Web sites are representative of the contemporary misuse of missing children statistics: Harrison K-9, "Frequently Asked Questions" (http://www.harrisonk9

.com/html/faq.cfm); Steadfast Enterprises SafeGUARD 1, "Missing Child Stats" (http://
www.safeguard-1.com/MISSING_CHILD_STATS.html); Alert Child, USA (http://
www.tbitdesign.com/portfolio/131/index.html). The findings of the Washington State
Attorney General's office are summarized in a May 13, 1997 news release (http://www
.atg.wa.gov/pressrelease.aspx?&id=4958), and more recent NCIC missing person statistics can be found on the FBI Web site (http://www.fbi.gov/hq/cjisd/missingper-
sons2009.htm).

20. Martin L. Forst and Martha-Elin Blomquist, *Missing Children: Rhetoric and
Reality* (New York: Lexington Books, 1991), 55.

21. Ibid., 62–63.

22. Gay Norton Edelman, "Kids and Kidnapping," *Parents* 60, no. 12 (December
1985): 81. In the same article, Dr. Lawrence Balter (a child psychologist) reminds us
that "a little fear is a good thing. Without it we wouldn't have caution." And Dr. Katherine Yost (a clinical therapist) suggests that "children are naturally prone to fear
because they're little and powerless." Fear is unproblematically naturalized in clinical
discourse.

23. To counter the rise of misleading and often conflicting figures on the number
and types of incidents, Congress mandated through the 1984 Missing Children's Assistance Act that the Office of Juvenile Justice and Delinquency Prevention (OJJDP)
periodically conduct studies to determine the national incidence rates for distinct categories of missing children. Researchers from the OJJDP developed the *National Incidence Studies of Missing, Abducted, Runaway, and Thrownaway Children* (NISMART).
NISMART-1 (1990) defined the major types of missing child episodes and estimated
the numbers of children who experienced episodes of each type, drawing on data col-
lected in 1988; while the report added methodological rigor to the incidence estimates
of child abductions, it was nonetheless criticized by social scientists for its method of
data collection and its often muddy classification system. The methodology and definitions were refined in subsequent studies. NISMART-2 (2002) surveyed a three-year
span, from 1997 to 1999, and is currently regarded as the most comprehensive and
methodologically sound data available for the missing children problem in the United
States. Still, many of the NISMART-2 findings have been taken out of context by child
protection organizations, and have been haphazardly reported in the popular press.

24. Forst and Blomquist, *Missing Children*, 65–66.

25. The same subject—missing children—was fodder for a number of distinct
television genres (each with its own conventions), some more grounded in fiction than
others; this slippage invites further study. Though not every episode was dedicated to a
missing child (the show's victims were drawn from a broader age range), *Without a
Trace* featured information pertaining to real-life missing persons at the end of most
episodes or included episode-specific public service announcements; the program ran
for seven seasons on CBS, premiering in the United States at the end of September
2002.

26. Senate Committee on Rules and Administration, *Printing Pictures of Missing
Children on Senate Mail*, 102d Cong., 2d sess., 25 June 1992, S. Rep. 102–303. Ap-
pendix D of the report includes an attachment listing the names of 190 missing children
recovered through pictures. The word "pictures" refers to a variety of media, including
posters, direct mail postcards, and both local (news) and national television programs.
The attachment indicates that many of the program types I have discussed (docudrama,

news, magazine, true-crime, and talk) were instrumental in the recovery of at least one missing child.

27. "Milk-Carton Hunt for Lost Children," *U.S. News and World Report* 98, no. 5 (February 11, 1985): 12.

28. Ironically, the first beneficiary of the milk carton program was a thirteen-year-old runaway (Doria Yarbrough), not an abducted child. Yarbrough's case was perhaps the inspiration for Caroline B. Cooney's book (for young adult readers) *The Face on the Milk Carton* (New York: Delacorte Press, 1990), which was followed by three sequels: *Whatever Happened to Janie?* (New York: Dell Laurel-Leaf, 1993), *The Voice on the Radio* (New York: Laurel-Leaf, 1996), and *What Janie Found* (New York: Laurel-Leaf, 2000).

29. It also has been suggested that the dairy campaign fell out of favor after parents began to complain that the milk cartons were frightening their children away from the breakfast table.

30. The company made a special appeal to the United States Postal Service to modify its regulations and allow nonvital information (the photos) to be placed on the address side of its cards.

31. Geoffrey Cowley and Karen Springen, "Faces from the Future," *Newsweek* 113, no. 7 (February 13, 1989): 62. In reference to this new technology and its beneficiaries, Barrows states: "This opens the files again. They can be considered alive again." More recently, Sony, IBM, and CompuAge have donated age-enhancing technology to the NCMEC. The initiative is supported by the Special Projects Unit of the Federal Bureau of Investigation and the Forensic Services Division of the U.S. Secret Service through their technical support of the NCMEC's video laboratory. Current age-progression techniques rely in part on data from heredity, using the photographs of parents and siblings and merging these gathered facial features with those of the missing child. In this act of convergence, it is possible that victim and victimizer may literally be mapped onto one another (if the case is one of family abduction), in an all-too-literal act of bodily co-optation.

32. Child Shield, U.S.A., *"It Couldn't Ever Happen to My Kid"* [Brochure], Titusville, 1994.

33. Blockbuster Video's service, sponsored by the NCMEC (and, in 1996, Marvel Comics), is registered as Kidprint; the Kidprint Identification Video, unlike the Child Shield video, is offered at no cost to parents (though the fees charged by Child Shield seem to be justified by the more-extended offerings of the contract—access to duplication and distribution).

34. John Tagg, *The Burden of Representation: Essays on Photographies and Histories* (Minneapolis: University of Minnesota Press, 1988), 74.

35. Ibid., 76.

36. Kevin Robins, "Will Image Move Us Still?" in *The Photographic Image in Digital Culture*, ed. Martin Lister (New York: Routledge, 1995), 34.

37. Tagg, *The Burden of Representation*, 76.

38. Child Shield, U.S.A., *How to Videotape Your Child* [Brochure], Titusville, 1994.

39. Gilles Deleuze, "Postscript on the Societies of Control," *October* 59 (Winter 1992): 6. I view Deleuze's work as a productive extension of Foucault's earlier treatment of the subject of power relations. Deleuze, in fact, notes that Foucault was cognizant of the transience of his model, which does indeed seem to be undone by the decompartmentalization of panoptic relations in contemporary capitalized,

globalized, and networked culture (wherein disciplinary bodies have less-discernible limits).

40. This commodity fetishism is all-too-readily assessable given the abundance of corporate sponsors that support the NCMEC's programs, all of whom would agree that their other products are a more desirable point of investiture (luxuries we could all enjoy if only the world were a better place).

41. The inappropriate consumption of the child's image is a risk that the NCMEC is willing to take in posting photos on the Internet. In any case, these photos all conform to a certain production code (a prescribed form and content—what is to be contained within the box of the photo and what must be excluded) that perhaps limits the possibility of an incorrect reading.

42. Edelman, "Kids and Kidnapping," 83. In the same sidebar, Edelman also gives the assailant a voice: "Abductors and molesters often play on a child's natural desire to help, by asking for directions or making up stories such as, 'I lost my dog and I need your help to find him.' . . . Another kidnapper's lure is to say, 'Your mommy is hurt and needs you.'"

43. The mother assumed the child was her natural granddaughter; she was not aware that her daughter had actually kidnapped a child and claimed her as her own.

44. Brian Massumi, "Preface," in *The Politics of Everyday Fear*, ed. Brian Massumi (Minneapolis: University of Minnesota Press, 1993), vii.

45. See, for instance: Dee Dee Halleck, "Towards a Popular Electronic Sphere, or Options for Authentic Media Expression beyond *America's Funniest Home Videos*," in *A Tool, a Weapon, a Witness: The New Video News Crews*, ed. Mindy Faber (Chicago: Randolph Street Gallery, 1990).

46. In one installment, Chris Hansen asks his subject, "Have you seen the show before?" "And what do you think of the stories?" "Did you ever think you'd be on one?"

47. Available at http://www.msnbc.msn.com/id/17601568/.

48. Available at http://www.msnbc.msn.com/id/11030951/.

49. The program's questionable ethics were made readily apparent in November 2006, when, during a field taping and arrest, the alleged predator (Louis William Conradt, Jr., an assistant district attorney in Texas) shot himself in the head as the *Dateline* crew and a team of police officers converged on his home. In June 2008, NBC Universal settled a $105 million lawsuit that was filed by Conradt's sister. Responding to continuing criticism, the network quietly suspended production of the series in December 2008.

50. Marilyn Ivy, "Have You Seen Me? Recovering the Inner Child in Late Twentieth-Century America," *Social Text* 37 (Winter 1993): 230.

CHAPTER 2: PRIVATE PHOTOS/PUBLIC TRAUMAS

1. Janny Scott, "Closing a Scrapbook Full of Life and Sorrow," *New York Times*, December 31, 2001, http://www.nytimes.com/2001/12/31/national/portraits/31PORT.html?pagewanted=1.

2. Allan Sekula, "The Body and the Archive," *October* 39 (Winter 1986): 8.

3. Ibid.

4. Marita Sturken, *Tangled Memories: The Vietnam War, the AIDS Epidemic, and the Politics of Remembering* (Berkeley: University of California Press, 1997), 8.

5. Ibid., 9.

6. Roland Barthes, *Camera Lucida: Reflections on Photography,* trans. Richard Howard (New York: Noonday Press, 1981), 91.

7. Stephen Heath, *Questions of Cinema* (Bloomington: Indiana University Press, 1981), 222–227.

8. Gilles Deleuze, *Difference and Repetition* (New York: Columbia University Press, 1994), 208–209.

9. Although United Airlines Flight 93 crashed into a field in rural Pennsylvania, the in-flight struggle between passengers, crew members, and hijackers is a notable part of its final narrative.

10. Sturken, *Tangled Memories,* 5.

11. Ibid., 7.

12. Deleuze, *Difference and Repetition,* 74–75.

13. Judith Herman, *Trauma and Recovery: The Aftermath of Violence—from Domestic Abuse to Political Terror* (New York: Basic Books, 1992), 155–156.

14. Thomas Elsaesser, "One Train May Be Hiding Another: History, Memory, Identity, and the Visual Image," in *Topologies of Trauma: Essays on the Limit of Knowledge and Memory,* ed. Linda Belau and Petar Ramadanovic (New York: Other Press, 2002), 67.

15. These three modalities, frequently used to conceive of trauma, are derived from Sigmund Freud's work on the techniques of psychoanalysis.

16. Linda Belau, "Remembering, Repeating, and Working-Through: Trauma and the Limit of Knowledge," in *Topologies of Trauma: Essays on the Limit of Knowledge and Memory,* ed. Linda Belau and Petar Ramadanovic (New York: Other Press, 2002), xv, xvii.

17. Sturken, *Tangled Memories,* 6.

18. John Tagg, *The Burden of Representation: Essays on Photographies and Histories* (Minneapolis: University of Minnesota Press, 1988), 76.

19. Marianne Hirsch, *Family Frames: Photography, Narrative and Postmemory* (Cambridge, MA: Harvard University Press, 1997), 10.

20. Ibid., 11.

21. Ibid., 12.

22. Deleuze, *Difference and Repetition,* 77.

23. Elsaesser, "One Train May Be Hiding Another," 70–71.

24. Hirsch, *Family Frames,* 199–200.

25. Ibid., 200.

26. Paul Levey, http://www.cnn.com/SPECIALS/2001/memorial/people/1807.html.

27. Jeremy, http://www.cnn.com/SPECIALS/2001/memorial/people/3071.html.

28. Mara, http://www.cnn.com/SPECIALS/2001/memorial/people/2477.html.

29. Basil Fottis, http://www.cnn.com/SPECIALS/2001/memorial/people/3277.html.

CHAPTER 3: TRAUMA AND THE CELLULAR IMAGINARY

1. Motorola, "Motorola Makes Seamless Mobility Real at the 2004 Analysts Meeting," *Motorola Media Center,* http://www.motorola.com/content.jsp?globalObjectId=2738 (accessed October 20, 2007; site now discontinued).

2. Motorola, "Motorola Seamless Mobility Solutions," *Motorola Service Provider Solutions,* http://www.motorola.com/content.jsp?globalObjectId=2364-8176 (accessed March 26, 2008; site now discontinued).

3. Since the time of my original research, most of the execution footage has migrated to YouTube or can be found across Google Video and YouTube (as well as on several ancillary video-hosting services). And while Google Video began showing the number of views for each of its hosted videos in September 2006, it no longer posts such data, reverting instead to a less-transparent popularity rating. The transient nature of Internet video makes documenting a working URL a difficult task. As of June 2009, the clips discussed in this chapter could be found at the following addresses: "Unedited Saddam Hanging" (http://video.google.com/videoplay?docid=6404914135939160727); "Swinging Saddam Execution Video" (http://video.google.com/videoplay?docid=6185219928333240724); "Hanging Saddam" (http://video.google.com/videoplay?docid=-4660889599328574037). The "Ken Burns effect" is a common video editing tool that simulates camera movement and gives subtle motion to still images. Apple adopted the effect as a standard software component in 2003, with the release of iMovie 3.

4. Lev Manovich, *The Language of New Media* (Cambridge, MA: MIT Press, 2001), 46.

5. Apple's negotiation between a closed and open system is reflected in its approach to third-party application development for the iPhone. The launch of the company's iPhone App Store in July 2008 left independent developers with a difficult choice—to continue developing on their own or to come under the company's watchful eye. Apple's goal seems to be quality control—to maintain the stability of its platform. And while a partnership with Apple would guarantee that third-party developers see their tools finding a wider audience, it would also rule out certain otherwise functional applications. This calculated approach to development, both collaborative and responsive, seems key to making the iPhone a central lifestyle portal, capable of gaming, networking, and performing work-based, consumer-based, and leisure-based tasks. Many media providers have been quick to partner with Apple, including the major shareholders in online social networking: Facebook launched its iPhone-compliant mobile site just two months after the phone's release, a push that dropped the device into the ongoing flows of the network (and, acknowledging the network's importance, Apple has featured the Facebook application in its own advertising campaign).

6. The concept of embodiment, used several times throughout this chapter, has multiple inflections. My use is drawn from the work of phenomenologist Maurice Merleau-Ponty. In the *Phenomenology of Perception,* Merleau-Ponty distinguishes between embodiment as it relates to the actual shape and innate capacities of the human body (whose abilities are determined by its physical dynamics) and as it relates to affordance (what the body is called out to undertake or perform). In simplified terms, we may distinguish between the body's innate skills and those that are acquired, distin-

guishing between motor habits and culturally determined actions, both of which are nevertheless important in our experience of the world. I am suggesting that cellular technology can transform our understanding of the world at large, not simply as it mediates, but more significantly as it becomes integrated into our basic patterns of perception and knowing by shaping the body's actions. Understanding the material nature of new technologies (their engagement with the physical body) is just as important as understanding their psychosocial nature. See Maurice Merleau-Ponty, *Phenomenology of Perception*, trans. Colin Smith (New York: Routledge, 1962).

7. My play on words (singular/Cingular) is perhaps now obsolete; following AT&T's merger with BellSouth in December 2006, Cingular Wireless was solely owned by AT&T and was subsequently rebranded.

8. The concept of the subject is complex in critical theory, and there is a general tendency to complicate the notion of the autonomous individual capable of self-knowledge by introducing the shaping influences of discourse and ideology; such theories commonly suggest that the subject is best understood as a compromised position formed by the outward push of an innate root persona and the inward push of more universal cultural forces. Here, I suggest that technology must be added to the mix of decidedly exterior, cultural determinations that shape the subject. And with regard to the more specific terrain of trauma therapy, trauma psychology focuses on consciousness and commonly does so by considering both space and time as two distinct principles, in the first instance, space consciousness arises through the body's relationship to the environment, and in the second instance, time consciousnesses emerges through the experience of trauma work (through building psychic structures, engaging in the mental process of making sense of events). So in trauma theory, too, the individual/subject is not considered independent or autonomous but rather best understood as attached to the environment.

9. The concept of postindustrial logic can be counterposed with the industrial logic that precedes it. Industrial logic (associated with the rise of the industrial age) aptly describes a factory or assembly line mode of production and offers waiting consumers a rather homogeneous product. Postindustrial logic suggests production on demand, inviting consumers into the production process by promoting either customization or postassembly adaptation.

10. Jennifer Smodish, "Apple's Ad-ventures," *Macworld* (June 1, 2001), http://www.macworld.com/article/2223/2001/06/15appleads.html.

11. This convergence (of life and the photographic record) is even more pronounced in the burgeoning life-casting industry. The phenomenon is best understood as the continuous streaming of first-person video feeds using wearable technology. While the tactic has been used commercially and artistically, it has yet to find any concerted application in the field of citizen journalism.

12. E. Ann Kaplan, *Trauma Culture: The Politics of Terror and Loss in Media and Literature* (New Brunswick, NJ: Rutgers University Press, 2005), 1.

13. I use the terms "transience" and "being" here to convey the temporal dimension of trauma therapy, which charts the forward movement of a traumatized individual toward a point of synthesis. Time is of particular interest in the study of trauma because admitting the sovereignty of time—and its movement with or without us—is, in itself, a potentially threatening act that exposes the limits of the ego. I am suggesting that traumatized individuals may seek stopgap measures to achieve synthesis; this

is an easy point of entry for the commodity fetish, and the results may not be authentic.

14. Marsha Walton, "Cell Phones: A New Tool in the War-Zone Blogosphere," *CNN.com* (August 1, 2006), http://www.cnn.com/2006/TECH/internet/08/01/newblogs.

15. Yuki Noguchi, "Camera Phones Lend Immediacy to Images of Disaster," *Washington Post* (July 8, 2005), http://www.washingtonpost.com/wp-dyn/content/article/2005/07/07/AR2005070701522.html.

16. MSNBC hosts a citizen journalist component on its Web site; among other features, the site offers focused prompts from a virtual assignment desk and indexes select reports submitted from the field. The media organization urges readers to become an active part of the dialogue, soliciting both stories and images. As it shapes its consumers into producers, it embroils them in the network's interface. In 2005, MSNBC asked its London readers to share their experiences of the attacks on the city's transit system. Among these reports is citizen journalist Saira Kahn's diary of the London bombings. Kahn's narrative weaves together her personal experience with her impressions of the people of London. She suggests: "We are definitely a cosmopolitan city that hosts all different kinds of people that united today as humans as a family to help each other and share each others pain." Following journalistic convention, Kahn frames her minute-by-minute account as a larger tale of strength in unity, as she bookends her details with abstractions. And MSNBC situates Kahn's report alongside hyperlinks to the network's own coverage, viewable in the site's embedded (and commercially sponsored) media player. See Saira Kahn, "Bombings in London: Saira's Diary," *MSNBC.com* (September 23, 2005), http://www.msnbc.msn.com/id/8511900/ns/msnbc_tv-citizen_journalist. In 2007, MSNBC rebranded its citizen journalism pages with the launch of "FirstPerson." Editor in Chief Jennifer Sizemore introduces the feature with the claim: "We believe good journalism, no matter the topic, should seek to broaden the marketplace of ideas, deepen comprehension of the world around us and foster community." See Jennifer Sizemore, "Editor's Note: Welcome to FirstPerson," *MSNBC.com* (February 2007), http://www.msnbc.msn.com/id/16713129/ns/community-firstperson. MSNBC's public journalism project parallels ventures at other networks, including CNN's iReport; CNN launched its portal in 2008, although the news agency had been experimenting with Net-based, user-generated content since 2006. The 2005 London bombings have become part of a larger history of the rise of citizen journalism, and the breadth of citizen coverage from London is perhaps matched by the volume of reports that followed the December 2004 tsunami in Southeast Asia. The growth of citizen journalism and the circulation of independent footage across preexisting social networks have pushed the network news industry to develop its own conduits that weave the citizen journalist into a Web-savvy metanarrative (a commercially viable array that features all of the resources available to the corporation) and to pursue more nuanced interconnections (for example, FirstPerson can also be found on Facebook).

17. In contrast to what might be understood as the planned and orderly flow of commercial broadcasting (irrespective of any audience work that might complicate the path laid out by networks and advertisers), the concept of the supertext introduces the notion of clutter and suggests the need to consider a program in relation to various interstitial materials (ads, previews, promos, etc.), and associated forms of transmedia story-

telling, merchandising, and play. These fragments impinge on any attempt to simply deliver meaning (through a program's narrative), as they too make meaning. In the context of new media, I am suggesting that as the number of recombinatory elements increases, programming yields to interstice (the moments in between). The fragment becomes the norm as we navigate multiple media forms and pathways; meaning becomes an ever-more-unstable construct, and the master narratives that bind together the whole affair become quite messy, if they ever indeed truly materialize. Is there a big picture to be grasped or are we left with simply a series of disjointed communiqués and activities?

18. Susan Keith, Carol B. Schwalbe, and B. William Silcock, "Images in Ethics Codes in an Era of Violence and Tragedy," *Journal of Mass Media Ethics* 21, no. 4 (2006): 247.

19. Edward W. Soja, *Postmodern Geographies: The Reassertion of Space in Critical Social Theory* (New York: Verso, 1989), 23.

20. London Bomb Blasts Community, *Flickr*, http://www.flickr.com/groups/bomb.

21. Flickr's map function allows users to drag and drop their photos and videos onto a two-dimensional map to indicate each image's origin; these "geotagged" elements are reterritorialized, understood as an aggregate of geographic proximities with no marked temporal distance. The virtual geography of the Flickr map transcribes place in the absence of time. As I suggested in my earlier discussion of geopolitics, a virtual geography is not necessarily ideologically neutral; the proximal relations produced within Flickr can be very meaningful both in terms of what they highlight and what they erase, as the site's ever-widening catalog of images is reduced to a series of coordinates.

22. The origins and workings of folksonomies are discussed in greater detail in Chapter 6.

23. Susan Sontag, *On Photography* (New York: Anchor Books, 1990), 19–20.

24. Ibid., 17–18.

25. Manovich, *The Language of New Media*, 325.

26. As for the final two varied relationships to trauma, Kaplan lists: "4) reading a trauma narrative and constructing visual images of semantic data (news reader, three steps removed); 5) hearing a patient's trauma narrative." Kaplan, *Trauma Culture*, 91–92.

27. Ibid., 93.

28. Msoubra, "War on Lebanon (1) July 16, 2006—(AUDIO)," *YouTube* (July 18, 2006), http://www.youtube.com/watch?v=QvZ_qR8xwvo.

29. Nollie96, Reply to "War on Lebanon (1) July 16, 2006—(AUDIO)," *YouTube* (June 16, 2008), http://www.youtube.com/watch?v=QvZ_qR8xwvo.

30. Linda Belau, "Remembering, Repeating, and Working-Through: Trauma and the Limit of Knowledge," in *Topologies of Trauma: Essays on the Limit of Knowledge and Memory*, ed. Linda Belau and Petar Ramadanovic (New York: Other Press, 2002), xvi.

31. Ibid., xvii.

32. Patricia McKinsey Crittenden, "Toward an Integrative Theory of Trauma: A Dynamic-Maturation Approach," in *Developmental Perspectives on Trauma: Theory, Research, and Intervention*, ed. Dante Cicchetti and Sheree L. Toth (Rochester, NY: University of Rochester Press, 1997), 42.

33. Maria Puente, "Memories Gone in a Snap," *USA Today*, January 21, 2005, 1D.

34. William H. Whyte, *The Social Life of Small Urban Spaces* (New York: Project for Public Spaces, 2001), 16.

35. I use the term "postpraxis" to highlight those activities that are productive, but less explicitly producerly. I am referring to reactive second-order production practices that are more commonly associated with citing rather than authoring. While shooting and editing might be positioned as primary practices by YouTube's broadcast mandate, we also need to consider other facets of production, distribution, and exhibition that are equally meaningful (for example, embedding, hyperlinking, sharing, reading, and replying).

CHAPTER 4: *INTERVENTION* AND THE KODAK MOMENT

1. I borrow the term "discourse of sobriety" from Bill Nichols to highlight a common critical distinction between those programs that inform and educate (socially engaged programs that seem to operate in the public interest) and those that sensationalize and exploit. The distinction itself is often rather arbitrary and simply a reflection of a subjective critical attitude. It is much more difficult, and perhaps erroneous, to translate such a distinction into a rigid system of aesthetic and textual attributes. See Bill Nichols, *Representing Reality: Issues and Concepts in Documentary* (Bloomington: Indiana University Press, 1991), 3–4.

2. Susan Murray, "'I Think We Need a New Name for It': The Meeting of Documentary and Reality TV," in *Reality TV: Remaking Television Culture,* ed. Susan Murray and Laurie Ouellette (New York: New York University Press, 2004), 54.

3. Season 9 began airing in the United States in June 2010.

4. Ian Hodges, "Moving beyond Words: Therapeutic Discourse and Ethical Problematization," *Discourse Studies* 4, no. 4 (2002): 471.

5. Ibid., 457.

6. Mimi White, *Tele-Advising: Therapeutic Discourse in American Television* (Chapel Hill: University of North Carolina Press, 1992), 7.

7. Edward T. Linenthal, *The Unfinished Bombing: Oklahoma City in American History* (New York: Oxford University Press, 2001), 41–42.

8. Ibid., 43.

9. The original photomontage effect was reconfigured in Season 5. It now opens with twelve or so still images displayed on-screen; as the voice-over unfolds, select images move to the foreground, momentarily privileged and narrativized. These representations of different chapters in the subject's life move forward and separate along a z-axis, seeming to float in space and creating depth out of flatness. In addition, the initial collage exceeds the margins of the television screen, which suggests that the story is simply a fragment and the tapestry is larger and partially obscured from view. These changes still function as narrative shorthand and call out the ideological work performed by special effects. John Caldwell suggests that effects work "attempts to create visual analogues of feelings, products, surfaces, artifacts, and material pictures—representations of the stuff of mass culture itself." I am arguing that the photomontage operates as a doubly purposed hermeneutic act, introducing the semiological complexity of both the specific program (revealing and reviewing the central conflicts and enigmas) and the genre itself (as a shorthand guide to the textual strategies of documentary television). See John Caldwell, *Televisuality: Style, Crisis, and*

Authority in American Television (New Brunswick, NJ: Rutgers University Press, 1995), 192.

10. The final statement, "These are two of their stories," is used in early episodes of the series that feature two distinct cases in the same hour; the pronouncement is modified for episodes dedicated to one case.

11. The clinical data inserted into each episode (in the form of intertitles) performs a similar function; with structured attention to statistics and explanatory footnotes gleaned from such sources as the National Institutes of Health and the National Alliance on Mental Illness, the show moves from the personal to the public register (from the individual to the nation) and back again. These clinical details sit alongside other biographical intertitles and fill in the gaps in the subject's personal history.

12. This provocative style of titling (of morphing subject names into conflicted categories of being) was dropped in later seasons.

13. The series is able to maintain its critical perspective, even as it continues to become more open about its apparatus. The embedded broadcast technology is most commonly revealed at the outset of each prearranged intervention; the dramatic encounter between family and addict seems to activate the televisual gaze, and literally mobilizes the camera crew. As Tyler flees at the midpoint of his intervention (Season 8, Episode 116, May 2010), he crosses the axis of action, and momentarily confuses the steadicam operators who hover at the perimeter of the hotel room. While visual continuity is restored in the editing process, the spectacle reinforces the time-sensitive nature of events (the light stands are portable, the entire set is only temporary, and the intervention must happen now, at Tyler's rock bottom), and the difficulty of the call to order. The intervention is clearly a staged affair; yet its grammar is fluid, and it demands a particular stylistic response.

14. White, *Tele-Advising*, 182.

15. Michel Foucault, *The History of Sexuality, Volume I: An Introduction*, trans. Robert Hurley (New York: Vintage Books, 1978), 62.

16. Ibid., 61–62.

17. For a more thorough examination of reality television's possible relationship to neoliberalism, see Laurie Ouellette, "'Take Responsibility for Yourself': *Judge Judy* and the Neoliberal Citizen," in *Reality TV: Remaking Television Culture*, ed. Susan Murray and Laurie Ouellette (New York: New York University Press, 2004), 231–250. Ouellette's analysis is centered on courtroom procedurals, where the emphasis is on the resolution of microconflicts. By its very definition, trauma cannot be resolved through the same mechanisms; it cannot be contained by a simulated courtroom or worked through in such an abbreviated narrative arc. Moreover, its lessons are far less likely to be universalized and the disciplinary logic is, when correctly applied, nonhierarchical.

18. A&E added two new therapy programs to its schedule in 2009: *Hoarders* and *Obsessed*. I find these programs less satisfying than *Intervention* in their utilization of therapeutic (and photographic) discourse, as their narratives are far too truncated. In the case of *Hoarders*, each episode fails to produce a complete narrative trajectory; yet this lack of completion does not yield a sense of openness, of developing subjectivity. Instead, personal history, family entanglement, and therapeutic engagement are simply far less developed (and family photo albums are never used systematically, though they often function as a brief lead-in). Therapy itself is not cohesively represented; rather, it takes the form of ad hoc fieldwork, leaving the viewer uncertain of the program's commitment

to any serious and ongoing therapeutic exchange (although the producers note that each subject is offered aftercare). Moreover, therapy seems ancillary to organizational training. In each episode of *Hoarders*, clinical and nonclinical discourses are uneasily conjoined; the professional organizer is just as privileged as the psychologist. Yet the rules of this inverted hierarchy are never clearly articulated. But perhaps this is simply the nature of hoarding, a mental disorder that can be controlled but not cured. Within this framework, the show's central subjects never become sympathetic; their slovenliness is sensationalized. The narrative payoff, and the crisis of self-awareness, is commonly located in the moment that something shocking is found buried beneath the rubble—a dead cat, fecal matter, or a long-forgotten piece of nostalgia is unearthed inside the house of filth. Catering to our disbelief and exploring each grotesque landscape with a focused attention to detail, the show somehow maintains a degree of voyeuristic distance from its protagonists as they sort through their trash. Most of them never gain complete control over their disorders (given the sorter's two-day deadline), nor do they come through the therapeutic process to greater self-awareness. Never clearly locating the root cause of the condition, and never fully exploring the victim's backstory, the program fails to convey the life of the individual. Instead, the televised frame is filled with trash. There is simply too much to see here. Watching *Hoarders*, I find a certain irony in its misplaced engagement. Much in the same way that the program privileges its debris fields while displacing its central subjects, the hoarder also confuses these technologies of memory, this stuff, with subjectivity itself. Many hoarders displace themselves, as they are crowded out of their homes. The opening credits of the program tease viewers with the paranoid-inducing claim that "more than three million people are compulsive hoarders." And while this statement parallels the introductory gesture of *Intervention*, *Hoarders* never pushes beyond its declarative nature to fully explore the stories embedded within its episodic embrace. The series invests too much faith in the image. Still, I discuss *Hoarders*, if only in passing, as it introduces a unique form of media migration. In each episode, sorters move the hoarder's personal property outside and leave it on the front lawn. The home is turned inside out. Resting midway between domestic space and the dumpster, the hoarded objects become unstable texts; their irreconcilable status (as trash and treasure) becomes too much to bear. As their shelf lives expire, these objects begin to expose the narrative overload that haunts the hoarder.

19. Thomas Elsaesser, "One Train May Be Hiding Another: History, Memory, Identity, and the Visual Image," in *Topologies of Trauma: Essays on the Limit of Knowledge and Memory*, ed. Linda Belau and Petar Ramadanovic (New York: Other Press, 2002), 64.

CHAPTER 5: THE ARCHITECTURES OF CYBERDATING

1. Of course, place may reassert itself. Following a postindustrial logic of space, we have seen the birth of the use-neutral environment, constructed as a container for varying personal needs (a model "home away from home" or a place to telecommute) that might also lend itself to productive new forms of community building. Starbucks has positioned itself as a commercial developer of such third places (malleable arenas that are separate from work and home). The company's smart coffeehouses promote all forms of social networking (including electronically mediated forms) and are built for both work and play. In this manner, rather than becoming obsolete, we see places being

actively redefined to fit new cultural practices; and we see this not simply in the abstract but also as a strategic business model (that also speaks to the retooling of virtual destinations).

2. Michael Hardey, "Mediated Relationships: Authenticity and the Possibility of Romance," *Information, Communication & Society* 7, no. 2 (June 2004): 207.

3. Ibid., 212.

4. Launched in 2000, eHarmony offers its patented Compatibility Matching System as an assurance of connectedness. The site intends to forge lifetime partnerships among its members and, reflecting this orientation, it foregrounds its "scientific" textual markers (psychology-objectified) over the more abstract attachments of images. Its science also centers on heterosexuality, as the site only matches straight couples; the company claims it simply does not collect data on (or understand) gay relations. In mid-2007, Chemistry.com (a sister site of Match.com that launched in 2006) responded to eHarmony's exclusions by producing a number of humorous advertisements that courted gay consumers (and other eHarmony "rejects") interested in the compatibility market.

5. Theories of hyperpersonal communication suggest that we often form idealistic expectations when we are confronted with a restricted set of nonverbal cues. The less information we are presented with, the broader our assumptions and the more inflated our perceptions. The hyperpersonal nature of the online exchange can be mitigated by expanding the number of available cues. For a recent case study of these effects, see Samantha Henderson and Michael Gilding, "'I've Never Clicked This Much with Anyone in My Life': Trust and Hyperpersonal Communication in Online Friendships," *New Media & Society* 6, no. 1 (August 2004): 487–506.

6. Match.com is a membership-based content provider that launched in 1995, and, according to its own statistics, now features more than twenty million members.

7. UsingMyVoice, "UsingMyVoice said . . ." (May 13, 2007), http://matchceo.blogspot.com/2006/12/sneak-preview-of-all-new-matchcom.html (accessed November 15, 2007; site now discontinued).

8. Julie, "Julie said . . ." (June 20, 2007), http://matchceo.blogspot.com/2006/12/sneak-preview-of-all-new-matchcom.html (accessed November 15, 2007; site now discontinued).

9. David Phillips, "Modern Vision," *Oxford Art Journal* 16, no. 1 (1993): 137.

10. Kevin Robins, "Will Image Move Us Still?" in *The Photographic Image in Digital Culture*, ed. Martin Lister (New York: Routledge, 1995), 45.

11. IAC, "Overview," *IAC—Overview* (2007), http://www.iac.com/overview.

12. Linda Singer, "Recalling a Community at Loose Ends," in *Community at Loose Ends*, ed. Miami Theory Collective (Minneapolis: University of Minnesota Press, 1991), 125.

13. Allan Sekula, "The Traffic in Photographs," *Art Journal* 41, no. 1 (Spring 1981): 15.

14. While truth and pleasure are not necessarily at odds with one another, the critical distinction being made is one of rigor, where pleasure by its very nature escapes categorization and is always marked by excess.

15. Sekula, "The Traffic in Photographs," 15.

16. Celia Lury, *Prosthetic Culture: Photography, Memory and Identity* (New York: Routledge, 1998), 7.

17. Ibid. Italics in the original.

18. Site participants seem to know that they will become the subjects of secondary narratives. Members who write longer biographical entries and provide more contextual cues seem to be trying desperately to control any act of fantastic projection.

19. Lury, *Prosthetic Culture*, 19.

20. Despite this apparent neutralization of what are fundamentally human properties (as they take on the semblance of mathematical terms), one of the guiding principles of database construction is that relations should not be static but should instead abstract some portion of the real world that may itself change with time. For a more detailed consideration of database logic, see David Maier, *The Theory of Relational Databases* (Rockville, MD: Computer Science Press, 1983).

21. Lury, *Prosthetic Culture*, 19.

22. Edmond Bayle, "The Scientific Detective," *American Journal of Police Science* 2, no. 2 (March–April 1931): 158–159.

23. Sekula, "The Traffic in Photographs," 18.

24. Bayle, "The Scientific Detective," 169.

25. Miriam Hansen, "Mass Culture as Hieroglyphic Writing: Adorno, Derrida, Kracauer," *New German Critique*, no. 56 (Spring–Summer 1992): 51. Italics in the original.

26. Ibid., 51–52.

27. BigMuscle.com was launched in February 1999 and is a free, independently operated site based in San Francisco; its operating costs are offset by donations from its members, although profilers are not required to donate to the site. The terms of usage prohibit the posting of photos depicting sexual acts, although full or partial nudity is promoted. In fact, the terms state: "I understand that if I post photos to my profile that a photo will be of a muscle type photo with my shirt off or wearing a tank-top."

28. Manhunt.net launched in 2001 as a local venture courting the Boston market, but quickly gained a national subscriber base by sending its creative team to launch events in other cities and by advertising in community publications. Though commonly understood by gay men as a place to find partners for late-night, casual sex, Manhunt. net also has other social-networking tools.

29. Despite my general remarks about Gay.com, the site's personal ads include men, women, and transsexuals. In an interesting inversion of more popular commercial sites such as Match.com, gay sexuality is the naturalized position here, though one can select a more detailed search to reorient the search engine. Gay.com is owned by Planet-Out, a media company that has a variety of LGBT (lesbian, gay, bisexual, transgender) holdings, including the print brands *The Advocate*, *Out*, and *Out Traveler*. Given this synergy, it is not surprising that Gay.com places its personals in a tabloid format that draws from the company's other resources, though Gay.com was initially launched as a chat service in 1996.

30. The majority of the profiles on Dudesnude.com feature photos and videos of amateur and professional models. In the absence of truly insightful biographical details (and instead, showcasing sexual content), these men are simply to be looked at; the emphasis is on exhibitionism or sexual play. In fact, the site has been a launchpad for several amateur porn actors.

31. Physical type and content type are the two largest search categories on Dudesnude.com; again, these taxonomies refer most directly to an image (to an expectation

that is attached to the visual field) and are only secondarily applied to a profile. The roster of physical types includes: dude next door, fit jock dude, big muscle dude, bear, chub, leatherman, daddy men, sex pig, couples, and POZ (HIV-positive) dude. And the roster of content types includes: face, body (clothes on), body (clothes off), underwear, butt, cock, action, and duo/group.

32. "About Match.com," *Match.com* (2008), http://www.match.com/matchus/help/aboutus.aspx (accessed August 22, 2008; site now revised).

33. Jean-Luc Nancy, *The Inoperative Community*, ed. Peter Connor, trans. Peter Connor et al. (Minneapolis: University of Minnesota Press, 1991), 25–27, 74–75.

34. "About Match.com," *Match.com* (2001), http://www.match.com/registration/aboutus.asp (accessed June 3, 2003; site now discontinued).

35. Don Slater, "Domestic Photography and Digital Culture," in *The Photographic Image in Digital Culture*, ed. Martin Lister (New York: Routledge, 1995), 131.

36. Ibid.

37. Andrew L. Shapiro, "The Net That Binds: Using Cyberspace to Create Real Communities," *The Nation*, June 21, 1999, 12.

38. Ibid.

39. Nancy K. Baym, "The Emergence of On-Line Community," in *Cybersociety 2.0: Revisiting Computer-Mediated Communication and Community*, ed. Steven G. Jones (Thousand Oaks, CA: Sage Publications, 1998), 51.

40. Ibid.

41. Bill Nichols, *Blurred Boundaries: Questions of Meaning in Contemporary Culture* (Bloomington: Indiana University Press, 1994), 92–106.

42. Nancy, *The Inoperative Community*, 31.

CHAPTER 6: THE SOCIAL FABRIC OF IMAGES

1. TiVo has had a similar impact on the television landscape; its swivel search can create a complex web of associations among seemingly unrelated TV programs using tags and other descriptive markers.

2. Seminal contributors to the field of social network theory include J. A. Barnes, Marlene Burkhardt, Mark Granovetter, Caroline Haythornthwaite, Stanley Milgram, and J. Clyde Mitchell. The general value of the field, which took root in the late 1960s, is its dual attention to structural analysis (reading the governing architecture of a network) and individual agency (acknowledging the unique characteristics of individuals within the network, though privileging their positions as an important variable in the strength of their individuated efforts). Network structures may be understood as modified and modernized organizational structures and, as such, can be subjected to similar forms of analysis. Yet contemporary network structures often reveal (and one can position Internet sites that follow social network principles within this rubric) that their power emanates from the possibility of disintermediation (removing the middleman); individuals can connect directly to one another, despite their dependence on privatized telecommunications pathways. Of course, disintermediation is also a buzzword in e-commerce, where the term is used to suggest the direct and cost-effective connections that can be made between Internet-based businesses and their customers (eliminating retail overhead). I draw attention to this commercial inflection of social networking

as a reminder that structural analysis should never be an end in itself; rather, the goal should be to understand what the network is doing (as a relative approximation of the relationships, ties, and generalizable investments that give voice to the efforts of individuals). Again, individuals gain their meaning and their agency through their positions in the network; individuality ultimately yields to positionality.

3. There is a certain danger in understanding persons simply as nodes in a network, and in reducing complex relationships into simplified lines of attachment (delimiting the most direct path from person A to person B and so forth); but the metaphor has its use if it can lead to rather specific considerations of the relationships in any single network and, by extension, to an understanding of the heuristic utility of the metaphor itself (which may lead to more accurate theories of social network architectures). J. Clyde Mitchell's contributions to social network analysis are especially useful in connecting social action to abstraction. See J. Clyde Mitchell, "The Concept and Use of Social Networks," in *Social Networks in Urban Situations: Analyses of Personal Relationships in Central African Towns*, ed. J. Clyde Mitchell (Manchester, UK: Manchester University Press, 1969), 1–50.

4. Steven G. Jones, "Information, Internet, and Community: Notes toward an Understanding of Community in the Information Age," in *Cybersociety 2.0: Revisiting Computer-Mediated Communication and Community*, ed. Steven G. Jones (Thousand Oaks, CA: Sage Publications, 1998), 21.

5. The term Web 2.0 gained popularity in 2004, at a conference hosted by O'Reilly Media and MediaLive International. Its early use at what was the first Web 2.0 conference privileged cocreativity, participation, and openness in the interest of harnessing collective intelligence to further the Web media marketplace and strengthen e-commerce; user-generated content and data trails could be used to foster more-focused business models tapping newly identifiable niche markets. Yet there have consistently been dual hyperbolic claims driving the concept of Web 2.0, with entrepreneurship being matched by socially conscious collaborative action (or simply collaboration without a self-evident economic return). At the same time, the concept of collective intelligence has a life of its own; though it has been casually tethered to Web 2.0, it is more pointedly developed in the field of mass communication by theorists such as Pierre Léyy. Lévy explores how networks may be used to construct intelligent communities (those defined by the successful realization of their social and cognitive potential) where the quantity of information available across the network is consistently read in relation to the quality of knowledge it produces.

6. Leslie Walker, ".com—Live," *Washington Post* (March 25, 1999), http://www .washingtonpost.com/wp-srv/business/talk/transcripts/walker/walker032599.htm.

7. Originally posted on a Friendster bulletin board in July 2003, *The Fakester Manifesto* was also republished on a variety of blogs, including: http://www.zephoria .org/thoughts/archives/2003/08/17/the_fakester_manifesto.html. The moniker Roy Batty is, of course, a reference to the renegade replicant of the same name in Ridley Scott's 1982 film, *Blade Runner* (a name also found, though with a modified spelling, in Scott's source material, the Philip K. Dick novel *Do Androids Dream of Electric Sheep?*); Batty's quest, to extend the lives of his fellow replicants and thus the narrative trajectory of the film, draws out the fundamental premise that the divide between human and replicant is rather tenuous and in this vein echoes the thematic concern of the

Fakester revolution, with its focus on the construction of and consequent fluidity of identity (and the appropriation of cultural memories as one's own).

8. Roy Batty, "An Open Letter to the Friendster Community and Management," *Friendster* (July 17, 2003). As with the manifesto, Batty's letter was originally posted on a Friendster bulletin board, and was republished on a number of blogs, including: http://www.zephoria.org/thoughts/archives/2003/08/17/open_letter_to_the_friendster_community_and_management.html.

9. Ibid.

10. Lessley Anderson, "Attack of the Smartasses," *SF Weekly* (August 13, 2003), http://www.sfweekly.com/2003-08-13/news/attack-of-the-smartasses.

11. Katharine Mieszkowski, "Faking Out Friendster," *Salon* (August 14, 2003), http://dir.salon.com/story/tech/feature/2003/08/14/fakesters/index.html.

12. Allucquère Rosanne Stone, "Will the Real Body Please Stand Up? Boundary Stories about Virtual Cultures," in *Cyberspace: First Steps,* ed. Michael Benedikt (Cambridge, MA: MIT Press, 1991), 94.

13. Ibid., 95.

14. Lawrence Lessig, *Code and Other Laws of Cyberspace* (New York: Basic Books, 1999), 30.

15. Mark S. Granovetter, "The Strength of Weak Ties," *American Journal of Sociology* 78, no. 6 (May 1973): 1373.

16. 100 Million Facebook Members for Democracy in Iran, "Basic Info—Description," *Facebook* (June 18, 2009), http://www.facebook.com/group.php?gid=105160039272&ref=search&sid=599579564.2977025891..1.

17. Facebook's default news prompt is now more open-ended and speculative, and encourages participants to enter the site's feed with the reflective inquiry, "What's on your mind?" In this manner, the feed accommodates both thought and action.

18. Though our posts may be original, they are nevertheless determined by a vernacular that governs the network's architecture, which urges us to privilege certain artifacts over others. My use of the term "ready-made" follows from a belief that personal artifacts are drafted from a number of shared conventions that circulate within the social network. I am following a model of symbolic interactionism that suggests human behavior is both individualized and social, the product of community life rather than simply the sum total of individualized properties. See Peter L. Berger and Thomas Luckmann, *The Social Construction of Reality: A Treatise in the Sociology of Knowledge* (New York: Anchor Books, 1967), 39.

19. Robert Prus, *Symbolic Interaction and Ethnographic Research: Intersubjectivity and the Study of Human Lived Experience* (Albany: State University of New York Press, 1996), 34.

20. Berger and Luckmann, *The Social Construction of Reality,* 39.

21. Prus, *Symbolic Interaction,* 80.

22. Zygmunt Bauman, "Consuming Life," *Journal of Consumer Culture* 1, no. 1 (2001): 13. Italics in the original.

23. Ibid., 17.

24. Ibid., 23.

25. Theodore John Rivers, *Contra Technologiam: The Crisis of Value in a Technological Age* (Lanham, MD: University Press of America, 1993), 9.

26. More generally, moblogging can be done from any mobile device, but those with camera-enabled cell phones are the largest group. These users publish their photos and videos direct to the Web, posting them to either an independent photo-sharing site or to a site hosted by their mobile carrier.

27. Software developers are responding to this possibility. Apple's recent introduction of "Places" into its iPhoto application leverages the power of Google Maps to add geotagging capabilities to its popular photo-management software, using the global positioning system (GPS) data from compliant cameras (or allowing end users to manually enter geographic data). By applying this organizational overlay, users can lay out their photos as pinpoints on a map.

28. The circumstances surrounding Arabi's death are still unclear, but reports suggest he died of a gunshot wound on June 15, although his body was returned to his family almost one month later; Iranian officials have claimed that seven people were killed during the protest that day.

29. Of course, tension is always visible at the microlevel, where it remains part of the transcript; I am not suggesting that networked groups push effortlessly forward to produce a seamless, authoritative metanarrative.

30. Smart mob tactics informed the street demonstrations that were held during the November 1999 World Trade Organization protests in Seattle.

31. Larry M. Edwards, "Local Firm Hopes to Turn Moblogs into Mo' Bucks," *SanDiego.com* (November 26, 2003), http://www.sandiego.com/option,com_sdca/target ,2151DFD5-AB55-4206-B134-D33C684C1ED1.

32. *TextAmerica.com* (2007), http://www.textamerica.com/moblogs.aspx?__y=1&_ media=I (accessed October 4, 2007; site now discontinued).

33. "About exTAmerica," http://www.flickr.com/groups/extamerica/ (accessed August 10, 2007; site now revised).

34. Daniel Terdiman, "Folksonomies Tap People Power," *Wired* (February 1, 2005), http://www.wired.com/print/science/discoveries/news/2005/02/66456.

35. Thomas Vander Wal, "Explaining and Showing Broad and Narrow Folksonomies," *Personal InfoCloud* (February 21, 2005), http://www.personalinfocloud.com/ 2005/02/explaining_and_.html.

36. Julian Dibbell, "Pic Your Friends," *Village Voice* (March 24, 2005), http://www .villagevoice.com/screens/0513,dibbell,62452,28.html.

37. David Buxton, *From* The Avengers *to* Miami Vice: *Form and Ideology in Television Series* (Manchester, UK: Manchester University Press, 1990), 15.

38. As one form of response and boundary marking, Facebook promotes collective autobiographical practices; members can tag each other in photos and push these into their respective repositories. In this way, tagged photos reside alongside profile pictures and album photos; images produced by others enter a personal narrative that might otherwise be meticulously constructed. Though tags can be removed and intruding photos excised, such cocreativity (collective profile authoring and group nostalgia) is distinct from a more controlled form of self-expression that is revealed, for instance, in the selection of one's profile image.

39. Alice Mathias, "The Fakebook Generation," *New York Times* (October 6, 2007), http://www.nytimes.com/2007/10/06/opinion/06mathias.html?_r=1.

40. Steven Levy and Brad Stone, "The New Wisdom of the Web," *Newsweek* 147, no. 14 (April 3, 2006): 50.

41. Ibid., 52.

42. Pierre Lévy, *Cyberculture,* trans. Robert Bononno (Minneapolis: University of Minnesota Press, 2001), 147–148.

43. James Jay Carafano, "All a Twitter: How Social Networking Shaped Iran's Election Protests," *Backgrounder* 2300 (July 20, 2009): 12.

44. The phrase is a popular translation of Isaac Newton's third law of motion, originally presented in the first book of his *Philosophiae Naturalis Principia Mathematica* (1687).

45. Google, "Google to Acquire YouTube for $1.65 Billion in Stock," *Google Press Center: Press Release* (2006), http://www.google.com/press/pressrel/google_youtube.html.

46. Herbert Marcuse, *One-Dimensional Man: Studies in the Ideology of Advanced Industrial Society* (Boston: Beacon Press, 1964), 22.

47. Ibid., 23.

48. In August 2007, reports began emerging that Comcast was preventing Bit-Torrent seeding, and suggested that the company was monitoring and interfering with peer-to-peer communications in a process known as traffic shaping. Comcast initially denied the claims, but subsequently changed its network management style.

49. Lev Grossman, "Power to the People," *Time* 168, no. 26 (December 25, 2006–January 1, 2007): 42.

50. In an earlier note to this chapter (note 27), I mention Apple's addition of geo-tagging to iPhoto 2009. Pushing further, Apple's addition of face detection and recognition technology to iPhoto allows users to reorganize the event-based database into a physiognomic map, borne out as a bulletin board pictorial. Space, place, and time yield to the familial register, in what is an inherently deterritorializing affair. The dynamism of tagging in the public sphere and the rapid evolution of Web-based interfaces has yielded parallel forms of dynamism in the private sphere, where individuals expect a similar degree of responsiveness and customization from the local interface. We have become rather savvy in the reterritorialization of our own media artifacts, to the extent that the pursuit of familiarity rips them out of more culturally valenced arenas. Perhaps this signals a marked return to privatization, and an industry acknowledgment of such a fantasy.

51. Michel de Certeau, *The Practice of Everyday Life,* trans. Steven F. Rendall (Berkeley: University of California Press, 1984), 123. Italics in the original.

52. Edward W. Soja, *Postmodern Geographies: The Reassertion of Space in Critical Social Theory* (New York: Verso, 1989), 6.

53. Ibid., 7, 122–126.

Bibliography

Adorno, Theodor W. *Negative Dialectics.* Translated by E. B. Ashton. New York: Seabury Press, 1973.

Althusser, Louis. "Ideology and Ideological State Apparatuses (Notes towards an Investigation)." In *Lenin and Philosophy and Other Essays,* translated by Ben Brewster, 127–186. New York: Monthly Review Press, 1971.

Alvear, Michael. "You've Got Male: How Did America Online Become the Bathhouse of the Internet? Size Matters." *Salon,* October 12, 1999, http://www.salon.com/tech/feature/1999/10/12/gay_aol.

Anderson, Benedict. *Imagined Communities: Reflections on the Origin and Spread of Nationalism.* London: Verso, 1991.

Anderson, Lessley. "Attack of the Smartasses." *SF Weekly,* August 13, 2003, http://www.sfweekly.com/2003-08-13/news/attack-of-the-smartasses.

Arnheim, Rudolf. *Visual Thinking.* Berkeley: University of California Press, 1969.

Badiou, Alain. "The Event in Deleuze," translated by Jon Roffe. *Parrhesia* 2 (2007): 37–44.

Baker, Tom, and Jonathan Simon, eds. *Embracing Risk: The Changing Culture of Insurance and Responsibility.* Chicago: University of Chicago Press, 2002.

Bakhtin, M. M. *The Dialogic Imagination.* Edited by Michael Holquist. Translated by Caryl Emerson and Michael Holquist. Austin: University of Texas Press, 1981.

Banet-Weiser, Sarah. "Surfin' the Net: Children, Parental Obsolescence, and Citizenship." In *Technological Visions: The Hopes and Fears That Shape New Technologies,* edited by Marita Sturken et al., 270–292. Philadelphia: Temple University Press, 2004.

Barnes, J. A. "Class and Committees in a Norwegian Island Parish." *Human Relations* 7, no. 1 (1954): 39–58.

Barthes, Roland. *Camera Lucida: Reflections on Photography.* Translated by Richard Howard. New York: Noonday Press, 1981.

————. *Image–Music–Text.* Translated by Stephen Heath. New York: Noonday Press, 1977.

Baudrillard, Jean. *Simulacra and Simulation.* Translated by Sheila Faria Glaser. Ann Arbor: University of Michigan Press, 1994.

Baudry, Jean-Louis. "Ideological Effects of the Basic Cinematographic Apparatus." Reprinted in *Film Theory and Criticism: Introductory Readings,* 5th ed., edited by Leo Braudy and Marshall Cohen, 345–355. New York: Oxford University Press, 1999.

Bauman, Zygmunt. "Consuming Life." *Journal of Consumer Culture* 1, no. 1 (2001): 9–29.

Bayle, Edmond. "The Scientific Detective." *American Journal of Police Science* 2, no. 2 (March–April 1931): 158–171.

Baym, Nancy K. "The Emergence of On-Line Community." In *Cybersociety 2.0: Revisiting Computer-Mediated Communication and Community,* edited by Steven G. Jones, 35–68. Thousand Oaks, CA: Sage Publications, 1998.

Belau, Linda. "Remembering, Repeating, and Working-Through: Trauma and the Limit of Knowledge." In *Topologies of Trauma: Essays on the Limit of Knowledge and Memory,* edited by Linda Belau and Petar Ramadanovic, xiii–xxvii. New York: Other Press, 2002.

————. "Trauma, Repetition, and the Hermeneutics of Psychoanalysis." In *Topologies of Trauma: Essays on the Limit of Knowledge and Memory,* edited by Linda Belau and Petar Ramadanovic, 151–175. New York: Other Press, 2002.

Beniger, James. "Personalization of Mass Media and the Growth of Pseudo-Community." *Communication Research* 14, no. 3 (1987): 352–371.

Berger, John. *About Looking.* New York: Pantheon Books, 1980.

Berger, Peter L., and Thomas Luckmann. *The Social Construction of Reality: A Treatise in the Sociology of Knowledge.* New York: Anchor Books, 1967.

Berlant, Lauren. *The Queen of America Goes to Washington: Essays on Sex and Citizenship.* Durham, NC: Duke University Press, 1997.

Best, Joel. "Missing Children, Misleading Statistics." *Public Interest* 92 (Summer 1988): 84–92.

Bhabha, Homi K. *The Location of Culture.* New York: Routledge, 1994.

Bock, Philip K. "The Importance of Erving Goffman to Psychological Anthropology." *Ethos* 16, no. 1 (March 1998): 3–20.

Bohman, James. "Practical Reason and Cultural Constraint: Agency in Bourdieu's Theory of Practice." In *Bourdieu: A Critical Reader,* edited by Richard Shusterman, 129–152. Malden, MA: Blackwell Publishers, 1999.

Bolter, Jay David, and Richard Grusin. *Remediation: Understanding New Media.* Cambridge, MA: MIT Press, 1999.

Bott, Elizabeth. *Family and Social Network: Roles, Norms, and External Relationships in Ordinary Urban Families.* London: Tavistock Press, 1957.

Bourdieu, Pierre. *The Field of Cultural Production: Essays on Art and Literature.* Edited by Randal Johnson. New York: Columbia University Press, 1993.

————. *The Logic of Practice.* Translated by Richard Nice. Stanford, CA: Stanford University Press, 1990.

————. *Outline of a Theory of Practice.* Translated by Richard Nice. Cambridge: Cambridge University Press, 1977.

———. *Photography: A Middle-Brow Art.* Translated by Shaun Whiteside. Stanford, CA: Stanford University Press, 1990.

———. "The Social Conditions of the International Circulation of Ideas." In *Bourdieu: A Critical Reader,* edited by Richard Shusterman, 220–228. Malden, MA: Blackwell Publishers, 1999.

Branwyn, Gareth. "Compu-Sex: Erotica for Cybernauts." In *Flame Wars: The Discourse of Cyberculture,* edited by Mark Dery, 223–235. Durham, NC: Duke University Press, 1994.

Burkhardt, Marlene E. "Social Interaction Effects following a Technological Change: A Longitudinal Investigation." *Academy of Management Journal* 37, no. 4 (August 1994): 869–898.

Buxton, David. *From* The Avengers *to* Miami Vice: *Form and Ideology in Television Series.* Manchester, UK: Manchester University Press, 1990.

Caldwell, John. *Televisuality: Style, Crisis, and Authority in American Television.* New Brunswick, NJ: Rutgers University Press, 1995.

Carafano, James Jay. "All a Twitter: How Social Networking Shaped Iran's Election Protests." *Backgrounder* 2300 (July 20, 2009): 1–12.

Certeau, Michel de. *The Practice of Everyday Life.* Translated by Steven F. Rendall. Berkeley: University of California Press, 1984.

Chapman, Gary. "Taming the Computer." In *Flame Wars: The Discourse of Cyberculture,* edited by Mark Dery, 297–319. Durham, NC: Duke University Press, 1994.

Chun, Wendy Hui Kyong. *Control and Freedom: Power and Paranoia in the Age of Fiber Optics.* Cambridge, MA: MIT Press, 2006.

Collins, Douglas. *The Story of Kodak.* New York: Harry N. Abrams, 1990.

Cooney, Caroline B. *The Face on the Milk Carton.* New York: Delacorte Press, 1990.

———. *The Voice on the Radio.* New York: Laurel-Leaf, 1996.

———. *What Janie Found.* New York: Laurel-Leaf, 2000.

———. *Whatever Happened to Janie?* New York: Dell Laurel-Leaf, 1993.

Cowley, Geoffrey, and Karen Springen. "Faces from the Future." *Newsweek* 113, no. 7 (February 13, 1989): 62.

Crary, Jonathan. *Techniques of the Observer: On Vision and Modernity in the Nineteenth Century.* Cambridge, MA: MIT Press, 1990.

Crittenden, Patricia McKinsey. "Toward an Integrative Theory of Trauma: A Dynamic-Maturation Approach." In *Developmental Perspectives on Trauma: Theory, Research, and Intervention,* edited by Dante Cicchetti and Sheree L. Toth, 33–84. Rochester, NY: University of Rochester Press, 1997.

Culler, Jonathan. *Framing the Sign: Criticism and Its Institutions.* Norman: University of Oklahoma Press, 1988.

Curtin, Michael. *Redeeming the Wasteland: Television Documentary and Cold War Politics.* New Brunswick, NJ: Rutgers University Press, 1995.

Davis, Joshua. "The Secret World of Lonelygirl15." *Wired* 14, no. 12 (December 2006): 232–239.

Degenne, Alain, and Michel Forsé. *Introducing Social Networks.* Thousand Oaks, CA: Sage Publications, 1999.

Deleuze, Gilles. *Difference and Repetition.* New York: Columbia University Press, 1994.

———. "Postscript on the Societies of Control." *October* 59 (Winter 1992): 3–7.

Deleuze, Gilles, and Felix Guattari. *A Thousand Plateaus: Capitalism and Schizophrenia.* Translated by Brian Massumi. Minneapolis: University of Minnesota Press, 1987.

———. *What Is Philosophy?* Translated by Janis Tomlinson and Graham Burchell III. New York: Columbia University Press, 1996.

Dibbell, Julian. "Pic Your Friends." *Village Voice,* March 24, 2005, http://www.village-voice.com/screens/0513,dibbell,62452,28.html.

Doheny-Farina, Stephen. *The Wired Neighborhood.* New Haven, CT: Yale University Press, 1996.

Durkheim, Emile. *The Division of Labor in Society.* Translated by W. D. Halls. New York: Free Press, 1997.

Dyson, Esther. *Release 2.1: A Design for Living in the Digital Age.* New York: Broadway Books, 1998.

Edelman, Gay Norton. "Kids and Kidnapping." *Parents* 60, no. 12 (December 1985): 81–84.

Edwards, Larry M. "Local Firm Hopes to Turn Moblogs into Mo' Bucks." *SanDiego.com,* November 26, 2003, http://www.sandiego.com/option,com_sdca/target,2151DFD5 -AB55-4206-B134-D33C684C1ED1.

Elsaesser, Thomas. "One Train May Be Hiding Another: History, Memory, Identity, and the Visual Image." In *Topologies of Trauma: Essays on the Limit of Knowledge and Memory,* edited by Linda Belau and Petar Ramadanovic, 61–71. New York: Other Press, 2002.

Enzensberger, Hans Magnus. *The Consciousness Industry: On Literature, Politics and the Media.* New York: Seabury Press, 1974.

———. "A Theory of Tourism." *New German Critique,* no. 68 (Spring–Summer 1996): 117–135.

Ewald, François. "Two Infinities of Risk." In *The Politics of Everyday Fear,* edited by Brian Massumi, 221–228. Minneapolis: University of Minnesota Press, 1993.

Faber, Mindy, ed. *A Tool, a Weapon, a Witness: The New Video News Crews.* Chicago: Randolph Street Gallery, 1990.

Feldman, David B., and Katrin Julia Kaal. "Vicarious Trauma and Assumptive Worldview: Beliefs about the World in Acquaintances of Trauma Victims." *Traumatology* 13, no. 3 (2007): 21–31.

Fernback, Jan. "The Individual within the Collective: Virtual Ideology and the Realization of Collective Principles." In *Virtual Culture: Identity and Communication in Cybersociety,* edited by Steven G. Jones, 36–54. Thousand Oaks, CA: Sage Publications, 1997.

Finkelhor, David, Heather Hammer, and Andrea J. Sedlak. "Nonfamily Abducted Children: National Estimates and Characteristics." *National Incidence Studies of Missing, Abducted, Runaway, and Thrownaway Children* (NCJ 196467). Washington, DC: Office of Juvenile Justice and Delinquency Prevention, Office of Justice Programs, U.S. Department of Justice, October 2002.

Forst, Martin L., and Martha-Elin Blomquist. *Missing Children: Rhetoric and Reality.* New York: Lexington Books, 1991.

Foucault, Michel. *The Archaeology of Knowledge and the Discourse on Language.* Translated by A. M. Sheridan Smith. New York: Pantheon Books, 1972.

———. *The Birth of the Clinic: An Archaeology of Medical Perception.* Translated by A. M. Sheridan Smith. New York: Vintage Books, 1973.

———. *The History of Sexuality, Volume I: An Introduction.* Translated by Robert Hurley. New York: Vintage Books, 1978.

———. *Madness and Civilization: A History of Insanity in the Age of Reason.* Translated by Richard Howard. New York: Vintage Books, 1965.

———. *The Order of Things: An Archaeology of the Human Sciences.* New York: Vintage Books, 1970.

Freedman, Eric. "The Architectures of Cyberdating: Personal Advertisement Photography and the Unworking of Community." In *Community Media: International Perspectives,* edited by Linda K. Fuller, 175–184. New York: Palgrave Macmillan, 2007.

———. "'Have You Seen This Child?' From Milk Carton to *Mise-en-Abîme.*" In *Hop on Pop: The Politics and Pleasures of Popular Culture,* edited by Henry Jenkins, Tara McPherson, and Jane Shattuc, 689–700. Durham, NC: Duke University Press, 2002.

———. "Public Access/Private Confession: Home Video as (Queer) Community Television." In *The Television Studies Reader,* edited by Robert C. Allen and Annette Hill, 343–353. New York: Routledge, 2004.

Freud, Sigmund. *Beyond the Pleasure Principle.* Translated and edited by James Strachey. New York: W. W. Norton, 1975.

Frow, John. "Tourism and the Semiotics of Nostalgia." *October* 57 (Summer 1991): 123–151.

Fuller, Linda K. *Media Mediated Relationships: Straight and Gay, Mainstream and Alternative Perspectives.* New York: Haworth Press, 1996.

Galloway, Alexander R. *Protocol: How Control Exists after Decentralization.* Cambridge, MA: MIT Press, 2004.

Gardiner, John M., and Alan Richardson-Klavehn. "Remembering and Knowing." In *The Oxford Handbook of Memory,* edited by Endel Tulving and Fergus I. M. Craik, 229–244. New York: Oxford University Press, 2000.

Garfield, Bob. "The YouTube Effect." *Wired* 14, no. 12 (December 2006): 222–227, 266.

Garnham, Nicholas. *Capitalism and Communication: Global Culture and the Economics of Information.* London: Sage Publications, 1990.

Gemünden, Gerd. "Introduction to Enzensberger's 'A Theory of Tourism.'" *New German Critique,* no. 68 (Spring–Summer 1996): 113–115.

Germain, Carel Bailey. *Human Behavior in the Social Environment: An Ecological View.* New York: Columbia University Press, 1991.

Giroux, Henry A. *Beyond the Spectacle of Terrorism: Global Uncertainty and the Challenge of the New Media.* Boulder, CO: Paradigm Publishers, 2006.

Glassner, Barry. *The Culture of Fear: Why Americans Are Afraid of the Wrong Things.* New York: Basic Books, 1999.

Godwin, Mike. *Cyber Rights: Defending Free Speech in the Digital Age.* Revised and updated edition. Cambridge, MA: MIT Press, 2003.

Goffman, Erving. *Frame Analysis: An Essay on the Organization of Experience.* New York: Harper & Row, 1974.

———. "Picture Frames." *Studies in the Anthropology of Visual Communication* 3, no. 2 (Fall 1976): 78–91.

————. *The Presentation of Self in Everyday Life*. New York: Anchor Books, 1959.

Granovetter, Mark S. "The Strength of Weak Ties." *American Journal of Sociology* 78, no. 6 (May 1973): 1360–1380.

Grigely, Joseph. *Textualterity: Art, Theory, and Textual Criticism*. Ann Arbor: University of Michigan Press, 1995.

Gross, Larry. "Life vs. Art: The Interpretation of Visual Narratives." *Studies in Visual Communication* 11, no. 4 (Fall 1985): 2–11.

————. "Somewhere There's a Place for Us: Sexual Minorities and the Internet." In *Technological Visions: The Hopes and Fears That Shape New Technologies*, edited by Marita Sturken et al., 255–269. Philadelphia: Temple University Press, 2004.

Grossman, Lev. "Power to the People." *Time* 168, no. 26 (December 25, 2006–January 1, 2007): 42–58.

Habermas, Jurgen. *The Structural Transformation of the Public Sphere: An Inquiry into a Category of Bourgeois Society*. Translated by Thomas Burger and Frederick Lawrence. Cambridge, MA: MIT Press, 1991.

Hansen, Chris. *To Catch a Predator: Protecting Your Kids from Online Enemies Already in Your Home*. New York: Dutton, 2007.

Hansen, Miriam. "Mass Culture as Hieroglyphic Writing: Adorno, Derrida, Kracauer." *New German Critique*, no. 56 (Spring–Summer 1992): 43–73.

Hardey, Michael. "Life beyond the Screen: Embodiment and Identity through the Internet." *Sociological Review* 50, no. 4 (November 2002): 570–585.

————. "Mediated Relationships: Authenticity and the Possibility of Romance." *Information, Communication & Society* 7, no. 2 (June 2004): 207–222.

Haythornthwaite, Caroline. "Social Network Analysis: An Approach and Technique for the Study of Information Exchange." *Library and Information Science Research* 18, no. 4 (Autumn 1996): 323–342.

Haythornthwaite, Caroline, and Barry Wellman, eds. *The Internet in Everyday Life*. Oxford: Blackwell Publishers, 2002.

Heath, Stephen. *Questions of Cinema*. Bloomington: Indiana University Press, 1981.

Henderson, Samantha, and Michael Gilding. "'I've Never Clicked This Much with Anyone in My Life': Trust and Hyperpersonal Communication in Online Friendships." *New Media & Society* 6, no. 4 (August 2004): 487–506.

Herman, Judith. *Trauma and Recovery: The Aftermath of Violence—from Domestic Abuse to Political Terror*. New York: Basic Books, 1992.

Himmelstein, Hal. "Kodak's 'America': Images from the American Eden." In *Television: The Critical View*, 6th ed., edited by Horace Newcomb, 183–206. New York: Oxford University Press, 2000.

Hirsch, Marianne. *Family Frames: Photography, Narrative and Postmemory*. Cambridge, MA: Harvard University Press, 1997.

Hirsch, Marianne, ed. *The Familial Gaze*. Hanover, NH: Dartmouth College, 1999.

Hodges, Ian. "Moving beyond Words: Therapeutic Discourse and Ethical Problematization." *Discourse Studies* 4, no. 4 (2002): 455–479.

Huyssen, Andreas. *Twilight Memories: Marking Time in a Culture of Amnesia*. New York: Routledge, 1995.

Ivy, Marilyn. "Have You Seen Me? Recovering the Inner Child in Late Twentieth-Century America." *Social Text* 37 (Winter 1993): 227–252.

Jakle, John A. *The Tourist: Travel in Twentieth-Century North America*. Lincoln: University of Nebraska Press, 1985.

James, David. "Lynn Hershman: The Subject of Autobiography." In *Resolutions*, edited by Michael Renov and Erika Suderburg, 124–133. Minneapolis: University of Minnesota Press, 1996.

Jameson, Fredric. *The Political Unconscious: Narrative as a Socially Symbolic Act*. Ithaca, NY: Cornell University Press, 1981.

———. *Postmodernism or the Cultural Logic of Late Capitalism*. Durham, NC: Duke University Press, 1991.

Jenkins, Henry. *Convergence Culture*. New York: New York University Press, 2006.

Johnson, Steven. *Interface Culture: How New Technology Transforms the Way We Create and Communicate*. New York: Basic Books, 1997.

Jones, Steven G. "Information, Internet, and Community: Notes toward an Understanding of Community in the Information Age." In *Cybersociety 2.0: Revisiting Computer-Mediated Communication and Community*, edited by Steven G. Jones, 1–34. Thousand Oaks, CA: Sage Publications, 1998.

Joseph, Miranda. *Against the Romance of Community*. Minneapolis: University of Minnesota Press, 2002.

Kahn, Saira. "Bombings in London: Saira's Diary." *MSNBC.com*, September 23, 2005, http://www.msnbc.msn.com/id/8511900/ns/msnbc_tv-citizen_journalist.

Kaplan, E. Ann. *Trauma Culture: The Politics of Terror and Loss in Media and Literature*. New Brunswick, NJ: Rutgers University Press, 2005.

Keenan, Catherine. "On the Relationship between Personal Photographs and Individual Memory." *History of Photography* 22, no. 1 (Spring 1998): 60–64.

Keith, Michael, and Steve Pile. *Place and the Politics of Identity*. New York: Routledge, 1993.

Keith, Susan, Carol B. Schwalbe, and B. William Silcock. "Images in Ethics Codes in an Era of Violence and Tragedy." *Journal of Mass Media Ethics* 21, no. 4 (2006): 245–264.

Kennel, Sarah. "Quick, Casual, Modern." In *The Art of the American Snapshot, 1888–1978: From the Collection of Robert E. Jackson*, edited by Sarah Greenough and Diane Waggoner, 73–145. Washington, DC: National Gallery of Art, 2007.

Krauss, Rosalind. "Photography's Discursive Spaces." In *The Contest of Meaning: Critical Histories of Photography*, edited by Richard Bolton, 287–302. Cambridge, MA: MIT Press, 1989.

Kristeva, Julia. *Desire in Language: A Semiotic Approach to Literature and Art*. Edited by Leon S. Roudiez. Translated by Thomas Gora et al. New York: Columbia University Press, 1980.

Leach, Edmund. "On Certain Unconsidered Aspects of Double Descent Systems." *Man* 62, no. 214 (September 1962): 130–134.

Lejeune, Philippe. *On Autobiography*. Translated by Katherine Leary. Edited by Paul John Eakin. Minneapolis: University of Minnesota Press, 1989.

Lessig, Lawrence. *Code and Other Laws of Cyberspace*. New York: Basic Books, 1999.

Lévy, Pierre. *Collective Intelligence: Mankind's Emerging World in Cyberspace*. Translated by Robert Bononno. Cambridge, MA: Perseus Books, 1997.

———. *Cyberculture*. Translated by Robert Bononno. Minneapolis: University of Minnesota Press, 2001.

Levy, Steven, and Brad Stone. "The New Wisdom of the Web." *Newsweek* 147, no. 14 (April 3, 2006): 47–53.

Linenthal, Edward T. *The Unfinished Bombing: Oklahoma City in American History*. New York: Oxford University Press, 2001.

Lunenfeld, Peter. *Snap to Grid: A User's Guide to Digital Arts, Media, and Cultures*. Cambridge, MA: MIT Press, 2000.

Lunenfeld, Peter, ed. *The Digital Dialectic: New Essays on New Media*. Cambridge, MA: MIT Press, 1999.

Lury, Celia. *Prosthetic Culture: Photography, Memory and Identity*. New York: Routledge, 1998.

Lyotard, Jean-François. *The Postmodern Condition: A Report on Knowledge*. Translated by Geoff Bennington and Brian Massumi. Minneapolis: University of Minnesota Press, 1984.

Maier, David. *The Theory of Relational Databases*. Rockville, MD: Computer Science Press, 1983.

Manovich, Lev. *The Language of New Media*. Cambridge, MA: MIT Press, 2001.

Marcuse, Herbert. *One-Dimensional Man: Studies in the Ideology of Advanced Industrial Society*. Boston: Beacon Press, 1964.

Massumi, Brian, ed. *The Politics of Everyday Fear*. Minneapolis: University of Minnesota Press, 1993.

Mather, Ronald, and Jill Marsden. "Trauma and Temporality: On the Origins of Post-Traumatic Stress." *Theory & Psychology* 14, no. 2 (2004): 205–219.

Mathias, Alice. "The Fakebook Generation." *New York Times*, October 6, 2007, http://www.nytimes.com/2007/10/06/opinion/06mathias.html?_r=1.

Mawston, Neil. "Camera Phones Outsell Digital Still Cameras in H1 2003 and Beyond." *Strategy Analytics*, September 1, 2003, http://www.strategyanalytics.net/default.aspx?mod=ReportAbstractViewer&a0=1773.

McCarthy, Anna. *Ambient Television: Visual Culture and Public Space*. Durham, NC: Duke University Press, 2001.

McGlotten, Shaka. "Queerspace Is the Space of the Screen." *Text, Practice and Performance* 3 (2001): 64–89.

McKenna, Katelyn Y. A., Amie S. Green, and Marci E. J. Gleason. "Relationship Formation on the Internet: What's the Big Attraction?" *Journal of Social Issues* 58, no. 1 (Spring 2002): 9–31.

McLuhan, Marshall. *The Gutenberg Galaxy: The Making of Typographic Man*. Toronto: University of Toronto Press, 1962.

———. *Understanding Media: The Extensions of Man*. Cambridge, MA: MIT Press, 1994.

Merleau-Ponty, Maurice. *Phenomenology of Perception*. Translated by Colin Smith. New York: Routledge, 1962.

Metz, Christian. "Photography and Fetish." *October* 34 (Autumn 1985): 81–90.

Meyrowitz, Joshua. *No Sense of Place: The Impact of Electronic Media on Social Behavior*. New York: Oxford University Press, 1985.

Mieszkowski, Katharine. "Faking Out Friendster." *Salon*, August 14, 2003, http://dir.salon.com/story/tech/feature/2003/08/14/fakesters/index.html.

Milgram, Stanley. *Obedience to Authority: An Experimental View*. New York: Harper & Row, 1974.

————. "The Small World Problem." *Psychology Today* 1, no. 1 (May 1967): 61–67.

Mitchell, J. Clyde, ed. *Social Networks in Urban Situations: Analyses of Personal Relationships in Central African Towns*. Manchester, UK: Manchester University Press, 1969.

Mitchell, William J. *E-topia: "Urban Life, Jim—But Not as We Know It."* Cambridge, MA: MIT Press, 1999.

————. *The Reconfigured Eye: Visual Truth in the Post-Photographic Era*. Cambridge, MA: MIT Press, 1992.

Moran, James M. *There's No Place like Home Video*. Minneapolis: University of Minnesota Press, 2002.

Morley, David. *Home Territories: Media, Mobility and Identity*. New York: Routledge, 2000.

Motorola. "Motorola 2004 Analysts Meeting." *Motorola Media Center*, July 27, 2004, http://www.motorola.com/content.jsp?globalObjectId=2622 (accessed October 20, 2007; site now discontinued).

Murray, Susan, and Laurie Ouellette, eds. *Reality TV: Remaking Television Culture*. New York: New York University Press, 2004.

Nancy, Jean-Luc. *The Inoperative Community*. Edited by Peter Connor. Translated by Peter Connor et al. Minneapolis: University of Minnesota Press, 1991.

Neal, Arthur G. *National Trauma and Collective Memory: Major Events in the American Century*. Armonk, NY: M. E. Sharpe, 1998.

Nichols, Bill. *Blurred Boundaries: Questions of Meaning in Contemporary Culture*. Bloomington: Indiana University Press, 1994.

————. *Representing Reality: Issues and Concepts in Documentary*. Bloomington: Indiana University Press, 1991.

Noguchi, Yuki. "Camera Phones Lend Immediacy to Images of Disaster." *Washington Post*, July 8, 2005, http://www.washingtonpost.com/wp-dyn/content/article/2005/07/07/AR2005070701522.html.

Nye, David E. *Image Worlds: Corporate Identities at General Electric, 1890–1930*. Cambridge, MA: MIT Press, 1985.

Olshaker, Mark. *The Instant Image: Edwin Land and the Polaroid Experience*. New York: Stein and Day, 1978.

Paradis, Kenneth. *Sex, Paranoia, and Modern Masculinity*. Albany: State University of New York Press, 2007.

Phillips, David. "Modern Vision." *Oxford Art Journal* 16, no. 1 (1993): 129–138.

Poister, Geoffrey. *A Cross-Cultural Study of Family Photographs in India, China, Japan and the United States*. Lewiston, NY: Edwin Mellen Press, 2002.

Prus, Robert. *Symbolic Interaction and Ethnographic Research: Intersubjectivity and the Study of Human Lived Experience*. Albany: State University of New York Press, 1996.

Puente, Maria. "Memories Gone in a Snap." *USA Today*, January 21, 2005, 1–2D.

Ratliff, Evan. "The Whole Earth, Changed: How Google Maps Is Changing the Way We See the World." *Wired* 15, no. 7 (July 2007): 154–159.

Reiss, Spencer. "His Space." *Wired* 14, no. 7 (July 2006): 142–147, 164.

Renov, Michael. "The Subject in History." *Afterimage* 17, no. 1 (Summer 1989): 4–7.

Rheingold, Howard. *Smart Mobs: The Next Social Revolution*. New York: Basic Books, 2003.

————. *The Virtual Community: Homesteading on the Electronic Frontier.* Revised edition. Cambridge, MA: MIT Press, 2000.

Rivers, Theodore John. *Contra Technologiam: The Crisis of Value in a Technological Age.* Lanham, MD: University Press of America, 1993.

Robbins, Bruce, ed. *The Phantom Public Sphere.* Minneapolis: University of Minnesota Press, 1993.

Robins, Kevin. "The Virtual Unconscious in Postphotography." In *Electronic Culture: Technology and Visual Representation,* edited by Timothy Druckery, 154–163. New York: Aperture Foundation, 1996.

————. "Will Image Move Us Still?" In *The Photographic Image in Digital Culture,* edited by Martin Lister, 29–50. New York: Routledge, 1995.

Russell, Catherine. *Experimental Ethnography: The Work of Film in the Age of Video.* Durham, NC: Duke University Press, 1999.

Ryan, Bill. "Millions of Cards in Pursuit of Missing Children." *New York Times,* July 14, 1996, http://www.nytimes.com/1996/07/14/nyregion/millions-of-cards-in-pursuit-of-missing-children.html?pagewanted=all.

Saltzman, Lisa, and Eric Rosenberg, eds. *Trauma and Visuality in Modernity.* Hanover, NH: Dartmouth College Press, 2006.

Saussure, Ferdinand de. *Course in General Linguistics.* Translated by Wade Baskin. New York: Philosophical Library, 1959.

Schiffer, Irvine. *The Trauma of Time: A Psychoanalytic Investigation.* New York: International Universities Press, 1978.

Scott, Janny. "Closing a Scrapbook Full of Life and Sorrow." *New York Times,* December 31, 2001, http://www.nytimes.com/2001/12/31/national/portraits/31PORT.html?pagewanted=1.

Sedlak, Andrea J., David Finkelhor, Heather Hammer, and Dana J. Schultz. "National Estimates of Missing Children: An Overview." *National Incidence Studies of Missing, Abducted, Runaway, and Thrownaway Children* (NCJ 196465). Washington, DC: Office of Juvenile Justice and Delinquency Prevention, Office of Justice Programs, U.S. Department of Justice, October 2002.

Sekula, Allan. "The Body and the Archive." *October* 39 (Winter 1986): 3–64.

————. "The Traffic in Photographs." *Art Journal* 41, no. 1 (Spring 1981): 15–25.

Sellen, Abigail, Andrew Fogg, Mike Aitken, Steve Hodges, Carsten Rother, and Ken Wood. "Do Life-Logging Technologies Support Memory for the Past? An Experimental Study Using SenseCam." In *CHI '07: Proceedings of the SIGCHI Conference on Human Factors in Computing Systems,* edited by Bo Begole et al., 81–90. New York: ACM, 2007.

Shachtman, Noah. "Murder on MySpace." *Wired* 14, no. 12 (December 2006): 240–245, 268.

Shapiro, Andrew L. "The Net That Binds: Using Cyberspace to Create Real Communities." *The Nation,* June 21, 1999, 11–15.

Silverman, Kaja. *The Subject of Semiotics.* New York: Oxford University Press, 1983.

Simmel, Georg. *On Individuality and Social Forms.* Chicago: University of Chicago Press, 1971.

Singer, Linda. "Recalling a Community at Loose Ends." In *Community at Loose Ends,* edited by Miami Theory Collective, 121–130. Minneapolis: University of Minnesota Press, 1991.

Sitney, P. Adams. "Autobiography in Avant-Garde Film." In *The Avant-Garde Film: A Reader of Theory and Criticism*, edited by P. Adams Sitney, 199–246. New York: Anthology Film Archives, 1987.

Sizemore, Jennifer. "Editor's Note: Welcome to FirstPerson." *MSNBC.com*, February 2007, http://www.msnbc.msn.com/id/16713129/ns/community-firstperson.

Slater, Don. "Domestic Photography and Digital Culture." In *The Photographic Image in Digital Culture*, edited by Martin Lister, 129–146. New York: Routledge, 1995.

Smith, Marc A., and Peter Kollock, eds. *Communities in Cyberspace*. New York: Routledge, 1999.

Smodish, Jennifer. "Apple's Ad-ventures." *Macworld*, June 1, 2001, http://www.macworld.com/article/2223/2001/06/15appleads.html.

Soja, Edward W. *Postmodern Geographies: The Reassertion of Space in Critical Social Theory*. New York: Verso, 1989.

Sontag, Susan. *On Photography*. New York: Anchor Books, 1990.

St. John, Warren. "Young, Single and Dating at Hyperspeed." *New York Times*, April 21, 2002, Section 9, 1–2.

Stolorow, Robert D. "Trauma and Temporality." *Psychoanalytic Psychology* 20 (2003): 158–161.

Stone, Allucquère Rosanne. *The War of Desire and Technology at the Close of the Mechanical Age*. Cambridge, MA: MIT Press, 1995.

———. "Will the Real Body Please Stand Up? Boundary Stories about Virtual Cultures." In *Cyberspace: First Steps*, edited by Michael Benedikt, 81–118. Cambridge, MA: MIT Press, 1991.

Stone, Brad, and Noam Cohen. "Social Networks Spread Defiance Online." *New York Times*, June 16, 2009, http://www.nytimes.com/2009/06/16/world/middleeast/16media.html.

Stone, Brad, Adam Rogers, and Kevin Platt. "Love Online." *Newsweek* 137, no. 8 (February 19, 2001): 46–51.

Sturken, Marita. "The Politics of Video Memory: Electronic Erasures and Inscriptions." In *Resolutions*, edited by Michael Renov and Erika Suderburg, 1–12. Minneapolis: University of Minnesota Press, 1996.

———. *Tangled Memories: The Vietnam War, the AIDS Epidemic, and the Politics of Remembering*. Berkeley: University of California Press, 1997.

Tagg, John. *The Burden of Representation: Essays on Photographies and Histories*. Minneapolis: University of Minnesota Press, 1988.

Terdiman, Daniel. "Folksonomies Tap People Power." *Wired*, February 1, 2005, http://www.wired.com/print/science/discoveries/news/2005/02/66456.

Tönnies, Ferdinand. *Community and Society*. Translated by Charles P. Loomis. New Brunswick, NJ: Transaction Publishers, 1988.

Trentmann, Frank. "Citizenship and Consumption." *Journal of Consumer Culture* 7, no. 2 (2007): 147–158.

Trotman, Nat. "The Life of the Party—The Polaroid SX-70 Land Camera and Instant Film Photography." *Afterimage* 29, no. 6 (May/June 2002): 10.

Turkle, Sherry. *Life on the Screen: Identity in the Age of the Internet*. New York: Touchstone, 1995.

Ulman, Richard B., and Doris Brothers. *The Shattered Self: A Psychoanalytic Study of Trauma*. Hillsdale, NJ: Analytic Press, 1988.

Urry, John. *The Tourist Gaze.* Second edition. London: Sage Publications, 2002.

Vander Wal, Thomas. "Explaining and Showing Broad and Narrow Folksonomies." *Personal InfoCloud,* February 21, 2005, http://www.personalinfocloud.com/2005/02/explaining_and_.html.

Walker, Leslie. ".com—Live." *Washington Post,* March 25, 1999, http://www.washingtonpost.com/wp-srv/business/talk/transcripts/walker/walker032599.htm.

Walther, Joseph B. "Computer-Mediated Communication: Impersonal, Interpersonal, and Hyperpersonal Interaction." *Communication Research* 23, no. 1 (February 1996): 3–43.

Walton, Marsha. "Cell Phones: A New Tool in the War-Zone Blogosphere." *CNN.com,* August 1, 2006, http://www.cnn.com/2006/TECH/internet/08/01/newblogs.

Wark, McKenzie. *Virtual Geography: Living with Global Media Events.* Bloomington: Indiana University Press, 1994.

Weissberg, Liliane. "Circulating Images: Notes on the Photographic Exchange." In *Writing the Image after Roland Barthes,* edited by Jean-Michel Rabaté, 109–131. Philadelphia: University of Pennsylvania Press, 1997.

Wensberg, Peter C. *Land's Polaroid: A Company and the Man Who Invented It.* Boston: Houghton Mifflin, 1987.

West, Nancy Martha. *Kodak and the Lens of Nostalgia.* Charlottesville: University Press of Virginia, 2000.

White, Mimi. *Tele-Advising: Therapeutic Discourse in American Television.* Chapel Hill: University of North Carolina Press, 1992.

Whyte, William H. *The Social Life of Small Urban Spaces.* New York: Project for Public Spaces, 2001.

Zgoba, Kristen M. "Spin Doctors and Moral Crusaders: The Moral Panic Behind Child Safety Legislation." *Criminal Justice Studies* 17, no. 4 (December 2004): 385–404.

Zimmermann, Patricia R. *Reel Families: A Social History of Amateur Film.* Bloomington: Indiana University Press, 1995.

Index

Linkletter, Art, 114
liquid media, 73, 77
Living Web, 168. *See also* Semantic Web
London Bomb Blasts Community, 87, 88, 165
looking, 4, 19, 27. *See also* gaze
Luckmann, Thomas, 155
Lury, Celia, 26, 121

Macintosh, 78. *See also* Apple
Madness and Civilization (Foucault), 25–26
Manhunt.net, 127, 128
Manovich, Lev, 60, 75–76, 91
Marcuse, Herbert, 169
marketing campaigns. *See* advertising
 campaigns
"mass-cultural hieroglyphics," 126
Massumi, Brian, 45
Match.com, 131–133; advertising campaign,
 115–118; gay and lesbian success stories,
 130–131; profile interface, 120–121; search
 engine, 120, 126; subcommunities, 130
Mathias, Alice, 167
McLuhan, Marshall, 6
meaning, 13
media, decentralization of, 85
media flow and trauma, 89–95
media frame, 74–75
media history, inauthentic, 65
mediation, 93, 139; systems of, 6
memorials, 59, 62–64, 69. *See also descansos*;
 roadside memorial markers; "September 11:
 A Memorial"
memory(ies), 3, 38, 41, 81, 85;
 autobiographical, 81; blocking, substitution,
 and erasure of, 60; bodies through which
 they are transmitted, 60; collective, 60,
 159; consciousness and, 121; cultural, 23,
 59–61, 63, 67, 85, 159; cultural terrain and,
 12; images/representations and, 59, 94, 113;
 mechanics of imaging becoming
 subservient to machinations of, 4; narrative
 and, 11, 94, 121; national, and moving
 images, 53–59, 66–72 (*see also* trauma);
 photography and, 59, 60, 82, 91; *punctum*
 and, 11; representation and, 94–95;
 sharing, forming, and terminally
 depositing, 60; technologies of, 60, 190n18.
 See also forgetting
memory images, photographs as, 11
memory objects, 60, 63
memory processes of knowing, 81–82
Merleau-Ponty, Maurice, 184n6
Metzenbaum, Howard, 35
microblog, 145. *See also* blogs and blogging

Microsoft Research, 81. *See also* SenseCam
migratory patterns, 106–110
Milgram, Stanley, 143
milk cartons, 28, 30, 31, 35, 44, 181nn28–29
missing children, 31–34; campaign to recover,
 27–30; categories of, 42; codes of fear
 production and, 38–45; fear in the archive,
 45–48; manufacturing fear and, 30–31;
 statistical knowledge and, 33–38, 42;
 stories of, in magazines, 34; television and,
 34–35 (*see also Dateline: To Catch a
 Predator*); threat levels and, 31–33
missing children campaign, 27, 32, 35–39
Missing Children's Assistance Act of 1984,
 42, 180n23
Missing: Have You Seen This Child? (TV
 program), 34
missing persons, 65–66; from 9/11, 54–56, 59
 (*see also* "America's New War: Missing")
Mitchell, J. Clyde, 194n3
MobileActive, 152
mobile phones. *See* cellular imaginary
mobility and movement, 157, 173
moblogs and moblogging, 157–158, 160, 170,
 196n26. *See also* blogs and blogging
Motorola, 73, 74
Murdoch, Rupert, 169
Murray, Susan, 98
MySpace, 145, 169

Nancy, Jean-Luc, 131–132, 139
narrative: desire in, and trauma, 14–20;
 memory and, 11, 94, 121; vs. story, 4. *See
 also* progressive narrative; redemptive
 narrative; storytelling; toxic narrative
narrative fixity, 63, 166
narrative impulses, 11, 20, 51, 62
narrative responses to traumatic events,
 103–104
narratives of excess and recovery, 22–24
narrativity, 61, 64
narratology, 15
narrowcasting, 136
National Center for Missing and Exploited
 Children (NCMEC), 27, 29, 35, 36, 45
nation(al) signifiers, 60, 63, 66–68
national symbolic, 68
national trauma, 62, 83, 98, 159. *See also*
 September 11, 2001 attacks; trauma, public
nation(s), 54, 83–85, 159; individual, family,
 and, 66–72; trauma and, 92 (*see also* trauma)
new media, 60–61, 75, 84; destructive powers,
 49; fear and, 52; technologies and, 83;
 trauma and, 91. *See also* technology, new

Eric Freedman is an Associate Professor in the School of Communication and Multimedia Studies at Florida Atlantic University.